PROBLEM
EMPLOYEES

PROBLEM EMPLOYEES

HOW TO IMPROVE THEIR BEHAVIOUR AND THEIR PERFORMANCE

PETER WYLIE & MARDY GROTHE

PIATKUS

Copyright © 1991 by Dr Peter Wylie and Dr Mardy Grothe

First UK edition published in
Great Britain in 1993 by
Judy Piatkus (Publishers) Limited of
5 Windmill Street, London W1P 1HF

First Paperback Edition 1994

**The moral right of the authors
has been asserted**

*A CIP catalogue record for this book is
available from the British Library*

ISBN 0-7499-1227-8
ISBN 0-7499-1367-3 (pbk)

Edited by Carol Franklin
Designed by Chris Warner

Set in Linotron Plantin by
The Professional Data Bureau, London SW17
Printed and bound in Great Britain by
Mackays of Chatham PLC, Chatham, Kent

Contents

Preface

WE WROTE the first edition of this book more than a decade ago and we still get comments from managers and supervisors, saying the book has helped them resolve some pretty intractable performance problems with employees. Now, as we come out with this second edition, we'd like to mention a few things that've happened since we wrote the original version.

▶ In 1987 we wrote a book called *Problem Bosses: Who They Are and How to Deal With Them* (published in the United States in hardback by Facts on File and in paperback by Fawcett), where we talked about boss-employee problems from the other side of the coin. We described how difficult bosses can be and what employees can do to cope more effectively with them. In that book, we took the view that, in one way or another, *all* bosses are problem bosses to their employees. We still believe that.

▶ Over the years, though, we've decided that most of the trouble in the work world is caused by neither bosses nor employees, but by problem *relationships*. In our view, bosses and employees are in a very important *relationship* with each other; in many ways, similar to the relationship between spouses and romantic partners, parents and children, or good friends. However, most bosses, and many employees, don't see it that way. They say things like, 'What relationship? This is just business.' Well, business it may be, but bosses and employees don't leave their personalities at home when they come to work in the morning. And, because they're linked together by their respective positions in the organisation, it's impossible for them *not* to have a relationship with each other.

▶ Going a little further, we now see many employee 'performance problems' as symptoms of an underlying 'relationship problem' with a boss. That is, because of a not-so-hot relationship, the employee becomes demotivated and performance deteriorates. In our view, then, if bosses want to correct the employee's performance problem, they should focus on the relationship and do what they can to make it better. As the relationship with the employee improves, guess what? So does the employee's performance. We've tried to make this edition of the book reflect our greater realisation of the importance of this relationship focus.

▶ Finally, speaking of relationships, we've been very pleased to learn how many people have taken this book and tried to use its principles and techniques in their personal lives. We've had married couples tell us about some pretty dramatic relationship improvements as a result of using the process with each other. And our eyes have moistened as parents have told us how helpful the process was during difficult times with their teenage children. Even though we didn't have this 'personal' side in mind when we first wrote the book, it's very much in our minds now. So, please, explore the personal implications of this book as well as the professional ones.

We hope you enjoy *Problem Employees* and find it helpful. Please write to us care of the publisher if you have any questions or comments. We'd love to hear from you. Good luck!

Introduction

THE INFLUX of new groups of people into the labour force, along with the erosion of our acceptance of traditional standards and rules, have combined to make most workers more of a challenge to their managers and supervisors than they would have been as recently as twenty-five years ago. In a sense, all of us have become problem employees for the people we work for. And all of us have problem employees who work for us.

As management consultants, we've had about a decade's worth of exposure to scores of different organisational settings and to many different types of managers and supervisors:

▶ foremen and section supervisors in machine shops;
▶ executive vice-presidents of large and small corporations;
▶ head nurses and administrators of hospitals;
▶ owner-operators of small family businesses, such as restaurants, dry cleaners, shops, and catering services;
▶ principals and department heads in schools and colleges;
▶ directors of personnel or human resource development in private industry; and
▶ department managers in retail stores.

We've consistently found that most people who become supervisors and managers achieve these levels of responsibility because they've demonstrated considerable technical or conceptual ability, not because they have the skills to motivate people or to handle the predictable people problems they encounter in their positions. Such problems include:

▶ an employee who challenges a supervisor's authority in a group situation;
▶ a worker who maintains that, as a member of a minority group, he or she can't be fired;
▶ an employee who is obviously an alcoholic;

▶ a technician whose skills are superb but who frequently alienates co-workers and customers;

▶ a secretary who can't spell or distinguish a sentence from a phrase;

▶ a worker who's been on the job for twenty-five years and whose performance is on a gradual but steady decline;

▶ a young worker who's completely unwilling to stay after 5 p.m. and come in at weekends, even during peak periods when the pressure is on; and

▶ an overly dependent employee who seems to have no initiative and won't start any project without being told specifically to do so.

Our purpose in writing this book is to provide managers and supervisors with a simple, practical and straightforward approach to help all employees, especially problem employees, to significantly improve their work performance. Primarily, we offer guidelines for conducting a performance improvement interview—a process we've found to be effective in handling on-the-job people problems and in maximising the performance potential of most employees. Here's what *Problem Employees* features.

1. A course between covers. This book closely parallels a workshop we conduct for managers and supervisors. It's designed so that, as you read through and complete the practice exercises, you will, in effect, go through the process once, before you actually sit down with one of your employees.

2. A ten-step process. The book breaks down the process of conducting a performance improvement interview into ten steps that are very easy to follow. In the beginning, while learning how to conduct performance improvement interviews, the steps will act as a supportive guide through what can otherwise be a difficult and anxiety-producing process. After you've become more practised and confident, you'll carry out the steps without thinking much about them.

3. Listening and presentation skills. The book covers, in depth, two essential managerial skills: active listening and effective presentation skills. If you learn nothing else but how to be a better listener and how to present your ideas better, you'll have bought more than your money's worth. These skills will not only make you a better manager, but also will help you in some of your other private roles, such as parent, spouse, intimate partner or friend.

4. Alternative strategies.   Throughout the book we've tried to offer alternative strategies and techniques you can use when you run into problems. We haven't covered all of the contingencies, but at least you'll have a backup strategy if things don't go according to plan. When you're dealing with human beings, that's almost as much the rule as it is the exception.

We strongly believe that learning should be enjoyable, so we've tried to make our book as interesting as possible. It's written in the same language and tone we use in our workshops with managers and supervisors. It's very light on theory and very heavy on the application of specific techniques and skills. There are lots of examples and anecdotes, and we've really tried to share a little of ourselves with you. You can think of our book as a first-hand account; we've actually made all the mistakes we've written about!

We've read a lot of self-help books ourselves, and we've had many long discussions with others who've read them. We've concluded that a book's helpfulness is as much a function of how it's *read* as how it's written. This book in particular calls for a lot of active and thoughtful participation on your part. Therefore, we'd like you to get actively involved as a reader, complete the practice exercises, and try out the techniques we suggest with an employee *before* judging their validity. Make the book an enjoyable experience for yourself.

The Performance Improvement Process

Step One: Analyse Your Employee's Performance

Step Two: Ask Your Employee to Meet with You

Step Three: Begin the Performance Improvement Interview

Step Four: Find Out How Things Are Going

Step Five: Ask Your Employee 'The Question'

Step Six: Get Your Employee to Do a Self-Analysis

Step Seven: Present Your Analysis of Your Employee's Performance

Step Eight: Negotiate the Performance Agreement

Step Nine: Close the Interview

Step Ten: Follow Up

And...

'What Do I Do if None of This Works?'

Part I

The Problem of Problem Employees

Chapter 1

Who Are Problem Employees?

THIS IS a book about problem employees and how to deal with them. So, let's get right down to business.

Think of a problem employee, someone who causes you trouble, gives you some supervisory headaches or, in general, does not perform well on the job. If you're like most managers or supervisors, you'll have no trouble thinking of someone right away. More likely, several people will come to mind. But, for now, focus on just one person. Fix the individual clearly in your mind. *What makes this person a problem employee?* How does he create problems for you? What does she do or fail to do in her job that creates problems for you? How often, and under what circumstances, is he a problem? What negative effects does she have on other co-workers, on the organisation or work unit as a whole, and on you as her supervisor? (Note that we plan to use the pronouns he and she alternately to refer to employees and bosses throughout this book. This style may be a little confusing at first, but you'll quickly get used to it.)

As you think about the answers to these questions, record your thoughts below in as much detail as you can:

Name of employee _____

What makes this person a problem employee?

_____

_____

_____

_____

Everybody Has Problem Employees

Over the past few years, we've talked to many different types of managers about their experiences with problem employees. We've asked all of them to do the same thing we asked you to do a second ago—to think of a problem employee. Each one had little trouble thinking of somebody to fit that description. So, meet some of the problem employees your colleagues have told us about.

Sheila Ricks is a dentist in her mid-thirties. Having just taken over the practice of an older dentist she worked with for the last five years, Sheila also inherited a problem employee: Lyla Franks, her secretary and receptionist. As Sheila put it, 'Lyla's so unpredictable. One day she's friendly and outgoing, and the next day she's sullen and grouchy. I don't know which Lyla is going to walk in the door in the morning.' When asked about the negative effects of Lyla's behaviour, Sheila responded, 'This Jekyll-and-Hyde routine of hers is beginning to alienate some of my old patients and turn off some of my new ones. My dental hygienist ignores her completely. And I end up feeling confused half the time about what to do. They don't have a course in dental school on how to deal with people like Lyla.'

Charles Bickford is a fifty-year-old vice-president of marketing for a large corporation. He recently promoted a promising young regional sales manager, John Bailey, to assistant vice-president of sales for the eastern half of the country. 'John's good, but I'm having trouble getting him to see the big picture,' Charles said. 'He's still behaving like a sales manager, not a vice-president. He's too concerned about meeting monthly quotas and not concerned enough with our long-range goals. He thinks maybe only three months ahead. I need him to think five years ahead if we're going to have the kind of growth we've predicted for this part of the country. I've got to work out some way to get him on my wavelength.'

Barbara Stokes, twenty-nine years old, is a trained career counsellor. Last year, she was promoted to a supervisory position at an employment office in a large city. Her problem employee is Walter Williams, a fifty-three-year-old counsellor who's worked in the same office for over twenty years. 'I don't know whether it's an age issue, a sex issue or a race issue,' said Barbara, 'but I just haven't been able to get this man to come around. Often he just seems to be going through the motions, not really caring about his job or the people we're trying to help. His lack of interest shows in lots of ways—careless mistakes on forms, perfunctory reports and complaints from people about his lack of helpfulness. I don't know, his presence around here just seems to have a depressing effect on everybody. Especially me!'

Alan Smith is a forty-three-year-old section supervisor for a medium-sized machine tool company. Alan's been in this job for fifteen years and knows it inside and out. A couple months ago he hired a promising apprentice-trainee, Brian Turner. 'Brian's a hard worker, and he shows up every day,' said Alan, 'but he's slow to catch on to things. I've tried to explain stuff carefully to him, and he seems to understand. But I can tell he doesn't by the work he turns out. Some of the other workers are starting to complain that they don't want the responsibility of teaching him.' Turning his hands upward, Alan went on, 'I don't know what to do. Brian really wants to work, and that's rare these days. On the other hand, maybe he doesn't have what it takes to make it in this trade. I don't know.'

A Profile of Problem Employees

Based on our discussions with scores of bosses from all around the country, we've reached the following conclusion: problem employees are everywhere! They can be found anywhere people work for a living. No manager or supervisor is immune from them. What else do we know about problem employees? We've devoted the rest of this chapter to profiling them for you.

Problem Employees Come in All Colours, Shapes and Sizes

We haven't been able to detect any significant trends with respect to type of industry, level or status of job, race, sex, ethnicity, or any of the other variables that sociologists and psychologists look at when they do research on organisations. For example, we've found that chairpersons of large corporations are just as likely to have problem employees as first-line supervisors in small manufacturing firms. Professional employees with advanced education and training are just as likely to be problems to their bosses as workers with little education or those who punch a time clock. And in spite of widely-held stereotypes, we haven't been able to identify differences between men and women, minorities and whites, or younger and older workers in the tendency to be troublesome to supervisors.

Problem Employees Are Not a Clearly Identifiable Group

If given the task, census takers could probably get an accurate count on all Caucasian males in the country who are over twenty-one years of age and who have red hair and freckles. However, trying to count all the problem employees in the country would be an impossible task. Whether or not someone is *called* a problem employee—or in fact *is* a problem employee—depends on a number of factors.

1. Who's the boss? Although it may seem obvious, supervisors differ greatly in their opinions and evaluations of workers. More than once, we've seen two managers in the same organisation with diametrically opposed assessments of the same employee. In some respects, problem employees are like beauty: they're in the eye of the beholder.

As we said a few years ago in our book called *Problem Bosses: Who They Are and How To Deal With Them*, sometimes the *boss* is the problem, not the employee. The employee is only responding to the boss's management (or mismanagement) style. This becomes quite apparent if you spend a little time hanging around organisations, as we have. You quickly discover that some bosses are far more likely than others to have problem employees. Indeed, some bosses complain they have nothing but problem employees working for them, and that's the way it's always been. Are they just unlucky? Or are they doing something to bring out all this problematic and unproductive behaviour? As we say in our seminars: problem bosses often create problem employees. (A little later, we'll also talk about the critical importance of the 'relationship' between bosses and employees, and how that affects employee performance.)

Even when they're not 'bad' managers, bosses contribute to the problem of problem employees for other reasons. First, being a boss is a difficult job. You've got all kinds of employees, each with very different personalities and operating styles, reporting to you and expecting different things from you. And if you're like most managers and supervisors we know, you're probably reporting to a boss who has a long way to go when it comes to 'the art of managing people.' It's a tough position to be in. What makes it even tougher, though, is this: most bosses aren't selected for this very demanding job because of their ability to manage people. They're usually selected for some other reason, like excellent technical skills, a good record as an employee, an advanced degree, some kind of personal or family relationship with a 'big' boss, and so on. To make matters worse, most bosses get very little training for this very difficult job. For many of them, the only training they really get is reading books like this. Usually, they're just tossed into the waters of management and expected to sink or swim. No wonder so many of them run into problems when they try to make the transition from 'working' to 'managing'. As a result of this lack of training, one of the most important things bosses *don't* do is sit down periodically with employees and conduct a systematic review of the employee's performance. First, because they don't know how to do it (after all, nobody taught them), and second, because the prospect of doing it makes them nervous (who wouldn't feel that way?), they put it off and put it off— or they never do it at all. It's one of the major reasons we wrote this book.

2. Who's the employee? As we said earlier, all employees have distinct personalities. And how varied they are! For every cheerful and optimistic employee, there's a moody or depressed one. For every disciplined and hard-working employee, you can find a sloppy or lazy one. Many employees are a delight to work with, they make their bosses look good. But many of them are just the opposite. They were 'problem' employees in their previous jobs, 'problem' students when they were in school or college, and 'problem' family members to their parents and other relatives.

What's going on in the employee's personal life can also be a major factor. Even the best workers can become problem employees (at least temporarily) when they're contending with personal crises, like a divorce, the death or critical illness of a relative, a child who gets into trouble, or some other high-stress event. Looked at from this standpoint, all of us can be problem employees, and probably have been, at one time or another.

3. What job is the person in? If you travel around the country as much as we do, you quickly discover that there are a lot of people who should not be in the jobs they're in. Whether it's surly waitresses, rude salespeople, depressed desk clerks, or taxing taxi drivers, they don't do their 'customer service' jobs very well and they don't seem too happy in their jobs (not to mention the effect they have on us as consumers). It's a problem we complain to each other about all the time. Maybe you've recognised the problem as well.

Industrial psychologists have long stressed the importance of the 'fit' between the characteristics of the person and the demands of the job. Many people can be tremendously effective in one job and incompetent in another. Just because someone's a good machinist doesn't mean he'll make a good shop foreman. Just because someone's a good accountant doesn't mean she'll make a good business manager. Just because someone's a good vice-chairperson doesn't mean he'll make a good CEO. The right people can be in the wrong jobs. And when they are, you'll have problem employees to contend with.

4. What's the organisation like?   Just as people have different personalities and operating styles, so do organisations. Some organisations are wonderful places to work. The owners or top-level executives go to great lengths to make the work environment pleasant and tasteful, provide reasonable wage and salary levels, make sure that personnel benefits are adequate to the needs of employees, and so on. On the other hand, some organisations are terrible places to work. The owners are selfish, greedy people who care only about themselves, the work environment is nasty, and every wage increase or personnel benefit is given grudgingly. For obvious reasons, organisations like this have more than their share of problem employees.

Being a Problem Employee Often Has Little to Do with Ability

Problem employees can be very talented, competent people with more than enough ability to perform well on the job. But they can *still* be problem employees. Their bosses often complain about bad attitude, poor motivation, or the inability to get along with others. In fact, many managers put more emphasis on these factors than the employee's technical ability to do the job.

Here's what supervisors have told us about their 'unmotivated' employees:

'He does a great job when he's here, but he's often absent four or five times a month.'

'She'll frequently come in twenty minutes late, and I don't think I've ever seen her stay after 5 p.m.'

'He doesn't take any initiative. He almost never starts a project on his own. He seems content to do only what I ask him to, no more.'

'She always wants to study a problem to death. She doesn't seem to have any concept of deadlines.'

'I know he has to catch a commuter train at 5.20 p.m., but sometimes we have to work late around here to get proposals out. Sometimes I think he'd rather cut off his left hand than miss that train.'

'When she's finished with her work, she's ready to sit down and read a novel. I don't think I've ever seen her go around to see if she could help somebody else out.'

These are examples of what managers have told us about employees who have difficulty getting along with other people:

'He's always complaining to other people behind my back, but he'll never say anything directly to my face.'

'She's really touchy about any criticism of her work. I feel I always have to handle her with kid gloves.'

'He's very moody. One day he's all smiles and laughs, and the next day you can't get a word out of him. Nobody quite knows how to handle him.'

'She's a put-down artist, always going around insulting people. I have a hard job getting anybody to work with her.'

'He's really rough around the edges when it comes to dealing with customers. He never really listens to them. He's always telling them exactly what he thinks they need, without finding out what their problems are.'

'I can't get her to speak up at staff meetings. I know she's got a lot of great ideas, but you'd never know it. She just sits there and doesn't say "boo"'.

Problem Employees Are a Constant Source of Concern

Bosses spend a lot of time thinking and worrying about their problem employees. They ruminate about them in the car or train going to and from work. They complain to their spouses, friends, and peers about the difficulties they're having. They even begin to doubt their own competence as managers.

Supervisors also spend a lot of time cleaning up after their problem employees. This can mean redoing work the employee has screwed up or defending the foul-ups of these workers to others in the company. Managers also waste a lot of time figuring out ways to get around problem employees. They ask themselves questions like, 'How can I tell him I don't want him to make presentations without hurting his feelings?' or, 'Who else can I give this project to because I know she's going to mess it up?' or, 'How can I get somebody else in here to do all the things he can't do?'

A Quick Summary

Problem employees come in all colours, shapes and sizes. Depending on certain factors and situations, anybody can be a problem employee at one time or another—including you and us. Some of the key contributing factors include: who the boss is, who the employee is, what job the person is in and what the organisation is like. Problem employees are often as much of a problem in the areas of motivation and co-operation with other people as they are in their ability to do their work. Compared to other workers, problem employees are a constant source of concern to their bosses.

Chapter 2

How Do You Know a Problem Employee When You See One?

As WE were writing this book, we mentioned the term 'problem employee' to a manager or supervisor. Almost invariably, we'd hear the following remarks.

'Oh yes, I've got some of those. Like the older worker who's on active retirement. Or the young person just out of college, who only wants to work from 9 to 5, forget weekends.'

'I know what you're talking about. My receptionist is a great example; she's more interested in doing her nails than being polite on the phone or taking accurate messages.'

'What sales manager hasn't had a problem employee or two? Like one of my salespeople, who always blames the customer when he can't close a deal, refuses to make cold calls, and always turns in his sales reports a month after they're due.'

Most managers and supervisors feel they have a clear picture of who their problem employees are. However, our experience has shown us a couple of other things:

▶ Sometimes bosses fail to recognise a problem employee when they see one.

▶ Sometimes bosses *think* they have a problem employee when they really don't.

In this chapter we'll offer some suggestions for identifying less obvious problem employees and making certain a person you assume is a problem employee really *is* one.

Not Recognising Problem Employees When You've Got Them

Though most bosses *feel* they know who their problem employees are, they do occasionally fail to recognise when an employee really is a problem. We see a number of reasons for this.

1. Sometimes managers and supervisors don't want to admit they have a problem employee.   For many bosses, admitting that they've got problem employees is like admitting they're not good bosses. Even though the problems may be obvious to others, bosses like these seem to be saying, 'Problems? What problems?' This seems to be especially true with people who generally have trouble owning up to their mistakes and who aren't good at facing problems directly.

2. Some employees are so effective in some areas their bosses overlook or downplay their weaknesses.   For example, the systems analyst you couldn't live without, but who's brusque with people from other departments. Or the customer service rep who always takes less time than estimated to complete a repair, but whose paperwork is barely legible. The tendency to overlook weaknesses is understandable, but it's usually a mistake. As one owner of a small public relations firm told us about a talented *prima donna* employee: 'Listen, this man brings in 80 per cent of the business we do. Given his critical role in the organisation, I'm willing to turn the other way when it comes to some of his little idiosyncrasies.' What he didn't mention was that the employee's 'little idiosyncrasies' included a history of womanising in the firm, and that his escapades had already driven away several very talented younger employees and threatened the morale of the entire company.

3. Many supervisors accept the fact that some workers are weak in certain skills or habits.   They don't view these areas needing improvement as problems that necessarily need to be corrected. Given the somewhat philosophical attitude they adopt, they simply see performance deficiencies as a fact of life.

4. The supervisor overlooks weaknesses or performance problems because the employee is a friend, family member, or just a particularly pleasant person to be around. This is especially true in small, privately held firms and family businesses, but it can also happen in blue chip companies. The person working for you is a good friend, a relative, or just a really nice person, so your judgement is clouded. You may justify your inaction as you think, 'I don't want to be too hard on the person. Besides, it's not that big a problem.' It's understandable, but a mistake none the less.

5. The employee is slick. Unfortunately, some people are very good at forming a good impression with their bosses and still not turning out much work. Other employees see clearly what's going on, but the boss doesn't. Why? The boss has been 'conned'.

6. Managers get wrapped up in their own work. Some bosses are so focused on their own professional priorities—or their own personal agendas—that they simply ignore what their employees are doing. It's hard to think about other people when you're focused on yourself.

7. Some bosses get 'involved' with their employees. Novelists are always writing about it, so we might as well mention it, too. Occasionally a boss will form a romantic attachment with an employee. Or maybe just become infatuated with an employee, without any actual romance developing. This kind of involvement can, and usually will, obscure or distort the boss's perception of the employee's effectiveness.

8. Bosses occasionally go through their own personal crises. Like all human beings, managers have personal problems that may divert their attention from work and from how effectively their employees are performing.

To help you decide if—or recognise when—a worker is a problem employee, we've come up with a series of questions you can ask yourself. You'll find them in the Problem Employee Questionnaire on page 14. Read through the entire questionnaire as you think about a particular employee. We think a 'yes' answer to even one of these questions could mean you have a problem employee, especially if the question touches on an area that's particularly important to you. If you say 'yes' to two or more questions, there's no doubt about it.

For a few of your employees, you may have a tendency to answer 'yes, but ... ' to some of the questions. If you do, that probably means

Problem Employee Questionnaire

Read each question below. If you find yourself thinking **yes** in response to a question, put a tick in the space beside it. If the answer is **no**, leave it empty.

____ 1. Do you receive complaints from customers about his work or about his attitude toward customers?

____ 2. Do her co-workers complain to you about her rudeness, about her trying to dump work on them, and so on?

____ 3. Does your boss tell you about mistakes in his work?

____ 4. Do your peers complain to you about how she has treated them or their workers?

____ 5. If you don't check his work, will it often go out with major mistakes?

____ 6. When you give her an assignment, does it rarely come back done the way you wanted it?

____ 7. Do you often have to reschedule the work of your other employees at the last minute because he fails to show up?

____ 8. Do you frequently spend time doing work that you should be able to delegate to her?

____ 9. Does he rarely complete assignments on time?

____ 10. As soon as she finishes a task, does she wait until you assign her another one?

____ 11. After you give him an assignment, does he frequently return with a number of reasons why it can't be done?

____ 12. Do you receive reports that she has been complaining about you to other people?

____ 13. Are you always at least a little concerned he will say something to embarrass you in front of other people?

____ 14. Do you find it difficult to get your work done because of the time you spend on her problems and mistakes?

____ 15. When you decide to give an important assignment to someone, do you rarely pick him?

____ 16. Do you assign work that she should be able to do to other employees because you know they'll do it better and faster?

____ 17. When you point out mistakes he has made, does he almost always have an excuse or put the blame on someone else?

____ 18. Do you occasionally learn that she has lied to you, or at least stretched the truth?

you're having trouble accepting the fact that they're problem employees especially if you feel they have critical skills or are especially valuable members of your team. Our advice if that's the case? *Go ahead and accept the fact*. Then get on with the important business of helping them improve their performance.

When Is a Problem Employee *Not* a Problem Employee?

While some managers fail to recognise their otherwise obvious problem employees, it's also common for some bosses to assume they have a problem employee when all they really have is an employee with a different operating style.

We've found that it's awfully easy for bosses to confuse *process* with *outcome*. That is, it's easy to make the mistake of focusing too much on *how* an employee does the work and not enough on *what* the employee actually produces in terms of quantity, quality and timeliness.

Over the years we've noticed some common types of 'process concerns' on the part of bosses. We'll discuss them briefly below. Remember, a process concern has more to do with the way employees get their work done than it does with the actual work they produce.

1. Physical appearance. In spite of the relaxation in dress standards in business settings over the last twenty years, many managers still object to long hair, beards, jeans, and the like. They think men should wear ties and jackets and women should wear business suits or skirts and stockings. This attitude has been reinforced by the 'dress for success' fad in recent years. Clearly, there are many jobs that warrant or require someone to dress up. A salesperson who calls on customers who wear 'proper' business attire, a receptionist who greets the public, or a department store clerk all ought to dress appropriately for work. But we know of no evidence that a bra, a tie, and a cleanshaven face or legs ever contributed much to a worker's productivity on a job that doesn't have a lot of public contact or require a 'businesslike' image.

2. Flexibility of work hours. There's certainly nothing sacred about the eight-hour day, especially when it's rigidly sandwiched between 9 a.m. and 5 p.m. More and more organisations are experimenting with flexible schedules, or flexi-time, which permits employees to start work early and finish early or start late and finish late. If more managers and organisations adopted this flexible approach to work hours, the percentage of costly tardiness and absences in British industry would drop significantly.

3. Extra hours and weekends. Too many bosses equate long hours of work with high work productivity. Although there is some small correlation between the two, we think managers who consistently spend ten to twelve hours a day on the job are probably not using their time effectively. We've also noticed that these same managers often get upset when their employees don't put in equally long hours, even when it's apparent that the employees are much more efficient time managers than their bosses.

4. Participation in extracurricular activities. Almost all organisations have activities that aren't directly related to day-to-day business functions. Christmas parties, softball teams, football leagues, Friday afternoon 'staff meetings' at the local watering hole, and office picnics are but a few examples. We are pretty strong supporters of these kinds of activities because they can contribute significantly to worker morale. However, many employees steer clear of these functions; some even find them downright distasteful. As much as we may enjoy them, we think it's a mistake for bosses to hold employees' lack of participation in these activities against them. After all, people are being paid to turn out the work, not to socialise—even though it's great when the two can go together.

5. Differences in values, attitudes and lifestyles. People differ tremendously in their values, attitudes and lifestyles. Some people are staunchly religious, while others haven't been inside a church, chapel or synagogue in years. Some regularly smoke cigarettes (or marijuana) or drink alcohol; others strongly disapprove of these habits. Some people firmly believe that spouses should be completely monogamous; others approve of and engage in extramarital affairs. Some are politically very liberal and actively campaign for issues like the abortion question, equal rights or gay rights. Others are politically conservative and work just as hard for issues like a tightening of pornography and obscenity laws, or prayer in schools.

Occasionally managers will have employees who are so different from them it's difficult to take an objective view of the employees' actual work performance. Some bosses can't seem to separate what employees do on the job from what they do off the job, or from the views and opinions they occasionally voice on the job.

6. Demographic differences. In spite of the massive social changes of the last twenty or thirty years, some supervisors are still uncomfortable working with people who are 'different' from them. Many whites are ill at ease working with minorities, and vice versa. Many males are convinced women don't belong in certain roles and certain jobs. Older workers often view younger workers as selfish and irresponsible. Many younger workers see older workers as stodgy or as having retired on the job.

As with values, attitudes, and life-styles, it's difficult for some supervisors to look beyond an employee's skin colour, sex, age, and so forth to see the quality and quantity of work the individual actually produces.

To give you some practice in deciding whether a particular concern you have about an employee is a process or outcome concern, we've composed a list of ten sample concerns bosses might have about their employees. Fill in the form 'Process and Outcome Concerns' on page 18, then check your answers with ours.

Distinguishing between process and outcome concerns is a tough area for all managers, us included. A question we find helpful in making this distinction is: 'Am I focusing on results, or am I saying to the employee, "Why can't you be more like me?"'

By now, you're probably getting a better idea who your problem employees are, and who they aren't. In chapter 3, we'll take the focus off your employees and ask you to think a little about yourself. We'll discuss some common *ineffective* tendencies of bosses. Maybe you'll see some things that are familiar.

Process and Outcome Concerns

In the space next to each statement, put a **P** if you think it's a process concern and an **O** if you think it's an outcome concern. After you finish, compare your answers to ours.

___ 1. The employee has written a quarterly report that you feel is too long and disorganised. It needs to be rewritten.

___ 2. You suspect that the employee has been dating another worker in your office. You're bothered by this, and you've been seriously considering confronting her with your suspicions.

___ 3. The company vacation policy reads: 'All employees shall take their vacations in segments of no less than five days.' One of your employees has objected strongly to this policy. He's putting a lot of pressure on you to let him take his vacation days one at a time for a string of Mondays throughout the summer months.

___ 4. You happen to overhear your receptionist speak rudely over the phone to someone who is obviously a customer. You're wondering whether you should speak to her about it.

___ 5. The employee has made an arrangement with you to put his hours in on a flexible basis, some days working as few as three hours and others working as many as twelve or fourteen. You're beginning to find his schedule frustrating because you and several of your people are having trouble reaching him when you need to have the answers to important questions.

___ 6. The employee is an exceptional salesperson, but she hates paperwork. She's failed to turn in three of the last five weekly progress reports, and you're beginning to get some pressure from your boss to get them in.

___ 7. You strongly believe that neatness is an important part of high-quality performance. One of your account executives, who's been a consistently high producer, has an office that looks like it's been stirred with a stick. You're always teasing him about this, but he doesn't seem to take the hint. You're about ready to suggest that he neaten the place up so he can be even more productive.

___ 8. You have a younger person on your staff who frequently disagrees with positions you take. Her tendency to do this is especially strong at staff meetings. You're not bothered so much by what she says as how she says it. You're ready to speak to her about it.

___ 9. Several months ago you instituted a policy that calls for employees to fill in forms indicating how they spent their time on an hourly basis. One of your younger employees has said that he strongly objects to these forms and thinks they're a waste of time. He's filled in the forms conscientiously for the first month, but now he says he doesn't want to do it any more. You're confused about how you should deal with the situation.

___ 10. One of the managers who works for you frequently conducts group working sessions with her staff. It looks like a 'gossip session' to you and you have serious doubts about their effectiveness. You're seriously thinking of speaking to her about cutting down on the number of these work sessions.

Now look at the next page and compare your answers to ours.

Process and Outcome Concerns: Answers and Discussion

__O__ 1. *Disorganised quarterly report that needs to be rewritten*
This is an outcome concern because it is clearly related to the quality of the employee's work.

__P__ 2. *Employee dating another worker*
We see this as a process concern. Even though office dating can have a negative impact on an employee's work, you don't have any evidence of that here.

__P__ 3. *Employee objects to company vacation policy*
This is a judgement call. Depending upon work schedules and priorities, we think people ought to be able to take their vacations when they want to, not when the personnel department thinks they should.

__O__ 4. *Receptionist is rude on the phone*
Rude behaviour to customers is not a matter of individual style; it's inap propriate.

__O__ 5. *Employee on flexi-time schedule is unavailable when needed*
Flexible time schedules are one thing; not being able to reach employees when you really need to is quite another.

__O__ 6. *Salesperson not turning in reports*
Even though progress reports are frequently ignored by the people who ask for them, the fact that they're not being turned in regularly, in this case, is having a negative impact on your work. Something has to give. Either your boss has to change the policy or the salesperson has to get the reports in on time.

__P__ 7. *Account executive with messy office*
We think that people with neat offices are often better organised and more efficient than those with messy offices. But we think it's the employee's productivity that should govern your suggestions regarding the neatness of his office, not the office itself.

__O__ 8. *Younger member of staff disagrees in objectionable tone at staff meetings*
We think bosses not only should tolerate disagreement from their employees, but should encourage it. The problem here is not one of disagreement. It's the disrespectful way in which the disagreement is expressed. That you can't tolerate.

__P__ 9. *Younger employee who disagrees with time sheet*
Another judgement call. In general, we think time sheets are a big waste of time. In this case, the employee has given you some empirical evidence that supports our position. He's got better things to do with his time. This does not apply to organisations whose accounting divisions bill customers according to the number of in-house hours spent on a project. A publishing house or an advertising agency, for example, needs time sheets to assess accurately the service costs that have accrued on a job, in addition to the production and manufacturing costs.

__P__ 10. *Manager frequently holds group work sessions*
Here the focus is on the way she manages rather than the results she's getting. If the results aren't so hot, then it's time to take a look at how she's getting those results.

Chapter 3

How Not to Deal with Problem Employees: Common Ineffective Tendencies

IN CHAPTER 2 we alluded to a number of ways in which you, as the boss, might be contributing to the problem of your problem employees. In this chapter, we're going to delve into that topic in a bit more detail. We're going to describe four common ineffective tendencies we've noticed in bosses when dealing with employees, especially problem employees. These ineffective tendencies are:

▶ avoiding;
▶ overreacting;
▶ complaining;
▶ lecturing.

For each tendency we'll describe what it is, why people do it and why it's bad. We'll also offer suggestions on how to overcome each ineffective tendency. As we describe each of them, we'd like you to think to yourself, 'Which one of these is most like me?' If you're like most people, you'll think you do all of them from time to time. However, our experience has shown that one usually 'fits' better than the rest. That one will be your dominant ineffective tendency.

Taking a Look at Previous Bosses

Before we talk about these tendencies, though, think about bosses you've had in the past and how they dealt with employees, especially the more challenging ones. Focus on those who did a particularly bad job of handling their problem employees. Write down some of the things they did that were particularly ineffective. Be as specific as you can. For example, if you thought one of your bosses was too overbearing, you might want to write down something like this.

'He was always criticising his staff in front of other people.'

'She was always ordering this poor person around like a drill sergeant.'

'He literally followed the man around, checking up on him about every twenty minutes.'

If you thought a boss was not firm enough with the employee, you might write something like this.

'She seemed to ignore that the girl frequently came in twenty minutes late.'

'He was always letting this person talk him into special privileges, like extra days off, that the rest of us really resented.'

'I don't think that she ever told him he wasn't doing a good job.'

Ineffective Ways of Handling Problem Employees:

Supervisor 1 _____

1. _____

2. _____

3. _____

4. _____

5. _____

Supervisor 2 _____

1. _____

2. _____

3. _____

4. _____

5. _____

As you read through this chapter, compare the ineffective tendencies we'll be describing with what you just wrote down. And don't forget to take an honest look at your own ineffective tendencies as well.

Avoiding

Avoiding simply means putting off, postponing, or deferring the act of sitting down with a problem employee to discuss the person's work performance. Charlie Waters and June Sharp are good examples of managers who have this tendency.

Charlie Waters is the owner of a medium-sized insurance agency in the suburbs of Birmingham. For the past two months each of the agents who works for him has come to him complaining about the secretary who handles policy applications and claims. They say she doesn't pay enough attention to detail and makes careless mistakes that cause them all kinds of problems. Charlie's been meaning to sit down to talk with her for several weeks now, but never seems to be able to find the time to do it.

Jane Sharp is the manager in charge of customer relations for a bank in Bristol. One of the services of the bank is preparing payrolls for local businesses. A systems analyst who works for Jane is pretty abrasive and has antagonised some of the bank's business customers. Jane knows she should talk to the analyst, but for some reason she keeps putting if off. She shared her reluctance with us:
'I know I really need to sit down and talk with John. But at the same time I'm a little afraid he might leave. He's really good at the technical stuff he does, and systems analysts are hard to find these days. Besides, he's a bit touchy. Maybe I should wait a little longer. He may be having some personal problems he needs to work through.'

Why Do Managers Avoid?

Why do bosses avoid confronting their problem employees? There are a number of reasons.

1. They hate conflict. A lot of people out there, bosses included, are what we call 'Nicists.' A nicist is a person who wants everything to be ... *nice*. They hate conflict and disharmony of any sort. So they avoid getting into situations that might get out of hand, like sitting down and discussing unpleasant or 'touchy' subjects. These bosses are the 'conflict-avoiders' of the world.

2. It's anxiety-producing. This is closely related to the first reason. Sitting down and talking with an employee about work performance makes a lot of managers and supervisors nervous, more so in the case of problem employees. Most people avoid things that make them nervous. A famous American psychiatrist, Harry Stack Sullivan, once said, 'Anxiety rules!' And that just about sums it up.

3. They fear the worst. Many bosses are afraid that giving negative feedback will just cause employees to get defensive and possibly overreact or strike back in some way. Some managers fear the employee will actually resign. This is especially true in the case of employees who have highly technical jobs, where the demand for skilled people often exceeds the pool of available job applicants. The thinking process goes something like this:

'Yes, the person is performing poorly now, but if I sit down with him to talk about his performance, I might have an even bigger problem on my hands. If the person is a member of a union then the company, or even I, could get involved in litigation. Or it could backfire in another way. He could get touchy and defensive and do an even worse job than he's doing now. And another thing that could go wrong is ... '

This is called 'catastrophic thinking', for obvious reasons. And the fact that all these untoward events rarely happen still doesn't seem to stop bosses from doing it.

4. They don't think it'll do any good. Many bosses think sitting down and talking with employees is a waste of time. One of them told us:

'Look, what do you want me to do? I've spoken to her on a number of different occasions, and there hasn't been any change. Why do you think talking to her one more time is going to do any good?'

It's frustrating when repeated efforts don't lead to change. Understandably, a lot of managers conclude, 'I give up! I've got better things to do with my time.'

5. They don't know how to do it. Most people, including us, avoid tasks we don't feel competent to perform. The same holds true for many bosses when it comes to sitting down with a problem employee. As we said earlier, most bosses get no training, or very little training, for their jobs. Even those who do get training of some sort don't usually learn how to conduct a systematic review of an employee's performance. So they think, 'What exactly should I do? How should I do it?' Not knowing how, they do nothing at all.

Why Avoiding is Bad

As understandable as it may be, we think avoiding should be avoided. Here's why.

1. Avoiding the problem won't make it go away. Yes, the thought of sitting down with Johnson to review his work performance may make you nervous. However, the consequences of *not* confronting him will usually make you a lot more uncomfortable down the line, when your boss (and other important people in the organisation) feel the impact of his incompetence. Plus, if you don't sit down with Johnson, what's his motivation to change? He may even think you're pleased with his performance. Sitting down and talking is no guarantee he'll change. But *not* doing it is a guarantee he won't.

2. The problem is likely to get worse, not better. It's an unfortunate fact that people find it very difficult to change their behaviour. If you have any doubts about this, think back to when you tried to give up smoking or lose a few pounds. Changing behaviour is just plain hard work; quite frankly, work a lot of us would just as soon avoid. This certainly holds true for problem employees, who are usually people who've had a history of taking the easy way out. Without your help, the chances that a problem employee will change for the better are very small.

Moreover, if the person doesn't change, it just makes the situation worse. You become more frustrated. Other people who work with the employee become more frustrated and begin to feel resentful. The pressure to take action keeps mounting.

3. You lose respect and your credibility drops. You're not the only person who knows who the poor performers are; other employees know as well. In fact, problem employees often make their jobs more difficult. If these other employees see you avoiding the situation and not dealing firmly with the employee, guess what happens to your respect and credibility as a supervisor? Yes, it sinks really low. To make matters worse, some of the good performers may start thinking, 'Hey, why should I work so hard around here while they just mess about?' When that starts to happen, you've really got problems!

4. It makes 'firing' someone that much harder. Many problem employees must eventually be dismissed, and the process is much easier if they've had some warning. Most organisations cannot sustain the burden of the problem employee indefinitely. However, an employee who has not been confronted about performance shortcomings prior to termination can be very difficult to handle. The first reaction is often shock, followed by disbelief, and then anger. And then, of course, there are the potential legal problems.

We're not saying that the dismissal of problem employees always goes smoothly if they've been confronted prior to receiving notice. Not at all. Getting fired is tough for anybody. But the chances are it'll go more smoothly if they've been forewarned.

5. You lose respect for yourself. After a while, chronic avoiders themselves get disgusted with what's going on. Here are all these problems, many of them crying out for their attention and yet nothing is done. At some point they have to look in the mirror and say to themselves, 'What are you going to do, avoid problems *all* your life?'

Overreacting

While it's pretty unusual to see a manager or supervisor physically strike an employee, plenty of bosses verbally abuse their employees when they become frustrated, upset or angry. Overreacting is the unnecessarily harsh or emotional manner in which bosses dump their frustration or annoyance on employees. Tom Clark is a good example.

Tom Clark is in charge of maintenance for a large company. He has an engineer working for him named Bob Driscoll. Tom views

Bob as technically competent, but he's frustrated because Bob doesn't give him direct answers to his questions. Last week at a staff meeting Tom asked Bob to give a brief report on the progress the department was making on a particular test. He didn't make it brief and Tom exploded. Among other things, he slammed his paperweight down on the desk and called Bob 'The most long-winded fool I have ever met!'

That evening Tom told his wife what happened: 'Well, right away he started off on some tangent like he always does. Well, we were running late, and I decided I just wasn't going to put up with it any more. I suppose I lost my temper and yelled at him for telling me everything *but* what I wanted to hear. Looking back on it, I wish I hadn't done it. There was this embarrassed silence, and everybody at the table looked down. And Bob wouldn't even look at me for the rest of the day. I didn't mean to hurt his feelings, but you'd think he'd have learned by now that all I want when I ask for a brief report are straightforward, *brief* answers to my questions.'

Tom's staff meeting explosion is a pretty typical example of a boss overreaction. Sometimes the episodes are a lot milder than this. And sometimes they're a lot worse. For example, one boss we know actually tore a wall phone off the wall and threw it down the hall in a fit of rage, scaring the living daylights out of every employee in the place. The stimulus for this outburst? An employee had filled out a form the wrong way. Another boss we know got upset over some employee transgression and decided to put his fist through the wall in his employee's office. He thought it was a partition wall, but it wasn't. His fist hit the brick behind plaster board and he wore a cast for nearly six months.

Why Do Managers Overreact?

There are a number of reasons why bosses overreact to employees.

1. It's what they've learned to do. We hardly ever see an adult overreactor who didn't have a mother or father who was also an overreactor. That's what they saw when they were growing up and most of them learned their lessons well. Sometimes too well.

2. It offers a powerful outlet for frustration. The tension builds up and up and up and then, 'Poof!' it's gone. All of a sudden, you feel relieved. Losing your cool has a very cleansing, purging effect.

All that tension is gone, just like that. Because it's so reinforcing, it increases the chances it'll happen again in the future.

3. It seems so justified at times. Most of us feel we have a right to get angry when we repeatedly make reasonable requests of other people that never get fulfilled. It's not uncommon for bosses to say:

'Don't you think I have a right to shout at her after I politely ask her fifteen times to do something, and she still doesn't do it? Wouldn't you get frustrated with somebody like that?'

A belief that their actions are justified—often even appropriate— is extremely common among overreactors.

4. It seems to work. After an overreacting episode, many employees scurry around and do exactly what the boss wants—for a while. The changes may not last very long, but that's not what's going through the boss's mind at the time. The boss is thinking, 'Finally, a little action around here!'

5. It give some bosses a sense of power and control. Employees do some pretty predictable things when managers lose their tempers:

▶ they look startled and frightened;
▶ they look down and remain very silent;
▶ many of them will apologise (even if they don't know what they're apologising for);
▶ for a while, they treat their supervisors with deference.

For bosses who're 'into' exercising power and control, they feel successful.

Why Overreacting Is Bad

Because frustration and anger are such primary emotional responses, it's unrealistic to expect people to stop overreacting completely, especially if it's a well-established habit. But there are some compelling reasons to keep it down to a bare minimum.

1. It can have bad physiological effects. When you get angry, a number of things happen simultaneously in your body. Your pulse rate increases, your blood pressure goes up, adrenalin starts pumping, your pupils dilate, your throat dries and so on. In short, your body mobilises itself for a fight. There's more and more evidence nowadays that, if this mobilisation process occurs too frequently, you'll end up giving yourself ulcers, high blood pressure or any number of other physical ailments that are now associated with frequent emotional upset and poor temper control.

2. It doesn't really work. It's hard to explain why, but over-reacting doesn't have a lasting effect on employee behaviour. People do tend to scurry around after the eruption; but, usually within a day or two, they go right back to their old behaviour patterns.

3. Employees lose respect for you. With some exceptions, bosses who overreact on a regular basis eventually lose the credibility and respect of their employees. Here are some examples.

▶ Employees will start withholding more and more information; they'll begin to tell their overreacting bosses only the things they think their bosses want to hear.

▶ Some employees will become passive-aggressive. That is, they'll intentionally do things to 'get back' at the boss in some way, like saying things that make the boss look bad or ridiculous.

▶ We know one employee who 'accidentally' lets it slip whenever the boss leaves the office for a haircut, a dental appointment, or for other personal reasons. And, of course, the most common way for disgruntled employees to get back is by slacking off. If enough of them do it, it really comes back to haunt the boss.

▶ Most bosses who overreact just want employees to take more responsibility and initiative. That's all. Unfortunately, the opposite usually happens. In response, employees will spend more time trying to shift the blame on to other employees than on improving their performance. Or they'll shift coming up with excuses, alibis and other ways of deflecting the boss's wrath.

4. It sometimes has destructive effects on employees. In every organisation, there are some people who are particularly sensitive or vulnerable to overreacting bosses. Unlike a lot of employees who shrug it off and say, 'It's just another one of Pat's temper tantrums,' these people take what an overreacting boss says to heart. They end up believing all those things that were said in the midst of the tirade, even though the boss didn't mean half of it. They end up with a bruised and battered self-image and remain down in the dumps for long periods of time, and often don't realise their potential.

Complaining

Complaining means unloading your frustration over a problem employee on *somebody else*, not on the employee. Since we've been as guilty of it as most, we thought we might as well use ourselves as an example.

A number of years ago we were both in charge of a government-funded project to develop a series of instructional units on career development. The project lasted for several years, with the two of us responsible for hiring and supervising staff. Most of our staff members were problem employees in one form or another. Our secretaries either couldn't type or thought typing was beneath them; our instructional developers either couldn't write or were extremely defensive about any suggestions for improvement on their designs; our audio-visual people thought they knew everything, despite turning out sub-par work on a regular basis; and on and on. At times it seemed we were floundering in a sea of incompetence.

Even though *we* were completely responsible for the fix we were in, we didn't see it that way at the time. We'd spend hours every week commiserating with each other about how nobody could do anything right and how unfair it was for us to have to spend nights and weekends cleaning up after everybody else's mistakes.

Hindsight has given us a much clearer perspective on what was really happening. Yes, we had problem employees. There's no doubt about that. But we were problem bosses as well, guilty of all the ineffective tendencies we've been talking about, including complaining. And by complaining to each other, we were making the mistake all bosses make when they complain to other people about employees—we were talking to the wrong people. If we had spent only one-fifth of the time sitting down with staff to review their work performance as we did complaining to each other, we would have ended up with much more effective employees, and a lot more free time in the evenings and at weekends.

Why Do Managers Complain?

These are the main reasons we—and most other managers—complain.

1. Everybody complains once in a while. Unfortunately, complaining is a very common habit in our society. You can't be

around other people for an hour, much less a day, and not hear
someone complain about something: the weather, the crime rate,
corrupt politicians, giant corporations that place profits above everything else, selfish relatives, unappreciative kids, and so on. One of
our friends recently said: 'Complaining's a bad habit, like overeating
and smoking. People know it doesn't do them any good, but it's a
very tough habit to break.' We agree.

**2. It creates the illusion you're doing something about the
problem.** When you complain, you usually select someone who'll
give you a sympathetic ear, not someone who'll challenge your view
and defend the employee. No wonder you end up feeling better after
a good complaint session. Here's how it works: you express your
frustration, the other person listens attentively, and then says those
magic words, 'I understand exactly how you feel.' Once you get the
message that you have every right to feel the way you do, you walk
away feeling less upset. You feel like you've got a better angle on the
problem and you see things a little more clearly now. In reality, you
haven't changed a thing. But you certainly feel better.

3. You usually get some support for your opinions. This is
closely related to the previous point. When you complain about
employees, you're usually looking for support for your view—some
corroborative testimony, as it were. You're upset and puzzled by the
employee's behaviour. So, you're really asking the question, 'Is it just
me, or do you see the same things I do in Bob Johnson?' You're looking
for confirmation that your perceptions of the employee are accurate.
And you often get it, which increases the chances that you'll complain
again in the future.

Why Complaining Is Bad

There are several reasons why complaining to other people about
employees is ineffective.

1. You're talking to the wrong person. When you complain
to another person about a problem employee, you're talking to the
wrong person. It's the employee you should be talking to.

But be sure not to confuse complaining with seeking advice. If you
go to another person to seek help on how *you* can do a better job of
coping with an employee, that's not complaining because the focus
is on you, not the employee. When you complain, you're laying the

responsibility for the problem on the employee. However, when you seek advice or help from another person on how to deal more effectively with an employee, you're accepting some of the responsibility for the problem, and you're taking some positive action to solve it. It's a subtle distinction, but an important one.

2. People will eventually think less of you. There are two important factors to think about here.

▶ To whom are you complaining?
▶ How frequently are you complaining?

It's one thing to complain to a spouse or a trusted colleague about a problem. It's quite another, however, to complain to colleagues you don't know very well or to the employee's co-workers. Once you do either of these, trust and respect for you as a manager begin to erode. Perhaps the most negative consequence is that people will stop being open with you for fear you can't keep anything confidential. The more you complain, the lower your credibility drops. The more you complain, the more people see you as someone who's only interested in talking about problems, not solving them.

3. Complaining is a big waste of time. We honestly believe complaining doesn't move you even a fraction of a step closer to solving the problem. If anything, complaining just lets you temporarily reduce your frustration, and fools you into thinking you're doing something constructive. It's a seductive habit that's hard to break, but it's well worth the effort.

Lecturing

We define *lecturing* as telling employees—often in a condescending and patronising tone—what they already know or aren't ready to hear. It's such a common managerial practice that it's difficult to recognise. Dave Richards's boss is an example.

Dave Richards has submitted a draft quarterly report to his boss, Paula Pearson. The next day, as Dave and Paula are passing in the hall, Paula stops Dave and says, 'Dave, you've got to remember to include an executive summary and cost figures with your quarterly report. Those are the only things the CEO really looks at.' Dave, looking a little puzzled and then slightly annoyed, replies, 'Paula, give me a little credit, will you? I know that as well as you do. I just wanted to get your reactions before we sent the final copy up to the CEO.'

Here's another case:

Judy Morris is an up-and-coming account executive for a large distributor of business machines. She's just finished making a presentation of the company's newest product line to the senior members of the purchasing department of a large potential customer. Her boss, Tom Jones, has come along to see her in action. From the customer's response after the presentation, Judy has the feeling it went over very well, and she's obviously pleased. As they walk out of the building, Judy and Tom have the following conversation.

Judy: I think it went pretty well, I have a feeling we're going to get a big order from them.
Tom: I think it went pretty well, too. (*Pausing for just a second*) But I think you've got some things to learn about making a presentation ...
Judy: (*Startled and then frowning and looking down with a deflated expression but saying nothing.*)
Tom: For one thing, Judy, whenever you make a presentation, you've got to establish your credibility in the first five minutes. If you don't, you're in trouble. Now, you recouped today, but if you hadn't, we wouldn't have a snowball's chance at the sale. Another thing, you always have to try to close as soon as you can. So you need to have order forms already filled in, so all they have to do is sign.
Judy: (*Still frowning and looking down.*)
Tom: And another thing ...

In both situations, the managers made the mistake of talking before they were sure their employees were ready to listen. Both bosses just assumed their employees were ready to hear what they had to say, in spite of some pretty strong evidence to the contrary (e.g. Judy's frowning and looking down while Tom was talking). This is one of the reasons we sometimes define lecturing as 'talking to someone who's not listening to you.'

In the future, when you find yourself telling employees something and they start frowning, scowling, looking down, shaking their heads or arguing back, you can be pretty sure you don't have a receptive audience. In our listening skills chapter we'll talk about how to raise a person's receptivity to what you've got to say.

Why Do Managers Lecture?

There are two major reasons why bosses lecture their employees.

1. It lessens their anxiety.   Lecturing is a very common way for bosses to handle their anxiety when they see employees doing something ineffective or counterproductive. For example, the manager in a branch bank might observe a new teller respond brusquely to a rude customer. The manager begins to feel upset and anxious.

To bring down her level of anxiety, the manager immediately tells the employee what he's done wrong and why he shouldn't have done it. In our example, the manager waits until the rude customer leaves and then says to the teller: 'John, I know that customer was a bit of an idiot, but he is a depositor, and we can't afford to alienate our depositors. We've got to try to be nice to everybody in here, even the idiots. So, the next time ... ' Delivering the lecture makes the manager feel better. The fact that the employee didn't hear a bit of it doesn't seem to matter.

2. They don't know any better.   Maybe a more polite way to say this is that they don't have the skills to behave any differently. When we say skills here, we're talking about listening skills—something we'll be talking about later (see Chapter 8). Here, though, we just mean that bosses often don't know when to talk and when to listen. They don't know how to use listening skills to make other people more receptive to their feedback.

When you're nervous and intent on telling employees what they've done wrong, it's easy to ignore cues that they're not listening: they look down, appear embarrassed, start to get upset or angry, try to defend themselves and so on. To continue to talk *at* employees who are doing these things is a waste of time. It's far better to let them talk first, giving them a full opportunity to say what's on their minds, before you start talking. Does this take patience? And skill? Yes. But, it's the only effective way to deal with the problem of giving feedback to someone who's not receptive. We'll discuss this in more detail later.

Why Lecturing Is Bad

We could list lots of reasons why lecturing is ineffective, but most of them boil down to this: it's a big turnoff. All of us have been lectured to throughout our lives. It started with our parents. Then our teachers and college lecturers got into the act. Our coaches and religious leaders piled it on. And by the time we started working for a living, we were pretty tired of it.

Most employees resent bosses who lecture because they don't like being talked *at*. They want to be listened *to*. They want to believe their opinions and feelings are important to their supervisors. As one employee said to us, 'I realise the boss has the final say. But I would like him to extend the courtesy of asking me what I think before he makes a decision.' In our opinion, this is the single biggest thing bosses can do to treat employees with dignity and respect.

How to Control Ineffective Tendencies

The best way to eliminate ineffective tendencies is to replace them with the strategies and techniques we'll describe in the rest of the book. In the meantime, though, there are a couple of ways to help keep your ineffective tendencies under control.

1. Learn to recognise immediately when you're avoiding, over-reacting, complaining, or lecturing.
2. Try to get yourself to stop these tendencies as soon as you recognise them.

Recognise Your Ineffective Tendencies

To recognise when you're behaving ineffectively will take some practice. To help get you started, we've listed thirteen short descriptions of things you might catch yourself doing over the next week or so. Read over the form below and fill it in before you go on.

Ineffective Tendencies

In the space next to each description, write the letter:
A if you think it describes avoiding,
O if you think it describes overreacting,
C if you think it describes complaining, or
L if you think it describes lecturing.
Leave the space blank if you think the example describes some other behaviour.
Once you finish labelling each description, compare your answers to ours.

_____ 1. You say to yourself, 'I really have to speak to Terry about his tardiness. As soon as I get this report finished, I'm going to do it.'

_____ 2. You're sitting on a bus on the way to work and thinking about which one of your salespeople you're going to ask to make the presentation at Acme Tyres. Your thoughts turn to Keith because there's a lull in his schedule right now. But you know that Keith makes lousy presentations, so you start thinking about assigning it to Rachel or even doing it yourself.

_____ 3. You're driving home with the manager from another department. You say 'Do you want to hear what Celia did today? Remember I told you that I had asked her at least five times to stop sending those purchase orders out? Well guess what ... '

_____ 4. You're at a cocktail party talking to a friend whose judgement you respect. You say, 'Pat, I'm having a problem with one of my people at the office. Maybe you could give me some advice on how to handle it because everything I've tried so far hasn't worked.'

_____ 5. You've just finished reading an evaluation that one of your employees has written on the market prospects for your product line in the southeast. Although you think the evaluation has some merit, you see a lot of ways it could be improved. You take the evaluation into the employee's office, and after a little chat, you say, 'Bill, I'd like to give you some feedback on the evaluation you wrote. (_You pause as Bill nods and leans forward._) Okay, let me start off with some of the really positive aspects of what you wrote ... '

_____ 6. You've just been told off by your boss for something that one of your workers has done. You're about to get up and do the same thing with your employee, but you catch yourself. You stick your head inside your secretary's office and say, 'Terry, I have to go outside for a while; I'll be back in a quarter of an hour.'

_____ 7. You've made a commitment to yourself to meet with one of your minority employees who has not been performing effectively. The next day you read in the newspaper that a large corporation has had to pay damages to a group of minority workers who claimed that they had been discriminated against by their company. As you read the article, your anxiety starts to rise and you begin to have second thoughts about speaking to the employee.

_____ 8. You've just tried to reach one of your salespeople on the intercom, but there's no answer. You need to see him right away, so you try buzzing him five minutes later. Still no answer. Annoyed, you call your secretary in and say, 'Sally, do you know where the hell Jack is? I can never find him when I need him.'

_____ 9. You're the foreman in a precision machine-building company. You're having a conversation with one of your toolmakers about one of his co-workers. You say, 'Pat, what do you think is wrong with Bill, anyway? He's got a good head on his shoulders, and he's a damn good mechanic, but he doesn't listen to anything I tell him. Like just last week, he did the exact opposite of what I ... '

_____ 10. You're the chief at a university teaching hospital. One of the junior doctors on your staff neglected to give you an update on a patient who's recovering from a complicated appendectomy. You're very upset about this. As soon as you see the doctor in the hall, you stop her and say, 'What were you thinking about last night? Forgetting to tell me about Mrs Thompson's condition is inexcusable! I don't ever want that sort of thing to happen again!'

_____ 11. You supervise fifteen customer account representatives for an air freight company. One of your representatives is sitting in your office telling you about how upset he is over an argument he had this morning with a fellow representative. As soon as he finishes describing the argument, you say, 'Tom, the first thing you've got to realise is that there are many different kinds of people in the world. Why, I remember years ago when I first started working in this business ... '

_____ 12. A fellow manager tells you that one of your workers has been complaining about you behind your back to a number of other people in the company. As soon as you hear this, you call the employee into your office, and before he even sits down, you say, 'John, what's this I hear about you complaining to other people about me? If you've got something to say about me, say it to my face. Don't go complaining to everybody else in the plant!'

_____ 13. In a staff meeting, one of your up-and-coming managers said something that upset and threatened one of your senior managers. The next time you see the younger manager you say to her, 'Karen, I think you came on a little strong with Bob Wilson the other day. Let me tell you some things about him that you may not be aware of. For one thing, he's a lot older than you, even though he doesn't have your raw talent. Another thing is, even if you don't feel a lot of respect for him, you've got to ... '

Now look at pages 37-38 and compare your answers to ours.

Ineffective Tendencies: Answers and Discussion

A 1. *You decide you'll speak to Terry after you've finished your report.* Even though you appear to be making a commitment to deal with Terry, you're avoiding by not setting an immediate date.

A 2. *Although Keith has the time, you decide to give the assignment to someone who makes better presentations.* You've identified a major area that Keith needs to work on—making better presentations. By focusing your attention on Rachel or yourself as replacements, you're avoiding the problem of how to help Keith improve his presentations skills.

C 3. *You complain to a colleague in another department about your employee, Celia.* Your colleague is probably getting pretty tired of hearing about Celia, especially since he can't do anything to help her change.

____ 4. *You ask a friend whose judgement you respect for advice on how you can handle a problem with an employee.* This might sound like complaining, but it's not. You're asking Pat for some thoughts on what you can do about the problem. When you complain, your focus is almost always on the other person.

____ 5. *You want to give your employee some suggestions on how to improve a report he wrote. When he nods, you begin noting some of the positive aspects.* This might sound like lecturing, but we don't think it is. In this case, you got a clear signal from Bill that he was interested in hearing your feedback.

____ 6. *Your boss has just blamed you for an employee's mistake. You take a 15-minute break before dealing with the problem.* You almost overreacted, but you stopped yourself and took time to get your thoughts together before speaking to the employee.

A 7. *You have second thoughts about speaking to a minority worker about the person's ineffective performance after reading about a discrimination case.* This is a clear example of avoiding. You're allowing possible (but not very probable) negative consequences to stop you from facing a problem that has to be dealt with.

C 8. *When you're unable to reach an employee, you express your exasperation to your secretary.* If you wrote an O, we probably wouldn't argue with you. However, we think this is a better example of complaining. Your secretary can't change Jack's behaviour. You only lose respect in her eyes by running down Jack in that way.

C 9. *You criticise one of your toolmakers in a conversation with his co-worker.* This is a clear example of complaining. It's especially bad because you're complaining to Pat, Bill's co-worker, who's very likely to relay your comments back to Bill.

O 10. *You shout at a junior doctor who forgot to bring you up to date on a patient's condition.* You certainly told her off, didn't you?

L 11. *You offer some 'words to the wise' to one of your representatives who is still upset over an argument with a co-worker.* Even though your advice to Tom may be very good, he's not going to listen to what you have to say right now. There's no sense in giving him suggestions until he's shown you that he's ready to listen to them.

O 12. *You tell off an employee who has been talking behind your back about you..* Same as 10!

L 13. *You chide one of your younger workers for intimidating a senior manager, then offer her some advice.* Again, your advice here may be very sound. But Karen has given you no evidence that she's ready to hear it. Unless you're sure that she's receptive to what you have to say, you're probably lecturing.

Stop Your Ineffective Tendencies

As soon as you catch yourself starting to engage in one of the ineffective tendencies, tell yourself to *stop* before you actually 'commit the crime'. Just imagine a huge hand appearing before your face that says:

 **Hold it!**

Using the *Hold It!* cue will buy you some time to:

▶ think about a more effective strategy if you're about to lecture an employee or complain to somebody else about an employee;
▶ go outside to cool off if you're about to overreact; or
▶ make a commitment to do something about the problem right away if you're in the process of avoiding.

In this chapter we've taken an in-depth look at a number of common, but ineffective, ways of dealing with employees, especially problem employees. We've also tried to get you thinking about which of the ineffective tendencies is most characteristic of you.

In the next chapter, we'll take a look at problem employees from a slightly different perspective—a 'relationship' perspective.

Chapter 4

Problem Employees or Problem Relationships?

IN CHAPTER 1 we talked about problem employees and who they are. One of the things we said there was that problem employees are not a clearly identifiable group. We also said that whether or not a person is called a problem employee depends on a number of factors: (1) who the boss is; (2) who the employee is; (3) what job the person's in; and (4) what the organisation is like.

In this chapter we want to talk about problem employees from a different point of view—what we call a 'relationship' perspective. We want to say that another reason people become problem employees is because they're struggling in a relationship with another person, that other person being their boss. Let us explain.

Over the past ten years, we've noticed that many so-called problem employees weren't performing poorly because of the typical reasons: personal problems, negative attitudes, being in the wrong job, and so on. These employees were performing poorly because they weren't getting along with their bosses. In fact, the boss and the employee had a pretty bad *relationship* with each other. Maybe the boss treated the employee with contempt or disdain, and the employee had no respect or affection for the boss. Even though it's a boss and employee who are struggling with each other, the situation looks suspiciously like a bad marriage.

In many ways, it was. Just think for a minute about a marriage you know that hit the rocks and finally ended. When you step back from the heat of the battle, you can see that both people were pretty miserable. Generally, you also see that both people were contributing to the problems in the relationship. But that's not the way the individuals in a bad marriage view the situation. The wife thinks she has a 'problem' husband, and can easily come up with examples to bolster her case. The husband thinks he has a 'problem' wife, and he too has considerable documentation. Caught up in the struggle, both people see the other one as primarily responsible for the 'fix' they're in. The husband blames the wife, and vice versa.

This tendency to blame the other person is called 'externalising'. Rather than look inward and accept some of the responsibility, it is shifted or externalised—to the other person. The black hat is placed on the other person—where it seems to belong—and the white hat on ourselves. It's something all people do when they're struggling with one another. We've certainly done it enough times ourselves when we've run into problems in our relationships.

It's pretty much the same thing with bosses and employees who are struggling with each other: the employee blames the boss, and vice versa. The boss thinks he has a problem employee. The employee thinks she has a problem boss. When we step back and try to take an objective look at the situation, what do we see. A problem boss? A problem employee? Often, neither of these. What we often see is a *problem relationship.*

In this chapter we want you to think about your problem employee from a 'relationship' point of view. We'll discuss several concepts that may help you see things from a new perspective. For example:

▶ A concept we call the 'vital signs' of a relationship.
▶ A new approach where you try to improve an employee's performance by concentrating on the things you can do to improve the *quality of your relationship* with that person. In contrast to the well-known expression 'people management,' we call this approach 'relationship management'.
▶ Some thoughts about what you can do to become a better 'relationship manager' in your dealings with employees and other important people in your life.

The 'Vital Signs' of a Relationship

One of the best ways to 'get a handle' on this somewhat elusive subject is to compare good relationships to bad ones. Think for a minute about people you know who have a healthy relationship. Try to identify what it is about these people and their relationship that makes it good? Then think of people who have an absolutely lousy relationship with each other. What is it about them and their relationship that makes it bad? While you're thinking about these good and bad examples, we'd like to introduce you to a concept we call the 'vital signs' of a relationship.

We believe a relationship is a lot like a human body—both have 'vital signs' you can look at to determine how healthy or sick they are. For a body, the vital signs are things like temperature, pulse, blood pressure, and respiration. If the vital signs get too weak, the body is in danger and death may result.

For a relationship, the vital signs aren't as clear. However, we've come up with four which have stood the test of time. They are trust, respect, affection, and confidence. (We've given them the acronym TRAC to help you remember them.) When these signs get too low, a relationship, like a body, can expire.

Since coming up with the concept, we've asked thousands of people to rate each other on TRAC. First we ask them to imagine a scale from zero to ten, in which zero is as low as you can go and ten is the highest. Then we ask them the following four questions—on a scale from zero to ten:

▶ how much do you *trust* the other person?
▶ how much do you *respect* the other person?
▶ how much basic *affection*, or liking do you feel for the other person?
▶ how much overall *confidence* do you have in the other person?

What we've discovered is what you'd expect. People in unhappy and unproductive relationships give each other low TRAC ratings. And people in happy and productive relationships give each other high TRAC ratings.

Now we'd like you to TRAC-rate an employee. Actually, we'd like you to do three things.

1. Think of an employee you've been struggling with, someone you consider a 'problem' employee. Frame that person clearly in your mind's eye. Then, on a scale from zero to ten, rate the person on Trust, Respect, Affection, and Confidence. Don't worry too much about how to define these terms. Just go ahead and make the ratings.

2. When you finish, think about *why* you rated the employee as you did. Let's say you rated your employee 5—7—8—4 on the four dimensions of TRAC. These numbers just didn't come out of nowhere. They're based on things the employee does (or doesn't

do), either occasionally or on a regular basis. Think about those things and jot them down on a sheet of paper if you like. Do this for each of the four dimensions.

3. Think about what the employee would have to do differently to get higher ratings from you on each of the four dimensions. Try to describe these things as specifically as you can. (By the way, we've only seen a few examples of people giving each other 10s across the board; and every single time it was a couple during the 'honeymoon' period of their relationship. We've *never* seen a boss and an employee give each other all 10s, regardless of the stage of their relationship.)

Now that you've TRAC-rated your employee, we'd like to tell you some of the things we've learned about TRAC and TRAC ratings over the years.

1. TRAC ratings change over time. TRAC ratings are dynamic, even volatile. The ratings you just gave your employee may be quite different from those you would have made six months ago, and they may be quite different from the ones you'll make a year from now.

2. The general trend for ratings is slowly downward over time. If you look at most relationships, personal and professional, the general trend is for TRAC ratings to go down slowly over the years. Sometimes, they go down so slowly the participants don't even recognise it when it's happening. Then, after a year or so, they notice the difference and it surprises them.

3. Sometimes TRAC ratings drop precipitously. While the general trend is slowly downward, sometimes a TRAC rating will drop precipitously. In the romantic arena, this can happen when one spouse finds out the other one has had an affair—when a rating on trust can drop from 10 to 0 overnight. In the work arena, the same thing happens after an employee makes a major mistake or error of judgement. The boss's trust or confidence ratings drop like a stone and the boss says things like, 'I've completely lost confidence in him' or 'I just don't trust her any more'.

4. It's hard to build ratings back up once they've gone down. Once ratings have gone down, especially when they've dropped precipitously, it takes a long time and a lot of effort to build them back up. Take the wayward spouse example above. Let's say the husband who had the affair sees the error of his ways. He ends the affair, gets into marriage counselling with his wife, and works hard over the next six months to 'save' the marriage and recapture what he and his wife once had with each other. It's now six months later and he's absolutely sure he'll never cheat on his wife again. What's his current rating on trust? He thinks he deserves a 7, maybe an 8. What's he actually getting from his wife? He's lucky if it's back up to 3 or maybe 4. She's been 'burned' and she doesn't want to be taken for a fool again. His 'sentence' is a lot stiffer than any judge would hand out. And he's going to be on probation for a *very* long time.

The same kind of thing happens with your employees when they make mistakes, especially when it's a big-time error. Once they've fallen from grace—and seen a trust or a confidence rating from you drop—it's hard for them to get back into your good graces. Like the wife above, you've been burned. And you're going to be *very cautious* as you think about the future, despite the employee's protestations that it'll never happen again.

5. TRAC-rating is a two-way street. You may not have been thinking about it when you were rating your employee earlier, but guess what? While you were rating the employee, the employee was rating you. Because people are so 'locked in' to their own perspective, they tend to forget this fact when they're TRAC-rating their spouses or romantic partners, their children, their employees, and even their customers. (In fact, we think most businesses would be far better off if they occasionally asked their customers to TRAC-rate the company and its key employees—and then paid attention to what the customers said as they explained their ratings.) In a barely conscious way, all people are constantly TRAC-rating each other.

6. Bosses aren't good at 'guesstimating' the TRAC ratings they get from employees. We've asked managers to think about how their employees would TRAC-rate them and we often get a smug response—one that goes something like this: 'Well, I think I know my people pretty well. And I think I've got a pretty good handle on how they'd rate me on TRAC.'

It's not uncommon for these bosses to 'guesstimate' that they're probably getting 7s, 8s, and 9s on the four dimensions of TRAC. However, when we sit down with the very employees who work for these bosses and say, 'Look, we're not going to say anything to your boss; this is strictly between you and us', guess what happens? What kind of TRAC ratings do they actually give these very same bosses who expected high ratings? Usually it's closer to 3, 4 and 5 than it is to 7, 8 or 9. (And, quite frankly, we almost always see a few 2s, 1s, and 0s thrown in.) We usually offer the following advice to bosses: Once you've estimated how your employees would TRAC-rate you, subtract two or three points from each estimate and you'll probably be closer to the true figure.

7. People, especially bosses, are usually surprised by the TRAC ratings they get.   A few years ago, a man who attended one of our seminars was 'taken' with the idea of TRAC. He went back home and asked all eighteen people who worked for him to rate him. He even developed a confidential rating form and instructed his secretary to gather up the forms so the anonymity of the employees would be guaranteed. Apparently, this man considered himself a pretty good manager, so he was expecting some high ratings. However, when the secretary finally tallied up the forms, his average TRAC scores were between 4 and 5 and there were quite a few very low ratings.

According to his secretary, who called us and told us what happened, his first reaction was total shock. But, after a few days, he recovered and called another meeting of the entire staff. He looked around the conference table and said in a firm tone, 'OK, we're going to do this again!' He paused for just a second and added, 'And this time, we're going to do it right!' Like many other bosses we've known—and like us, if the truth be told—he viewed the lower than expected ratings as wrong or flawed in some way.

8. Low TRAC ratings and poor performance almost always go together.   This may be the most important thing we've learned over the years. And perhaps the most important thing we want to say here. Whenever we see people performing ineffectively, we look for low TRAC ratings. Before we talk about how this works with employees, let's look once again at how this plays itself out in the personal domain.

Let's go back to our wayward husband for a moment. We'd probably all agree that his is a good example of 'poor' performance on the part of a husband. However, if we went back and looked at the TRAC ratings he gave his wife just prior to the affair, we wouldn't be surprised if he gave *her* pretty low TRAC ratings. In fact, if he had rated his wife high, he probably wouldn't have had the affair in the first place. The whole thing raises some good questions about how to look at something like an affair. Is it the contemptible act of a vile person? Or is it a manifestation of a troubled relationship?

Let's take another personal example, an adolescent who's almost flunking out of school, or one who is in trouble with the authorities. These are good examples of 'poor' performance on the part of teenagers. But what if we went to that same teenager and said, 'We'd like you to rate both of your parents on TRAC.' We guarantee you that one (or both) parents would get very low marks. So what do we have here? A bad child? Or a teenager who's struggling in a relationship with some pretty significant people in his or her life?

It's often quite similar with employees. They start off a new job full of enthusiasm, hoping this will be the job where they can really begin to soar. However, after a while, they begin to have some 'boss problems'. Maybe the boss is excessively critical or a bit of an overreactor. Or maybe she's an avoider who gives only the blandest feedback and who never confronts critical problems on the job. Maybe he's so concerned with his career that he never gives any help to employees. Or maybe the boss is an over-controlling type who must have everything done her way. What happens in these cases? Gradually, the employee becomes demotivated, and this shows up clearly in the boss's lowered TRAC ratings. At about the same time, the employee's performance begins to deteriorate a bit. What do we have here? A problem employee? Yes, in part. A problem boss? Yes, that too, in part. Or, do we really have a problem relationship?

More and more, we've begun to see 'performance problems' as symptoms of an underlying 'relationship problem'. So, if bosses want to correct what they see as an employee performance problem, they should do whatever they can to improve their relationship with the employee. As the relationship improves, so will the employee's performance. Usually. (Remember, the last chapter of this book is called, 'What Do I Do If None of This Works?')

Improving Employee Performance by Improving Your Relationship with Employees

Our message is pretty simple: if you want to see an improvement in an employee's performance, improve the quality of your relationship with that person. But how do you improve a relationship? What, specifically, should you do to make it better? The most important advice we can give you is this: *try out the ten-step performance improvement process.*

In the second part of this book we'll present a ten-step 'performance improvement process' you can use with your employees. When we came up with it more than ten years ago, we thought of it as a good *problem solving* and *performance-improving* process. And experience proved that it worked pretty well. However, what we pleasantly discovered over the years was that it's also a very good relationship-improving process. That is, when bosses used it with the specific goal of improving an employee's performance in mind, they achieved another goal as well: a better relationship (i.e. their employees began to rate them higher on trust, respect, affection, and confidence). In a way we couldn't see ten years ago, we now know *why* this is true.

As you'll see when you get into the book, the heart of the ten-step process is a face-to-face meeting with your employee. In this meeting, you'll do several important things:

First, *you'll listen* to the employee in a way you've probably never done before. You'll draw the employee out—fully and completely—on such topics as:

▶ how things are going in general on the job;
▶ any problems the employee is currently experiencing on the job;
▶ what you could do to make his job less frustrating and more satisfying in the future, and
▶ what the employee thinks he's doing particularly well on the job *and* the areas where he thinks he could stand to improve.

After listening, *you'll talk* to the employee in a way you may not have before. You'll give the employee direct and specific feedback on:

▶ things you think the employee is doing particularly well on the job, and;
▶ areas where you think the employee could stand to improve.

You'll form a performance agreement in which *both of you, not just the employee,* will set some specific goals for the immediate future, including:

▶ what the employee is going to be working on to improve her work performance; and
▶ what you're going to be doing to help the employee improve *as well as* what you'll be doing to make her job more satisfying and less frustrating in the future.

By doing these three things—and a few others we'll be suggesting—you'll meet some important employee *needs*. Identifying and meeting key employee needs goes to the heart of what 'relationship management' means. We talk about these needs at various points throughout the book. For now, though, the major ones are:

- ▶ the need to be listened to;
- ▶ the need for helpful, constructive feedback;
- ▶ the need to be treated with dignity and respect;
- ▶ the need to feel somebody 'cares'; and
- ▶ the need for mutuality and reciprocity in a relationship.

When bosses meet needs like these, they almost automatically improve their relationships with employees. It's that simple. And with an improved relationship, they often see an improvement—sometimes a dramatic one—in employee performance.

We want to be very clear about one thing before we go on. You don't necessarily have to 'agree with' all the relationship stuff we've been talking about in this chapter. You can still achieve the goal of improved employee performance by just using the performance improvement process. That's classic 'people management' thinking, and we have no quarrel with it. However, if you want to go a bit further, there are several other things you can do to improve your 'relationship management' skills, as follows.

1. Recognise that you *are* in a 'relationship' with your employee. If you're like most managers and supervisors, you probably don't see yourself as being in an important relationship with your employee. You may even be thinking, 'Hey, this is just business.' But, even if that's the way it *seems*, you and your employee have a very important *relationship* with each other. It may be different in some key ways from your personal or family relationships, but it's similar to them in many ways as well. The two of you spend a good deal of time with each other and you're inextricably linked together as a result of your positions in the organisation. The question isn't whether or not you have a relationship with each other, but what kind of relationship it is.

2. Think about how 'relationship-orientated' you are. Forget about your employee for a moment and think about how important relationships are to you in general and how much you think about them on a day-to-day basis. We call this 'relationship orientation.'

Think about your spouse or romantic partner. Think about your children, if you're a parent. Think about your family and other close friends. In general, how important are these key relationships to you?

More important, how much time do you spend on a daily or weekly basis thinking about and 'working on' your relationships with these people? (Hint: if you *say* these relationships are important, but never seem to find the time to focus on them because of more pressing matters, that's important evidence to pay attention to; it probably means you have a low 'relationship orientation'. Because of the way people are conditioned in our culture, relationships are generally something women place more importance on than men (although there are lots of exceptions to this general rule). However, it's an area *everybody* can improve in if they set their minds to it.

3. Think about how well you handle your relationships. Here are some questions that will help you decide how good you are at managing your relationships.

▶ when a problem or 'touchy' subject arises in a relationship, how do you typically handle it? Are you good at sitting down quickly to discuss the matter, before it gets out of hand? Or do you avoid the problem and delay discussion until it becomes so bad you finally have to face it?

▶ when you sit down to discuss a relationship problem or 'touchy' subject, how good a listener are you? Do you give other people a chance to express their thoughts and feelings? Or are you a nonstop talker who's always saying what's on your mind and rarely listening to what others have to say? Are you an interrupter? When you disagree with people, do you let them say what's on their minds or do you jump on them right away?

▶ when you talk about your thoughts and emotions, do you express yourself in a clear and organised way, so the other person knows exactly what you're thinking and feeling? Or are you so disorganised, emotional or inarticulate that you hardly ever get your points across as well as you'd like?

These all involve important relationship *skills*. We'll be discussing skills like these throughout the book. For now, though, think about the question: 'How skilfully do I handle my relationships?' Ask a few very close friends for their honest opinions as well. The answers may surprise you.

4. Think about making 'relationship management' a higher priority. It's easy for us to take our important relationships for granted and *not* do the things we know we *should* do. Like:

▶ spending time with our children, even though there's football on TV or that quarterly report is coming up soon;

▶ sitting down and listening patiently to things that are important to our intimate partners, even though they may not be all that important to us;

▶ every now and then, doing something special for a child, a spouse, or a friend, without a 'hidden agenda' or expectation the favour will be returned;

▶ making sure we've asked for the employee's view of a problem at work before offering our own opinion; and

▶ asking an employee the question: 'What can I do to make your job here more satisfying and less frustrating?'

In our view, a relationship is like a garden. People plant seeds in the hopes of reaping a bountiful harvest and enjoying the fruits of their efforts. But once those seeds are planted, people vary enormously in how hard they work on their gardens. Some forget about the maintenance work completely. The garden becomes overgrown with weeds and the seedlings never become healthy and hearty plants. What they had once dreamed about becomes a big disappointment. Other people work hard at their gardens. They put in a lot of time watering the soil, picking out weeds, adding nutrients, protecting the garden from pests, and so on. What they had once only dreamed about becomes a reality.

One of our good friends always reminds us that a priority is not what people say is important to them, but what they actually spend time on. If he's right—and we believe he is—making relationships more of a priority simply means finding more time for those relationships. If you can't find the time, maybe it's not as much of a priority as you thought.

5. Think about how you can improve your TRAC ratings, personally and professionally. This is something we'd like you to just *think* about now. You can *do* something about it after you finish the book, when you've had a chance to digest what we've said fully.

As we said earlier, the TRAC ratings you're currently getting from your employees are probably nowhere near what they could be. So spend a little time thinking about the question, 'what would I have to do to get higher TRAC ratings from all the people who work for me?'

Don't stop there, though. Find someone who knows you and your work situation well. Make sure it's someone you trust and who has the guts to be honest with you. Explain the concept of TRAC to this person and then ask this question 'Based on everything you know about me as a person, and as a boss, what are some things I could start doing right away to get higher ratings from my employees on each of the four dimensions of TRAC: trust, respect, affection, and confidence?'

When the person starts talking, use the listening skills we cover in Chapter 8. Don't interrupt, counter, argue or get defensive. just listen, without responding. Let the advice 'incubate' in your mind for several days. If you can, interview more than one person. Your goal is to identify a number of specific things you need to work on to be better at 'managing your relationships' with employees.

We're going to suggest you *don't* directly ask employees to rate you on TRAC, for several reasons. First and foremost, by asking 'The Question' we mentioned above, you'll already get most of the information about what you need to work on to improve your TRAC ratings. Second, since we don't suggest anywhere that you *formally* rate employees on TRAC, we don't think it's necessary for them to rate you. Third, we always get a little nervous when it comes to confidential ratings—they always seem to have a way of becoming public or falling into the wrong hands. And, finally, we don't really think of TRAC as a psychometric test, but more as a thought-provoking concept. So use it to stimulate your thinking, not to gather data.

Also think about the other important roles you play besides that of boss—spouse, romantic partner, parent, son or daughter, good friend, etc. Think about what you could do to get higher TRAC ratings from people in each of these relationships.

Here, you can also use the 'interview a close friend' technique. However, we think it would be better if you actually went to the people you have a 'personal' relationship with and asked 'The Question' of them: 'What could I do to make our relationship more satisfying and less frustrating for you?' Once again, use good listening skills to get people to respond openly and candidly.

We've now come to the end of Part I of the book. In this section we've tried to do a number of things.

- ▶ In Chapter 1, we talked about 'Who are Problem Employees?' and tried to profile them for you.
- ▶ In Chapter 2, we talked about how you know problem employees when you see them. We focused on the problem of confusing

process with *outcome* and suggested some ways for making sure someone you consider a problem employee really is one.

▶ In Chapter 3, we described four common ineffective tendencies of bosses—avoiding, overreacting, complaining, and lecturing—and asked you to identify which were most characteristic of you.

▶ In this chapter, we suggested that a 'problem relationship' may be at the core of an employee's performance problem. We talked about the 'vital signs' of a relationship and offered some ideas for improving employee performance by becoming better at 'relationship management'.

In the second half of the book we'll lay out a ten-step 'performance improvement process' you can use with problem employees *and* your other employees. It all begins in the next chapter, where we'll talk about how to analyse your employees' performance.

Part II

The Performance Improvement Process

Chapter 5

Step One: Analyse Your Employee's Performance

BEFORE YOU sit down to meet with your employee, we think it's a good idea to prepare for the meeting. And a good way to prepare for the meeting is to spend some time thinking about the employee's work performance. In this chapter, we'll introduce you to a simple but effective way to analyse your employee's performance, the first step in the performance improvement process.

By the time you finish the chapter, you'll have learned:

▶ a valuable technique for shifting your concern from your employee's problem behaviour to a behaviour change goal;
▶ a method for helping you specify the behaviour change goals you have in mind for your employee; and
▶ a procedure for identifying and capitalising on the work-related strengths of your employee.

Before getting into Step One, though, let's take a look at some mistakes managers and supervisors can make in getting ready to meet with employees.

Common Mistakes in Preparing for Performance Improvement Interviews

Managers and supervisors often make at least one of several mistakes when preparing for a performance improvement interview with an employee.

1. They don't see an obvious need to analyse the employee's

performance.

2. They spend too much time speculating on the reasons for the employee's poor performance and not enough time focusing on the performance problem itself.
3. They think about the employee's performance in abstract rather than concrete terms.
4. They focus only on what the employee is doing wrong.

No Obvious Need to Analyse Performance

When we talk to bosses about this first step of the process, they often respond, 'Why should I analyse the performance of my problem employees when I already know what they're doing wrong?' Here's an example we looked at before.

Sheila Ricks is a dentist with a small but growing practice in a middle-class, suburban town. She identified her problem employee as Lyla Franks, her secretary and receptionist. As Sheila put it, 'Lyla's so unpredictable. One day she's friendly and outgoing, and the next day she's sullen and grouchy. I don't know which Lyla is going to walk in the door in the morning. This Jekyll-and-Hyde routine of hers is beginning to alienate some of my old patients and turn off some of my new ones.' In our interview with Sheila, we asked her what further information she felt she needed about Lyla's work performance. Her answer? 'I know all I need to know about her work performance. She's unpredictable. I know what she's doing wrong. What I don't know is why she behaves that way or how I can change it.'

Speculating on the Reasons for Poor Performance

Even though they think they know what the employee is doing wrong, many bosses are confused and bewildered by an employee's poor performance. Because they feel puzzled, they tend to speculate about *why* the employee is behaving ineffectively.

'I don't know what it is, but something is certainly bothering her these days.'

'He must be having problems at home.'

'It could be a drug or alcohol problem, I'm not sure which.'

'She's been under so much pressure lately, it's beginning to show.'

'I don't know, maybe it's because he didn't get that promotion he was expecting.'

Speculating on what's motivating people can sometimes be helpful, but it's usually a big waste of time. In addition, by focusing on the reasons the employee is performing poorly, you can lose sight of the real problem—the poor performance itself.

Thinking Too Abstractly

When thinking about any employee's performance, it's very common for managers to use language like:

'Poorly motivated';
'Not enough confidence';
'Lack of credibility';
'Unco-operative with other departments';
'Bad attitude';
'Not poised enough in making presentations'; and
'Undependable'.

Abstract concepts like attitude, motivation, dependability, and cooperativeness are useful for categorising different aspects of an employee's performance. They don't, however, convey much useful meaning to an employee; they're too vague. Later in the chapter we'll talk about how you can translate these concepts (or 'fuzzies') into concrete descriptions of observable behaviour. The more specific you can be, the more helpful you'll be to an employee.

Emphasising what an Employee is Doing Wrong

When it comes to analysing employee performance, another strong tendency of bosses is focusing on the negative. They're much more likely to think about what employees do wrong than what they do right.

Regardless of why employers tend to zoom in on the negative, we're convinced that emphasising what employees do wrong has a very demotivating effect. Even employees who ask for criticism of their performance want to hear what they're doing right.

How to Analyse Employee Performance

One of the best ways to prepare for a performance improvement interview is to analyse the employee's performance. This doesn't have to be a complicated, time-consuming process. If you break down the process into these three tasks, it should go pretty smoothly:

1. formulate some positive behaviour change goals for your employee;
2. identify the specific behaviour changes you want your employee to make for each goal; and
3. identify several areas where the employee is performing effectively and give specific examples in each area.

Formulate Positive Behaviour Change Goals

Since supervisors often frame their concerns about problem employees in the negative, we suggest a slight but important shift in perspective. Rather than thinking in terms of what they're doing wrong, think in terms of what they need to do to *improve their performance*. Instead of saying, 'What is he doing wrong?' try asking the question, 'In what ways does he need to improve to function more effectively?' Let's see how this works with a couple of examples:

Rather than saying:	*Try saying*:
She's got a poor attitude.	She needs to improve her attitude.
He's got a very short fuse.	He needs better temper control.
She's not motivated.	She needs to be more motivated.
He's rigid.	He needs to be more flexible.
She's careless.	She needs to be more careful.

Now try it a couple of times yourself.

Rather than saying:	*Try saying*:
1. She's never on time.	1. _____
2. He's much too fussy.	2. _____

If for the first one you said, 'She needs to be more punctual' or 'She needs to come to work on time,' then you answered as we did. If for the second one you said, 'He needs to be better at telling the difference between important and unimportant matters on his job,' then you understand what we're trying to say.

Here's a rule of thumb that may help: In general, it's better to ask for more of something than less of something. For example, it's better to ask a person to be more flexible than less rigid. It's better to ask for a more positive attitude than a less negative attitude.

If you run into difficulty answering the question, 'What does the person need to do in order to improve?' try asking yourself, 'What is the person going to have to do more of in order to improve?'

Identify Specific Behaviour Changes for Each Goal

Just stating a positive behaviour change goal is not enough. Imagine, for example, that your supervisor set the following goals for you: 'You need to establish more credibility with your subordinates,' or 'You need to be more confident when you express yourself at staff meetings.'

Let's examine these two goal statements. They're certainly much better than negative statements like, 'You don't have the trust of your staff' or 'You're a bore at staff meetings.' And they ask for more rather than less. But do they clearly communicate the supervisor's intentions? We don't think so. You'd probably find yourself wondering what your boss really means by 'more credibility' or 'more confident'. You might even question whether bosses know what they mean when they use words or expressions like that.

The reason that phrases like these don't convey much meaning is they don't describe observable behaviour. For example:

A. You Can't See Someone:

▶ establish more credibility with her subordinates.

But You Can See Someone:

▶ look her subordinates in the eye when she talks to them.
▶ speak to her subordinates in a clear, concise manner.
▶ ask her subordinates for their ideas on how something ought to be done.
▶ openly praise her subordinates for a job well done.

B. You Can't See Someone:

▶ be more confident expressing himself at staff meetings.

But You Can See Someone:

▶ sit up straight when he talks.
▶ speak in an audible tone of voice.
▶ make suggestions that are different from those already proposed.
▶ disagree with the ideas and suggestions of other staff members without being apologetic.
▶ give specific reasons why the department ought to take a specific course of action.

Once you've established a behaviour change goal for an employee, the next step is to identify the specific behaviour changes the employee would have to make to convince you the goal has been achieved. That's how you can ensure the employee will know what you mean when you sit down and actually discuss future goals.

The entire process goes like this:

1. State the original problem.
2. State the behaviour change goal.
3. Answer the question: 'What will my employee have to do—in terms of observable behaviour—to convince me the goal has been achieved?'

Here's an example:

Original Problem: He never listens to me; he usually misunderstands what I want him to do.

The Behaviour Change Goal: He needs to be better at listening to me and following my instructions.

What will my employee have to do to convince me the goal has been achieved?

1. When I ask him to do something a certain way, he'll do it the way I ask (unless he checks with me in advance about doing it differently).
2. He'll look me in the eye when I'm talking to him (instead of looking down at the floor or all about the room).
3. He'll repeat, or read back, to me his understanding of an assignment before he actually begins it.
4. He'll ask for clarification of my instructions when he doesn't understand something (saying things like 'How do you mean

that?' or 'Can you give me an example of what you mean by that?').

Having seen how we've done it, why don't you give it a try? Imagine you're Sheila Ricks, the dentist we mentioned at the beginning of the chapter. Your problem employee is Lyla Franks, who can often be sullen and grouchy with your patients. After you've finished, compare your list to Sheila's.

Original Problem: She's unpredictable! One day she's nice and friendly to patients, and the next day she's sullen and grouchy.

The Behaviour Change Goal: Lyla needs to be consistently more courteous and friendly with all patients, both old and new.

What will my employee have to do to convince me the goal has been achieved?

1. _____

_____

2. _____

_____

3. _____

_____

4. _____

_____

Here's the list Sheila came up with:

1. Whenever a patient comes in, Lyla will look at the person directly, smile, and give the person an appropriate greeting (like, 'Hello! How are you today, Mrs Smith?').
2. When talking to patients, she will use their first names or formal names (like, 'How's that grandson of yours, Mrs Smith?').
3. Instead of arguing with patients who are angry or upset about something, she will acknowledge the person's feelings and refer them to me (for example, 'I can see you're very upset by this and I'll ask Dr Ricks to speak to you as soon as she's finished with the patient she's with now').
4. She will replace bad body language with good body language in

all dealings with patients (e.g. making good eye contact rather than rolling her eyes to the ceiling or shaking her head back and forth when disagreeing with someone).

How did your list compare with Sheila's? What did you think Lyla would have to do to become a more courteous and friendly person? Were all the items on your list concrete behaviours; things you could actually see Lyla do? Or were some of the items a little fuzzy and imprecise? (You'll notice that Sheila handled this problem by giving actual examples of the behaviour she wanted Lyla to exhibit.)

Your list may have been quite different from Sheila's. That's fairly common. When two people apply this process to the same goal statement, they invariably come up with different lists. People often mean different things when they're thinking of the same behaviour change goal. But if you follow the procedure outlined above, you'll make certain your employee knows what you mean when you sit down to talk about performance improvement.

Now that you've seen how the process works, try it for one of your employees. Using the same format as before, translate the original statement of the problem into a behaviour change goal. Then identify the specific behaviours that would convince you the goal has been achieved.

Original Problem _____

_____

The Behaviour Change Goal _____

_____

What will my employee have to do to convince me the goal has been achieved?

1. _____

_____

2. _____

_____

3. _____

_____

4. _____

_____

Identify the Areas Where Your Employee is Performing Effectively and Give Specific Examples

As we said earlier, it's a common mistake for bosses to concentrate on what employees are doing wrong and ignore what they're doing effectively. But employees need to hear about the good work, not just the areas that need improvement. It keeps them much more motivated and involved.

When you give employees feedback on what they're doing well, it's just as important to be precise and specific as when you talk about how they can improve. To give positive feedback effectively, answer these two basic questions.

1. What is the employee doing well?

2. What are some specific examples?

Here's an illustration.

What is the employee doing well? _He's pretty creative._

What are some specific examples? _1. He's come up with three good ideas this year for improving shop efficiency. These ideas have saved the company thousands of pounds. 2. He always has a couple of suggestions for different ways of doing a job._

What is the employee doing well? _She edits copy very well._

What are some specific examples? _1. She turned water into wine out of the material we gave her for the company's annual report. 2. She was invaluable in cleaning up the mess that our so-called public relations consultant left us with for the company brochure._

What is the employee doing well? _____

_____

_____

What are some specific examples? _____

_____

_____

_____

_____

_____

On page 65, we've included a Performance Analysis Form you can use when preparing for performance improvement interviews with your employees. The form integrates all the suggestions and concepts presented in this chapter. The first column focuses on employee strengths. For each employee strong point, the form asks you to come up with two specific examples. The second column focuses on areas where the employee needs to improve. For each of the areas needing improvement, the form asks you to identify the specific things the employee will have to do to convince you that performance has improved. This particular performance analysis form has been filled in to show you how it works. But an identical, blank form appears on page 66 that you can duplicate and fill in yourself.

We strongly recommend filling in a form like this before you meet with the employee. It's the best way to prepare for the meeting and it will help you *feel* prepared. This is especially important if you've avoided sitting down to talk with the employee, or if you're not terribly experienced at this sort of thing. By being prepared, you're on a solid foundation to move to the next step of the process—asking the employee to meet with you.

Performance Analysis Form

What is Your Employee Doing Well?	In What Ways Could He/She Improve?
1 HE DOES HIGH QUALITY WORK Example: He almost always checks his work before turning it in.	1. BETTER ATTENDANCE Specifically, the person will have to: a. Show up every day for six weeks
Example: I hardly ever have to ask him to do a job again.	b. Always call in if he's going to be late
2. HE'S PRETTY CREATIVE Example: He's come up with three good ideas this year for improving shop efficiency.	2. INCREASE PRODUCTIVITY Specifically, the person will have to: a. Meet all deadlines that we both agree on for the next six weeks.
Example: He always has a couple of suggestions for different ways of doing a job.	b. Let me know at least five days ahead of time if a deadline can't be met so that we can set a new target date.
3. HE GETS ALONG WELL WITH OTHERS Example: People say nice things to me about him all the time.	3. LISTEN AND FOLLOW INSTRUCTIONS Specifically, the person will have to: a. When I ask him to do something in a certain way, he'll do it the way I ask (unless he checks first)
Example: I don't know of anyone who really dislikes him.	b Look me in the eye when I talk and read back his understanding of the assignments c. Ask for clarifications as needed.
4. HE'S VERY SAFETY CONSCIOUS Example: He's always cleaning up his work area	4. NOT DISTURB OTHER EMPLOYEES Specifically, the person will have to: Confine his conversations with other workers to scheduled breaks for the next 6 weeks.
Example: He tactfully reminds others in the shop of safety procedures.	

Performance Analysis Form

What is Your Employee Doing Well?	In What Ways Could He/She Improve?
1. _____	1. _____
Example: _____	Specifically, the person will have to:
_____	_____
_____	_____
_____	_____
Example: _____	_____
_____	_____
_____	_____
_____	_____
2. _____	2. _____
Example: _____	Specifically, the person will have to:
_____	_____
_____	_____
_____	_____
Example: _____	_____
_____	_____
_____	_____
_____	_____
3. _____	3. _____
Example: _____	Specifically, the person will have to:
_____	_____
_____	_____
_____	_____
Example: _____	_____
_____	_____
_____	_____
_____	_____
4. _____	4. _____
Example: _____	Specifically, the person will have to:
_____	_____
_____	_____
_____	_____
Example: _____	_____
_____	_____
_____	_____
_____	_____

Chapter 6

Step Two: Ask Your Employee to Meet with You

NOW THAT you've done a careful job of analysing the employee's work performance, you're in a much better position to sit down and discuss the subject intelligently. From your perspective, you're ready to meet. However, even though you're prepared, the employee is not. This brings us to the second step of the performance improvement process—asking the employee to meet with you.

To most managers and supervisors, this step seems pretty simple and straightforward. And it is. But, like a lot of simple tasks, it's easy to foul it up if you don't think it through carefully.

In this chapter, we'll show you an effective, easy-to-follow method for arranging a performance improvement interview with an employee. It starts with a discussion of some typical mistakes bosses make when they ask their employees to meet with them. Then it goes on to describe a natural and effective way to do it. We'll end with a description of some things that can go wrong when you ask your employee to meet with you, and what to do about them.

Let's start off by looking at ways of asking employees to meet that don't work very well.

How *Not* to Ask Your Employee to Meet with You

Here are some common mistakes bosses make when asking employees to meet with them to discuss their work performance:

▶ they don't do it themselves—they ask their secretaries to do it;
▶ they don't speak to the employee face-to-face—they send a note or memo about the meeting;
▶ they combine the asking with the meeting;
▶ they say too little about the meeting to the employee;
▶ they say too much about the meeting to the employee;
▶ they make light of the performance improvement interview when asking the employee to meet;
▶ they wait until they're angry or upset to ask the employee to meet.

All these methods have one thing in common: none of them does a good job of *preparing* or *readying* the employee for this very important meeting. Let's look at each one in a bit more detail.

Don't Have Your Secretary Do It

To use their time effectively, or just to avoid doing it themselves, many bosses 'delegate' this kind of task to their secretaries. While understandable, it's a mistake. Here's what can happen.

> **Employee:** (*Answering telephone*) Sales Department. John Cole.
> **Secretary:** Hi John. This is Stella. How are things going?
> **Employee:** Fine, Stella, how are things with you?
> **Secretary:** Great! Busy, but just great. Listen, the reason I'm calling is because Sally wants to meet with you some time next week. Can you be free on Wednesday around 3.30 p.m.?
> **Employee:** Uh ... yes, I can be there. By the way, what's the meeting about?
> **Secretary:** I'm not exactly sure. I'll have to get back to you on that, John, but I think it's employee review time again. She scheduled a formal meeting with me for next week, too.
> **Employee:** (*Not saying anything for several seconds*) Well, I think I would have preferred her to ask me directly.
> **Secretary:** John, you know she's been very busy lately, with

the new merger and everything ...

Although having your secretary do the asking won't always turn out like this, it's generally not a good idea for several reasons.

▶ When you do the asking, you have complete control over the process. You say only what you want to say and don't have to worry about 'translation' problems if someone else does the asking. Plus, you can never be sure what hidden messages your secretary will send the employee. All you can be sure of is that some messages will get sent differently (at least a little) from the way you would have sent them.

▶ Your secretary will probably feel resentful at having to handle some of the questions the employee is likely to ask. This is understandable; it's not the kind of thing you find in a secretary's job description.

▶ The employee is probably going to feel confused and resentful at not having been asked directly.

Don't Send a Note or Memo

Imagine you came back from lunch and found a note on your desk that went something like this.

'Next Thursday, at 2.30 p.m., I'd like to meet with you in my office. The purpose of this meeting is to review your performance over the past six months and to set some goals for the future. Please let me know if the time and date are convenient for you.'

Even though notes and memos like this are sent frequently, they almost always backfire. They arouse anxiety because they sound so ominous and they cause resentment because they're so formal and impersonal.

If you're even tempted to ask an employee to meet with you via a note or memo, ask yourself, 'How would I feel if my boss did it to me?'

Don't Combine the Asking with the Meeting

Some managers make the mistake of not asking the employee to meet in advance; they see the employee walking down the hall and say:

'Charlie! Step into my office, would you? If you've got a few minutes, why don't we do your performance review now? What a coincidence you were walking by just as I was thinking about it.'

An approach like this is bad for several reasons.

▶ It takes employees completely by surprise. It also derails them from whatever else they were working on at the time, leading to predictable feelings of resentment.

▶ Chances are, the supervisor is not going to be well prepared for the meeting, and it certainly doesn't give employees much of an opportunity to get ready either. This means employees will be less thoughtful in analysing their own performance and less able to give helpful feedback to the boss.

Don't Say Too Little

Even when superiors directly ask employees to meet with them, things can still go wrong. Many bosses make the mistake of saying too little to the employee. For example:

'Tom, let's get together next week at 2.30 p.m. to have your annual performance review, OK?'

'Ruth, could I see you in my office at 11.30 tomorrow morning?'

'George, it's time for your annual review again. How about next Wednesday at 3 p.m.?'

When you make your request to meet this brief, the employee's likely to feel a little bowled over. Once the shock wears off, the person will probably wonder what's going to happen in the meeting, speculate about any 'hidden agenda' you might have, and so on. In the absence of more information, there's a good chance the employee will think things like:

'Let's see. What have I done wrong?'

'I wonder why he wants to meet with me. I don't know of anybody else who's getting reviewed now.'

'It can't be good news. She'd have said more if it were.'

The point is this: When you don't say enough, your message is ambiguous. And ambiguity often leads to anxiety. Discussions about work performance are anxiety-producing enough; it doesn't make sense to add even more by saying too little about the forthcoming meeting to the employee.

Don't Say Too Much

In anticipating their employee's concern about the meeting, some bosses err by saying too much. They try to reassure the employee that everything's fine and nothing bad is going to happen in the interview. This often backfires, leading the employee to expect the worst. Here's an example.

> **Supervisor:** Hello, James. I'd like to meet with you on Friday to review your work over the last few months, OK?
>
> **Employee:** Uh ... OK, that sounds all right with me.
>
> **Supervisor:** Great! Now, listen, there's nothing to worry about. Things look pretty good this time around. I'm looking forward to talking to you about the Smith deal and how you could have done an even better job than you did. And that's not meant to take anything away from a job well done, either.
>
> **Employee:** Thanks. I was pretty pleased with how it went myself
>
> **Supervisor:** You have a right to be. And I think I can offer you some suggestions for doing even better in the future. For example ...

Sometimes supervisors talk too much because they get dragged into responding to questions and comments about the interview from the employee. Later on we'll show you how to respond to questions and comments without entering into a prolonged discussion.

Don't Make Light of the Performance Improvement Interview

Some bosses make light of meetings where employee performance is discussed. They do things like walk up to an employee in the hall, slap him on the back, and say: 'Oh, Pete, next week we're going to have to sit down and do the old, half-yearly performance review. What do you think? Feeling up to it?'

Managers who do this are usually uncomfortable in their supervisory roles. In approaching the meeting in a lighthearted way, they attempt to send the message: 'Just because I'm your boss, I'm not trying to be any better than you. I just want to be one of the boys.'

Unfortunately, this lighthearted approach has several negative effects:

▶ the employee may misinterpret your remarks and think you view meetings like this as a joke;

▶ the employee may take your lead and fail to take the meeting seriously;

▶ by making light of a serious topic, you may lose credibility and respect as a manager.

Don't Ask to Meet when You're Upset with the Employee

While some bosses gloss things over when asking employees to meet with them, others are too blunt. This is especially true of managers who overreact with employees. These bosses make the mistake of asking employees to meet when they're feeling angry or upset about some mistake or foul-up. Even worse, they sometimes haul an employee on to the carpet when other employees are around.

A participant in one of our workshops told us about her first boss:

'He'd always want to talk with me after I'd done something wrong and never after I'd done something well. For him, a performance review meant a review of my screw-ups. And if that wasn't bad enough, he had this way of humiliating me in front of my co-workers by saying things like, "I want to see you in my office tomorrow at 8 a.m. sharp!"'

As tempting as it may be to read the riot act to someone after a mistake, it's no way to improve employee performance. The employee will only feel resentful, or intimidated, or both. And you'll end up having to undo a lot of unnecessary damage before you get down to improving the employee's work performance.

How to Ask Your Employee to Meet with You

Asking the employee to meet with you may be easy to do ineffectively, but it's not that difficult to do it well. Here are some important points to keep in mind:

▶ approach the person when there are not a lot of other people around;

▶ briefly and calmly explain the *purpose* of the meeting—that you want to meet with the employee to review his work performance. Also mention that you plan to do this with all the other people you supervise.

▶ tell the employee how you plan to prepare for your meeting—by thinking about (a) what the employee is currently doing well on the job and (b) those areas where the employee could stand to improve;

▶ suggest how the employee can prepare for the meeting—by thinking about what are her strong points as well as the areas in which she needs to improve;

▶ ask the employee to prepare for the meeting by thinking about one additional thing—what you can do, as his boss, to make his job more satisfying and less frustrating in the future. We call this 'The Question';

▶ arrange a specific date, time, and place to meet.

▶ ask if the employee has any questions, or anything else to say, about the proposed meeting.

▶ end on a positive note.

Before explaining these points in more detail, here's an example of a supervisor putting them into action:

Supervisor: (*To employee, out of earshot of others*) Pat, I'd like to arrange a time to meet with you at some point in the near future to review your work performance. (*Pause*) It's something I'm planning to do with everybody in the office.

Employee: Oh ... OK.

Supervisor: To give you a better idea about what I have in mind, let me tell you how I'm going to prepare for the meeting. (*Pause*) I plan to write down some of the things you've been doing really well on the job, and I think there are a few things there. I'll also come up with some areas where I think you could stand to improve, and I think there are a few examples of that, too. (*Pause*)

Employee: Uh-huh.

Supervisor: I'd like you to prepare for the meeting by doing pretty much the same thing. First, think about your good points, what you think you do especially well on the job. Second, think about some of the ways you think you could improve. (*Pause*)

Employee: OK ... I think I've got it.

Supervisor: I'd like you to prepare for the meeting by doing one more thing. (*Pause*) Think about some things I could do, as your boss, to make your job here less frustrating and more satisfying. OK?

Employee: Yes, all right. (*Smiling*) I'll be happy to think about that.

Supervisor: (*Smiling*) Great! How about next Wednesday at 2 p.m. in my office?

Employee: OK ... that sounds fine.

Supervisor: Good. Any questions? Or other thoughts? (*Pausing, looking directly at employee*)

Employee: Hmmm ... can't think of anything right now.

Supervisor: Fine. If you do, just ask. (*Pausing*) I'll look forward to seeing you next Wednesday.

Now let's take a closer look at each of these points.

Approach the Employee Privately

It's a good idea to approach the person when there are no other people around. This is very important. If there are others around, the employee may feel self-conscious or apprehensive. Further, if people are within earshot, they may begin to speculate about what's going on, a situation you definitely want to avoid.

Explain the Purpose of the Meeting

As briefly, calmly and firmly as you can, explain why you want to meet—to review the employee's work performance. Since the purpose of the meeting is to review job performance, it's best to say it simply and directly. Don't gloss it over or beat around the bush by saying something vague, like, 'Why don't we sit down in the next week or so to talk about how things are going around here?' By telling the employee exactly what you have in mind, you'll reduce the chances of a misunderstanding about the purpose of the meeting. The employee will also appreciate your candour and forthrightness if you use the direct approach. In addition, saying you plan to do the same thing with everyone you supervise will help reduce any anxiety the employee may feel about being singled out.

Suggest How to Prepare for the Meeting

Don't assume employees know what you mean when you say the purpose of the meeting is to review work performance. To make sure you're both on the same wavelength, tell the employee exactly how you plan to prepare for the meeting. Say you're going to write down some things the employee is doing well on the job as well as some ways he can improve. Then suggest the employee do the same thing to prepare for the meeting—consider some things she thinks she's doing particularly well on the job and, after that, areas where she thinks she could stand to improve.

By doing this, you'll make it clear what's going to happen during the interview and you'll send an important message about the employee's role in the process. The benefits are clear:

▶ You show that you know what you're doing and that you've thought this whole process through rather carefully. This inspires confidence in employees.

▶ You show that you expect the employee's active involvement in the process and that you think the interview will work best when both of you put your heads together.

▶ By showing that you want to discuss things the employee is doing well, you send an important message: this is not going to be just another gripe session where the employee gets hauled over the coals. In our view, talking about 'the positive aspects' is very important; employees generally have a strong need to know that their bosses notice and appreciate what they're doing well.

Ask the Employee to Think about 'The Question'

While on the subject of how to prepare for the meeting, it's a good idea to suggest one more way the employee can get ready for the session by thinking about 'The Question': 'What can I do, as your boss, to make your job here less frustrating and more satisfying?'

This is a simple, yet thought-provoking question with profound implications, which we'll explore later in the book. At this point, though, we'd like to point out that many bosses have strong reservations about asking employees this question. We frequently get a response like, 'No way! That's only going to open up Pandora's box, with the employee making all kinds of outrageous or ridiculous suggestions, like two-hour lunch breaks and six-week holidays.' While this is a common fear, this kind of thing happens so rarely it's not worth worrying about. When it does happen, it's often just an attempt to inject a bit of humour into the process, usually followed by 'real' suggestions.

Here are several other things to keep in mind when you suggest that employees should think about ways you can make their jobs more satisfying and less frustrating:

▶ Don't be surprised if the employee looks a little shocked, when you ask 'The Question'. You've probably never asked a question like it before and it may be the first time in the employee's working life that a boss has posed a question like this.

▶ It's natural to feel a little vulnerable when you ask somebody, especially an employee, to give you feedback on your own performance. After all, you're opening yourself up for criticism. That makes everybody a little nervous.

▶ When you ask 'The Question', you send employees an important message: that you're willing to accept feedback and you're open to suggestions from them. It is amazing how few bosses actually do communicate this to employees. However, if you expect the people who work for you to accept your feedback, it's a good idea to be willing to accept a little from them.

▶ Asking this question signals your belief that performance improvement is a two-way process. You're not just saying to the employee, 'You change and I'll continue on in the same way.' You're sending an important message that says, 'We're in this together and I'm willing to meet you half-way.'

Arrange the Time and Place to Meet

After suggesting how the employee can prepare for the meeting, agree on a specific time and place to meet. This may seem like a minor point, but it's an important one. It's no fun getting yourself prepared for a performance improvement interview only to learn that your employee is at the dentist on Thursday afternoon because she thought you meant Friday afternoon!

Ask If the Employee Has Any Questions

Before actually scheduling the time and place of the meeting, ask if the employee has any questions—or other comments or reactions—about the proposed meeting. Usually, employees will ask for more specific information, like, 'How long will the meeting last?' (We recommend setting aside an hour and a half.) Comments may be quite varied, but will generally be related to something you said, like:

'I'm glad we're finally going to meet; there are a few things I wanted to update you on.'

'I'm looking forward to thinking about how you could make my job better and more satisfying. No boss has ever asked me a question like that before.'

'I'm very glad we're going to focus on the things I do well as well as the things I do badly.'

Try to respond to questions and comments briefly but don't get dragged into an extended discussion. Your purpose here is to ask the person to meet, and that's it. At the end of the chapter, we'll offer some thoughts about how to respond to more difficult questions and comments.

End on a Positive Note

When asking the employee to meet with you, it's important to end on a positive note. This simply means smiling, possibly shaking hands, and saying something like, 'Good, I'll look forward to seeing you then.'

Practise Asking Your Employee to Meet with You

Here are some suggestions on how to practise asking the employee to meet with you. And, please, don't say to yourself, 'This sounds so easy I can just skip the practice and go on.' If you don't practise, you won't learn how to do it. That, we guarantee.

1. Review the main points and script on pages 72-5.
2. Mentally rehearse asking an employee to meet with you. Just sit back, close your eyes, and imagine yourself walking up to the employee and doing it.
3. After you've rehearsed it a couple of times silently, engage in more active practice. Try saying it out loud as you look at yourself in the mirror. Or tape record your practice attempts and listen to how well you do it.
4. Find someone to help you role play this step of the process. It might be another supervisor in your company, your spouse, a close friend, or somebody from the company's human resources or personnel department. As long as it's somebody you trust and feel comfortable with, it doesn't make any difference who it is. Simply ask the person to play the part of the employee.

After you've silently rehearsed and then role played this second step in the performance improvement process, check yourself on the following points:

_____ Did you imagine approaching the employee when there were no other people around?

_____ Did you explain the purpose of the meeting, mentioning specifically that it was to review the person's work performance?

_____ Did you say this was something you plan to do with all the people you supervise?

_____ Did you tell tell the employee how you plan to prepare for the meeting, mentioning that you plan to identify a number of things he's doing well on the job and also some areas where he could stand to improve?

_____ Did you suggest how your employee could prepare for the meeting, mentioning specifically that she should identify: (a) those things she thinks she's doing well on the job, and (b) some areas where she thinks she could stand some improvement?

_____ Did you ask the employee also to prepare for the meeting by thinking about what you could do, as his supervisor, to make his job less frustrating and more satisfying in the future?

_____ Did you agree to meet at a specific date, time, and place?

_____ Did you ask if the employee had any questions or reactions?

_____ Did you end the meeting on a positive note, by saying, 'OK, I'll look forward to seeing you then,' or an equivalent phrase?

If you answered no to any one of these questions or feel you could improve your approach, don't hesitate to practice as many times as you need to.

Possible Setbacks

If you follow the procedure outlined above, things should go without a hitch. Occasionally, though, you'll run into a problem. Usually, it'll have to do with some fairly predictable questions or remarks, and how employees ask those questions or make those remarks. Look at these two examples.

Janet, an employee who can be very abrupt and caustic, might respond this way after you've asked to meet with her: 'Well, just what do you plan to cover in this meeting, anyway? No one has ever done this sort of thing around here before, you know.'

Richard, who is somewhat emotional and lacks self-confidence, might say, 'What's the matter? Have I done something wrong? If I've done something wrong, why can't you tell me about it now?'

In situations like these, we think the best strategy is to:

1. acknowledge the employee's feelings (whether the employee is concerned, upset or angry);
2. repeat the purpose of the meeting, and how you and the employee can best prepare for it;
3. state calmly but firmly that you're willing to discuss things in more detail in the meeting, but you'd rather not do it right now.
4. repeat these steps as many times as necessary until the employee gets the message that you will not be dragged into an extended discussion of the nature, purpose or worthwhileness of the meeting.

Here's how this strategy would work with Janet:

'Janet, I realise this sort of thing hasn't been done here before and it probably comes as a bit of a surprise to you. As I mentioned before, though, the purpose of the meeting is to review your work performance, and the best way for both of us to get ready for that meeting is to begin thinking about some of the things you do well and some of the ways you could improve. I'd also like you to be thinking of some of the ways I could make your job less frustrating and more satisfying. I'd like to save the details for when we actually meet, though. OK?'

In response to Richard, you might say:

'Richard, you seem concerned that I want to meet with you to discuss what you're doing wrong. That's not why I want to meet with you. I'm talking about a meeting to review your overall work performance. As I mentioned, it's a meeting in which the two of us should come prepared to talk about what you're doing well on the job—and you are doing some things very well—as well as ways you can improve. I'd also like you to come to the meeting prepared to tell me how I can make your job less frustrating and more satisfying. We'll have plenty of time to talk things out when we actually meet. How does that sound?'

If Janet and Richard persisted in asking for more details, we'd recommend saying the same thing again (changing the words, but keeping the message the same) until they accepted the fact that you're not going to elaborate until you meet.

A Quick Summary

Let's briefly review the points we made in this chapter.

▶ Avoid some common mistakes managers make when asking employees to meet, such as having your secretary do it, sending a note or memo, combining the asking with the meeting, saying too little or too much, making light of the interview and asking to meet when you're angry.

▶ Begin by approaching the employee when there are no other people around.

▶ State clearly and directly why you want to meet: to review the employee's work performance. Mention you also plan to meet the other people who report to you.

▶ Tell the employee you plan to prepare for the meeting by identifying what he's already doing well on the job and some areas where he could stand to improve.

▶ Ask the employee to prepare for the meeting by analysing her performance in a similar way—by thinking of things she does well and areas where she thinks she could improve.

▶ Ask the employee to prepare for the meeting in one additional way—by thinking about some of the things you could do to make his job less frustrating and more satisfying.

▶ Ask if the employee has any questions. Respond to some of your employee's predictable questions and concerns, but don't get dragged into an extended discussion.

▶ Arrange for a specific time and place to meet.

▶ End on a positive note.

Now you're ready to meet with the employee.

Chapter 7

Step Three: Begin the Interview

Up TO this point you've analysed your employee's performance and you've asked the person to meet with you. Now comes what many managers and supervisors consider the tough part—actually sitting down face-to-face and discussing the employee's work performance.

In some ways, though, you've already completed the toughest part. You've made a commitment to deal with the employee, and you've acted on that commitment by asking the person to meet with you. Now your job is to begin the interview in such a way that you'll maximise the employee's involvement and co-operation. The purpose of this chapter is to show you how to do that. But first, let's talk about how not to begin a performance improvement interview.

How *Not* to Begin the Interview

Over the years we've often asked people to reflect on performance review meetings they've had with their bosses, especially meetings where they felt uncomfortable right from the start. We'd ask them, 'What did your boss do (or not do) that caused you to feel nervous, uncomfortable, or ill at ease?'
These are some typical answers:

'When I walked into his office, he said "Come in." But he didn't even look up from his desk when he said it. He just kept reading some report. I wasn't quite sure what to do.'

'She was talking on the phone when I arrived. She waved me into the room with her hand and kept talking for what seemed like an eternity. When she finally hung up, she didn't apologise or anything. I guess she didn't realise the effect it had on me.'

'When I got there, he was busy talking to somebody else. He said something like, "I'll be with you in a couple of minutes." I was just left standing there in the doorway while the two of them talked. I could tell the other person was very uncomfortable. And I just felt foolish.'

'She was cordial enough when I arrived, but as soon as I sat down, she said, "Let's get started," and she proceeded to get right down to business. I hardly had a chance to catch my breath from walking up three flights of stairs, and here we were off to the races!'

'I walked in and he asked me to sit down on this spindly little chair right in front of his desk. He was sitting in this very expensive looking executive chair behind this massive desk. There were pictures of his wife and kids, some kind of award he'd won, and a gold pen and pencil set. We were definitely on his ground! He was surrounded by things that made him feel comfortable. All I had was my ball-point pen!'

'I remember a meeting where, after about three minutes, there were people knocking at the door, telephones ringing, you name it. Not one of the interruptions lasted more than a minute, but each one threw us completely off track.'

How to Get the Meeting Off to a Good Start

Getting a meeting off to a good start is not complicated. There are only three basic points to keep in mind.

1. Set the stage for the interview by minimising distractions and potential interruptions.
2. Make the person feel comfortable and welcome.
3. 'Structure' the meeting for the employee. This means reminding the employee about the purpose of the meeting and describing briefly what's going to happen during the rest of the session. It also means suggesting how the two of you can get the most out of the session.

Let's look at each of these points in more detail.

Set the Stage

Before the interview begins, do whatever you can to make sure this will be a private meeting. Especially try to minimise potential distractions and interruptions. They have a negative impact on people, especially when they're already feeling nervous or when sensitive subjects like work performance are being discussed.

Unfortunately, too many supervisors think they can divide their attention between the employee and other matters that compete for their attention. But doing this just causes employees to feel irritated and resentful.

Here are some suggestions for minimising distractions and interruptions.

▶ If you have a secretary, ask that telephone calls be held until after the meeting.

▶ If your office has a door, close it (your 'open-door policy' shouldn't extend to private meetings with employees).

▶ If you share an office with others, ask them to leave while you're meeting with the employee. Find a private office, if necessary. This also applies if you work in an office with modular furniture and walls that go only half-way up to the ceiling.

▶ Clear your desk (and your mind) of the other pressing matters that normally compete for your attention.

▶ It's OK to refer briefly to notes or performance rating forms (including our own Performance Analysis Form), but don't make them the central focus of the meeting. Nothing is more distracting or disconcerting than a meeting that seems to revolve around a piece of paper.

The main thing to keep in mind when setting the stage for the interview is this: you need to meet in a room that is reasonably comfortable, free of major distractions, and most important, private enough so your conversations won't be overheard.

Make the Person Feel Comfortable and Welcome

When the employee arrives at your office (or whatever private place you've chosen to meet), give the person a warm and friendly greeting. You can do this by standing, walking out from behind your desk, smiling, and saying something like, 'Hello,_____ . Thanks for coming. Come in and have a seat.' It's important to do this as naturally as you can. If you're by nature a bubbly, effusive person, you'll do this reflexively. If you're more reserved or a little formal, push yourself a little, but don't go over the top. That just puts people off.

Try to sit down face-to-face with the employee, not across a desk or table. Desks and tables are nice things to hide behind when you're feeling anxious, but they create a psychological distance between people. If your office is designed so you have to sit at your desk, have the person sit at the side of your desk rather than across it, as the illustration indicates:

Bad   **Better**   **Best**

It's a good idea to put the person at ease with a little casual conversation to break the ice and get the conversational juices flowing. Make sure you select a subject that's interesting or relevant to the employee. Here are some examples:

'Your new baby must be about a year old now. How's she doing?'

'I hear you went to Disney World on your holiday. How did you like it?'

'Your son's in college now, isn't he? How's he enjoying college life?'

'Helen tells me you do power walks every morning. How did you get involved in that?'

'I hear your team won the local skittles league cup. Tell me about it.'

This kind of talk, especially about a subject of interest to the employee, can help relieve some of the predictable anxiety and discomfort that will exist at the beginning of the session. It also demonstrates that you're interested in more than just the employee's work performance.

However, sometimes an attempt at casual conversation can backfire. Here are several additional points to keep in mind:

1. Make sure the subject is of interest to the employee. If you bring up a subject you're intensely interested in (like football, aerobics or classical music), only to discover the employee hates it, you're worse off than when you started.

2. When the employee starts talking, pay attention! The worst thing you can do is ask a perfunctory question and then let your attention trail off during the person's answer.

3. Don't let things drag on for too long. That will only send the message that you want to avoid talking about the real purpose of the interview—the employee's work performance and how to improve it.

'Structure' the Meeting

At the beginning of any important meeting, two important questions are almost certain to be on people's minds: 'Why are we here?' and 'What's going to happen in this meeting?' Not answering these two questions early in the interview can have some negative consequences:

▶ if people aren't clear about why they're meeting or what's going to happen, they may get anxious or angry, or they may just switch off.

▶ if employees are preoccupied with thoughts about why they're meeting with you or what's about to happen, they won't hear much of what you're saying.

▶ if these questions aren't answered early in the interview, employees will probably ask them later on, often at the most inopportune time.

To answer these two questions for the employee, you need to explain (a) the purpose of the meeting and (b) what's going to happen during the interview. We call this 'structuring' the meeting because it provides a helpful structure or agenda to what is often an amorphous and ambiguous phenomenon—a meeting between two people. You can think of structuring as a good way to 'orient' the employee.

When you explain the purpose of the meeting, you should say that:

▶ the two of you are getting together to review the employee's work performance;

▶ periodically sitting down with employees to discuss their work performance is an integral part of your job as a supervisor;

▶ you're planning to meet with everyone you supervise (to keep the employee from getting the impression of being singled out).

When you explain what's going to happen during the session, say you want to cover a number of important topics. In this order, you want to:

1. find out how things are going at work for the employee, and especially about any problems she is having;
2. get the employee's ideas and suggestions about how you can make his job less frustrating and more satisfying;
3. hear what the employee thinks she does well at work and also how she thinks she can improve;
4. offer your thoughts about what the employee does well and also the areas needing improvement;
5. mutually agree on some specific goals for the future—things the employee will be working on to improve his performance and some things you'll be doing to make his job less frustrating and more satisfying.

When 'structuring' a meeting like this, it's also helpful to suggest what you and the employee can do to get the most out of the session. For example, you might say:

'I think there are several things the two of us can do to get the most out of this session. First and foremost, I think we should be as candid and forthright with each other as possible. If you hold back and don't say what's on your mind, we won't make any progress. I'll also try to be honest and straightforward with you. Second, I'd like both of us to try to listen to each other and respect each other's point of view. When you're talking, I'll try to be the best listener I can be. If you say something I disagree with, I won't interrupt or roll my eyes to the sky or anything like that. I'll just listen. I'd also appreciate your doing the same when I'm offering my thoughts and ideas. Finally, I'd like both of us to see this as a performance improvement meeting, not a gripe session. I'd like to focus on ways you can improve your performance and ways I could be a better, more effective manager.'

Now let's take a look at a manager getting a performance improvement interview off to a good start.

Walking through an Example

The following script is an example of how a supervisor might begin the interview by: (a) setting the stage, (b) making the person feel comfortable and (c) 'structuring' the meeting.

Supervisor: (*Sitting at her desk and hearing a knock on her office door*) Come in! (*Seeing that it's Janet, gets up from her desk and smiles warmly*) Hello, Janet. Good to see you. Please come in and have a seat.

Employee: (*Looking a little apprehensive*) Hello. Thanks. (*Sitting down*)

Supervisor: How's the jogging going, Janet?

Employee: (*Smiling*) You'll never believe this, Hannah, but I'm actually running three miles a day ... and enjoying it. And to think that a year ago I was smoking and in such terrible shape. (*Leaning forward slightly*) I'm even thinking seriously of running in a marathon this autumn

Supervisor: (*Smiling broadly*) That's great, Janet! I'm so impressed! You're an inspiration to us all!

Employee: (*Looking down slightly*) Thanks.

Supervisor: (*Leaning forward slightly*) Janet, let me explain why I asked you to meet with me today. As I mentioned the other day when we set up this meeting, the purpose of our getting together is to review your work performance. (*Pause*) I think it's a very good idea to sit down periodically with all the people I supervise to discuss how they're doing at work. As I said, I plan to do this with everyone in the office. (*Pause*)

Employee: (*Nodding*)

Supervisor: Janet, there are a number of things I'd like to cover in our talk today. Let me mention them briefly so you'll know what's coming. I'd like to begin by having you tell me how things are going in general at work and especially about any problems you may be having. Then I'd like to hear your ideas and suggestions about how I could make your job less frustrating and more satisfying. You'll recall that I asked you to think about that the other day when we set this meeting up.

Employee: (*Nodding*) Yes. I have been thinking about it too. I think it was the first time a boss ever asked me a question like that. (*Both smiling*)

Supervisor: Well, I'm glad I asked it and I'm looking forward to hearing what you have to say, even if it's not too flattering of me. (*Pause*) After that, I'd like you to tell me what things you think you do particularly well at work and then some areas where you think you could stand to improve. After you finish your analysis, I'll build on your thoughts by offering some of my own ideas about what you do well and where you could improve. Finally, I'd like to end up with the two of us setting some goals for the future. (*Pause*) And when I say goals, I mean goals for both of us—what you can do to improve your work performance and what I can do to make your job here more rewarding and satisfying. I think it'd be helpful if we even write down some of the specific things both of us will be doing in the weeks and months ahead. (*Pausing, looking at employee, saying nothing more*)

Employee: I think I've got a clear idea about what you've got in mind. And it makes a lot of sense to me.

Supervisor: Good! (*Pause*) Oh yes, one more thing about how to get the most out of this meeting. One, I'd like you to be honest and frank with me. Don't hold back for fear of hurting my feelings or because you might get in trouble if you say something negative or critical. My job is to listen to what you've got to say, and that's what I plan to do. I'm open to any suggestions you have for how I can be a better boss and what I can do to make your job more satisfying. And I'd like you to be open to how you can improve your performance as well.

Employee: That sounds all right to me. Where do we start?

Supervisor: Well, before we get started, I'd like to answer any questions you may have about why we're here today or what we're going to be doing ...

Practise Beginning the Interview

Now for a little practice. Since this step is more complicated than asking the employee to meet with you, try to get somebody (another supervisor, a close friend, your spouse) to help you go through it before doing it with an employee. It's a good idea to mentally rehearse this step a few times before finding somebody to practise with. When you role play it, use a tape recorder so you can hear how well you did.

When you're ready, imagine you're sitting in your office and the employee is knocking on the door. Close the book and begin the interview. If you make a few false starts, don't let it bother you. Just start again. Try to run all the way through until you get to the point of asking if the employee has any questions. When you've finished, reopen the book.

Whether you practised alone or with somebody else, check yourself on the following points:

▶ Did you give your employee a warm, friendly greeting? Specifically, did you stand up, walk out from behind your desk, and say something like, 'Hello,_____ . Thanks for coming. Please have a seat.' If you used a tape recorder, listen to how you sounded. How would you feel sitting down and talking to someone who sounds like you?

▶ Did you sit down face-to-face with the employee, not across a desk or table? How did this make you feel? If you're not used to doing this, you can expect a little discomfort at first.

▶ Did you engage in some appropriate conversation to put your employee at ease? What subject did you select? Were you able to keep it brief? Were you really listening?

▶ How well did you 'structure' the meeting? When you explained the purpose of the meeting did you (a) say the purpose was to review the person's work performance and (b) mention that sitting down periodically with employees was a good thing and something you plan to do with all the people you supervise?

▶ When you gave the employee a preview of what was going to happen in the meeting, did you (a) say you wanted to begin by learning, in general, how things were going in her job and especially about any problems the person might be having (b) say you especially wanted to hear about suggestions for how you could make the employee's job more satisfying and less frustrating (c) mention that you wanted to learn what the employee thinks he does well in his job as well as areas where he thinks he could stand to improve (d) add that you also wanted to mention what you think the employee is doing well and the things she could do to improve and (e) say you wanted to end by setting some goals for improving the employee's work performance and making his job less frustrating and more satisfying? Did you also mention that it would be wise to write down the specific things both of you would be doing in the future to achieve these goals?

▶ After you explained what was going to be covered during the interview, did you suggest how the two of you could get the most out of the session?

▶ Did you find out if the person had any questions before you got started by saying something like, 'OK, before we go any further, I'd like to answer any questions you may have.'

If you left out any of the points on the list, don't hesitate to practise until you're satisfied you've mastered this step.

If you find yourself getting a little discouraged when it doesn't come as smoothly or as easily as you'd like, think back to the times when you tried to learn some other complex task, such as driving a car, or hitting a backhand in tennis. Although interpersonal skills don't require the finely honed motor co-ordination of most physical skills, they're at least as difficult to master. The only secret to learning both kinds of skills is consistent, determined practice.

Respond to Your Employee's Questions and Concerns

After 'structuring' the meeting, invite the employee to ask any questions before you continue. Most of the questions you'll get are likely to fall into one of these categories:

1. neutral questions;
2. questions expressing concern; and
3. hostile questions.

Neutral Questions

Neutral questions are simply requests for clarification about the purpose of the interview or what you'll be discussing. Look at the examples below:

'I do have one question. What do you mean by goals?'

'How long do you think this meeting will take?'

'Will we also be discussing salary issues at this meeting?'

'Do you mind if I refer to some notes I've brought with me?'

If the employee asks you a neutral question, you shouldn't have much difficulty. Simply answer these questions as honestly and directly as you can, and then move to the main part of the interview. Here's how we'd answer the question about whether the interview would include a discussion of salary:

'That's a good question, Sheila. No, we won't be talking about salary today. I'd like to save our discussion about salary until a future meeting, when we can talk about that, and only that. Today, I want to concentrate fully, and solely, on the things we can both do to improve your work performance and what I can do to make your job less frustrating and more satisfying.'

Questions Expressing Concern

Questions that express some concern on the part of the employee often have to do with the possible negative consequences of the interview. Although they're phrased as questions, they 're really statements that are based on some reservation or apprehension the employee feels. Some examples include:

'What effect is this going to have on my salary and chances for advancement in the company?'

'Is everything we talk about going to be placed in my personnel folder?'

'If I talk about other employees, will any of it get back to them?'

'Does all of this just mean you're not happy with my performance?'

When the employee asks you a question that expresses some concern, try the following.

1. Acknowledge the feeling. Say something that reflects your understanding of the employee's concerns, pausing to give the person a chance to expand on what they've said. (We go into more detail on the technique of 'reading back' in Chapter 8.)
2. Respond directly to the concern. Say something that responds to the person's question. As you would with neutral questions, answer as honestly and as succinctly as you can.
3. Get the employee's reactions. Ask how responsive you've been to the employee's original concern. If you have, move on to the

main part of the interview. If not, make another attempt.

Here's how this approach works with a relatively common employee question:

Employee: (*With a suspicious tone*) What effect is this going to have on my salary and my chances for advancement?

Supervisor: (*Slowly*) Joe, you sound a little concerned that what we discuss here may be used against you when it comes to time for a promotion or a pay rise. (*Pause*)

Employee: (*Jumping in quickly*) Exactly! That kind of thing has happened around here in the past, you know. Not that you've done it, but I know other managers have. (*More slowly now*) I suppose that's what's making me wonder about it now.

Supervisor: Yes, I'm sure it has happened before, and I appreciate your concern. But that's not what I intend to do here. Not at all. As I said before, my only purpose is for the two of us to find some ways to help you improve your work performance and make your job here more satisfying. (*Pausing for a moment as employee looks thoughtful*) How well have I answered your question?

Employee: (*Looking more comfortable*) Pretty well. I feel better now ...

Either by yourself or with the help of your role-play partner, respond to the question below. If you don't have a partner, write in below how you would respond, using the 'read back' strategy, where you try to paraphrase or summarise the person's concern in your own words.

Employee: Yes, I do have a question. Is everything we talk about going to be placed in my personnel folder?

You: _____

_____

_____

_____

Employee: Yes, that's exactly how I feel.

You: _____

_____

Did you begin by reading the person back—saying something that showed you understood the underlying feeling or concern? Did you pause after your read back, so the person had a chance to talk further?

After acknowledging the person's feeling, did you say something that addressed the concern directly? Did you do this briefly and succinctly? Here's how we would have handled it:

> **Employee:** Yes, I do have a question. Is everything we talk about going to be placed in my personnel folder?
>
> **Supervisor:** Lee, it sounds as though you're worried that what goes on here will be recorded permanently in your files. (*Pause*)
>
> **Employee:** Yes, I am. Those files have the reputation of being like the Public Record Office—they last for ever. And I don't want something to show up five, ten years down the line that I may regret.
>
> **Supervisor:** So, your concern is that something that might get recorded here today could come back to haunt you at some point in the future? (*Pause*)
>
> **Employee:** Yes, that's it exactly! And another thing ... I'm not sure how confidential those files really are. I don't want everything I say to be available to other people in the company, too.
>
> **Supervisor:** (*Continuing to read back*) That is, you want this to be a private session between you and me, and not something that everybody in the company knows about. (*Pause*)
>
> **Employee:** Yes, that's exactly how I feel. (*Leans forward to hear supervisor's response*)
>
> **Supervisor:** I'm glad you raised the issue, Lee. It's an important one. (*Pause*) The only things that are going to find their way into your personnel folder are the goals that we eventually set for improving your work performance and the things that I'll be doing to make your job here more satisfying. Everything else that happens here today is strictly between you and me. (*Pause*) Now, how responsive have I been ... ?

Hostile Questions

Hostile questions or remarks often come when the employee is feeling threatened or angry about having to talk with you. Often these questions have a smoke-screen effect, since they divert attention from the employee and the real purposes of the interview. They bring to mind the expression, 'The best defence is a good offence,' because the person asking hostile questions, really does seem to be on the offensive. Here are several examples:

'Well, if you're going to talk to everybody, why are you seeing me first? Do you think I'm the worst of the lot?'

'I'm glad we're going to talk about how you can improve too, because there are a lot of things you can do to improve!'

'Let's be serious! Do you really think this is going to do any good?'

'Look, I've been through five supervisors in this company. They all start out gung ho, just like you. Then they begin to relax.'

When employees ask hostile questions or make remarks that have a hostile or angry tone, we recommend the following:

1. Do not respond directly to the question. Remember, it's probably not a question anyway, but a statement disguised as a question.
2. Read back the essence of the remark or question and attempt to draw out the employee even further. If you need to, ask follow-up questions like, 'What would you add to that?' or 'Tell me a little more.' Continue to either read back or ask follow-up questions until the employee finishes talking.
3. Respond calmly and rationally by reminding the employee of the purpose of the session, but don't get dragged into an argument or extended discussion. Tell the employee that your only purpose is, as you said earlier, to review her work performance and to get some suggestions and feedback. This is called the 'broken record' technique, because all you're doing is repeating what you said earlier. You can repeat this as often as necessary after you've read back a hostile question.

Here's an example:

Employee: (*In an angry tone of voice*) Well, if you're going to talk to everybody, why are you seeing me first? Do you think I'm the worst of the lot?

Supervisor: (*Calmly*) You sound a bit angry that I'm starting with you, James, maybe because I see you as someone who particularly needs to improve? (*Pause*)

Employee: (*Slightly taken aback by non-defensive tone of supervisor*) Ah ... well, I don't quite know what I think. But I just have this feeling that you called me in here to pick on me, and I don't think that's fair. There are plenty of other people out there you should be talking to instead of me.

Supervisor: (*Continuing to read back*) So, instead of talking to some other employees who may need it more, you feel I may be singling you out to give you a hard time? (*Pause*)

Employee: Right. (*Voice a little softer now*) Is that what's going on? (*Leans forward*)

Supervisor: No, not at all. And I'm sorry you have that impression. I asked you to meet with me for exactly the reasons I mentioned earlier—so that both of us could put our heads together to find some ways to improve your work performance and make your job here less frustrating and more satisfying. As I mentioned earlier, I plan to do this with everyone who reports to me, not just you. But I'm glad you told me what was on your mind. (*Pause*) I'd like to hear about any other concerns you have before we go on. (*Leaning forward slightly*)

Employee: (*Softer now*) No, I think that's it.

Supervisor: Good. OK, let's move on ...

The technique for dealing with hostile or angry questions is very similar to the one for dealing with questions that express worry or concern. In both cases, it's important to give employees a chance to fully express their feelings before you respond with thoughts of your own.

A Quick Summary

Let's recap what's been covered in this chapter, which was devoted to the topic of beginning the interview. First, you set the stage for a private meeting by minimising distractions and potential interruptions. Second, at the beginning of the session you make your employee feel comfortable and welcome, including greeting the person in a warm and friendly manner, engaging in a bit of casual conversation before getting down to business, and sitting down face-to-face with the employee, not across a desk or table. Thirdly, you 'structure' the meeting by briefly describing the purpose of the meeting, previewing what's going to happen in the remainder of the session and offering a few thoughts on how to get the most out of the session. And, finally, you respond to any questions and concerns before moving on to the main body of the interview.

In the next chapter, we'll discuss some valuable listening skills for getting employees to talk openly and freely.

Chapter 8

Get Your Employee to Talk: Listening Skilfully

LET'S REVIEW for a moment where you are now in the overall performance improvement process. In Step One, you analysed your employee's performance. Then you moved on to Step Two and asked the person to meet with you. In Step Three, you learned how to get the interview off to the best possible start.

Now we're going to take time out from this step-by-step process to introduce some skills that will help you get the employee to talk fully and freely. These skills will come in very handy in the next few steps of the process.

An awful lot of what we do for a living involves teaching people how to listen more effectively. Unfortunately, we've discovered that most bosses, like most people, are poor listeners. They're not very good at paying attention (especially when they're distracted or feel rushed), keeping quiet (especially when they disagree or have thoughts of their own), and patiently staying on the other person's wavelength.

We define listening as 'helping another person think out loud'. Being a good listener is absolutely essential if you're going to be an effective problem-solver, especially when the problems have to do with how you're getting along with other people, like employees (or spouses, romantic partners, children etc.).

For the performance improvement process to work, it's very important that you be a reasonably good listener. That's why we've written this chapter. In it, we shall:

- ▶ talk about why listening skills are so important;
- ▶ describe a variety of listening skills you can use to draw another person out;

▶ present an example of these listening skills in action; and

▶ give you some practice in using some of the skills.

The listening skills we'll be describing are pretty straightforward and simple to learn, but they're very hard to put into practice. Part of the reason for this is they often run counter to what you really want to do when you disagree with someone or have a strong reaction to what they're saying—and that is to *talk*, not to listen. To become proficient at listening will require a lot of practice, until you feel comfortable and natural. But if you work at it, the rewards will be worth it. You'll be a much better supervisor. And it'll pay off in your personal life as well.

Why Listening Skills Are So Important

Think for a moment about a supervisor you've had who wasn't a very good listener. Fix the person clearly in your mind and think back to a time when the two of you sat down to talk about your job performance. What made your boss a poor listener? What did your boss say or do that communicated the message, 'I'm not listening to you', or 'I don't really care about your ideas or feelings'?

Now think about how you felt. What effect did your supervisor's poor listening behaviour have on you? Record your thoughts below:

What did the supervisor say or do? _____

_____

_____

How did you feel as a result? _____

_____

Here's a sampling of responses we've heard:

'I could never tell if he was listening to me or not, because he was always doing something else when we'd meet, like checking over last month's sales figures or going over invoices. What I had to say just didn't seem very important to him. I suppose it made me feel rather trivial.'

'The person I'm thinking of was a non-stop talker. I mean how can a person listen when they're talking all the time? Even though we were supposed to be in a conversation, I could hardly get a word in edgeways. We used to call her 'motor mouth' behind her back. How did it make me feel? Totally uninvolved, as if I weren't there at all. I'd just switch right off!'

'I had this supervisor who would interrupt me whenever he disagreed with me. Not only would he butt right in, he'd also put me down by saying things like, "That's a stupid idea!" or "I can't believe you could say such a thing!" He turned me off completely. I could never produce for a person like that!"

'I had a supervisor once who would always misinterpret—or even distort—what I said. After we'd agree on something, he'd go out and do just the opposite. Then when I'd point this out to him, he'd look really innocent and say something like, "Well wasn't that what we agreed on?" This happened so often I got to the point where I almost tape recorded our meetings just to prove to myself I wasn't going crazy. I felt completely confused and bewildered by his behaviour. I completely lost faith in him as a supervisor.'

Clearly, a supervisor with poor listening skills can have a very negative impact on an employee. But what benefits can you expect from good listening skills? Why are listening skills so important? Here's why:

1. You'll show employees you care about them. When we interview groups of employees and ask what they want from their bosses, one of the items that's always near the top of the list is: 'I want my boss to be better at listening to my thoughts and ideas.' As a manager or supervisor, when you listen you send the message: 'I care.' In our view, attentive and patient listening is the single best way to meet your employee's basic need to be treated with dignity and respect as a human being. Think about it. Isn't that what you want from *your* boss?

2. You'll show employees you're not just concerned with yourself. Another common complaint is that bosses are selfish and self-absorbed—over-concerned with *their* priorities and over-focused on *their* goals and objectives. It's easy to see why employees feel that way because bosses are often so wrapped up in themselves they don't stop to think about things from the employee's perspective. The message they send is: 'I care about me!' However, when you try to learn what employees are thinking and see things from their vantage point, you send another message: 'I don't just care about me. You're important too.'

3. You'll give employees the opportunity to fully express themselves and gain some new understanding or perspectives. We define listening as 'helping another person think out loud'. This is something we all need to do from time to time, especially when we're wrestling with important problems or weighty issues. In a performance improvement interview, you'll want to get the employee's best thinking on a number of important topics: (a) how things are going at work; (b) problems at work you should be aware of; (c) ways you could improve as a manager or supervisor; and (d) the employee's view of his or her own performance. The single best way to to get people to talk freely and fully about important topics like this is by skilful listening. Yes, people want to talk, but only if they feel you are willing to listen.

4. You'll often find out why employees haven't been performing well. There's often a good reason behind a person's poor work performance. Sometimes it has to do with a problem at home. Sometimes it has to do with a company policy that's been misunderstood. Sometimes it has to do with another employee who's stirring up trouble. Sometimes it has to do with you and your relationship with the employee. If you listen carefully, you might find out why. And that puts you in a much better position to begin the process of improving your employee's performance.

5. You'll find out things that will help make you a better manager. You certainly don't see yourself the same way your employees do. You see yourself from your perspective. That's why we recommend you ask employees the question, 'What can I do to make your job less frustrating and more satisfying?' If you're smart, you'll pay attention to the perspective of employees, who are often quite good at identifying things about you that you may be completely unaware of or oblivious to—unrecognised strengths, annoying or irritating personal habits, simple little things you could do to be a better boss, and so on. In our view, your employees (and also your close friends and family members) are 'experts' on you. Paying attention to all that expertise by good listening will help you grow as a person.

6. You'll learn about organisational problems before they get out of hand. As a boss, you can't be everywhere, so you can't notice every little developing problem and nip it in the bud. But your employees are out there, and they can be your eyes and ears if you listen to what they've got to say. By periodically sitting down and drawing them out on how things are going at work and what problems they're noticing, you'll learn about all kinds of things requiring corrective action. In many ways, employees can be like a 'distant early warning system' for you. If you hear about little problems early on, you can do something before they become big problems or crises, not just for that employee, but for the company as a whole. Good listening has a preventive aspect that can't be denied.

7. It motivates and involves employees. Listening is not only a great way to get information, it's also a wonderful way to get people involved and keep them involved. If you do all the talking, employees will become demotivated because they'll think you don't care. If you actively listen to them, you'll make them active participants in a collaborative problem-solving process.

8. You'll greatly increase the chances that employees will listen to you. You want your employees to listen to you. What boss doesn't? But if you want your employees to listen to you, you've got to be prepared to listen to them first. Here's why. A person's level of receptivity—his willingness to listen to you—varies from extremely high to extremely low and depends to a large extent on what you do and how he sees you. If you have good listening skills, you'll raise an employee's level of receptivity; if you don't, you'll drive it down. It's that simple.

In the remainder of this chapter we'll introduce you to three very important listening skills* that will help you achieve these benefits. They are:

▶ attending behaviour;
▶ question-asking and information-gathering techniques; and
▶ 'reading back'.

---

*While our approach to listening skills has been influenced by many people, we'd especially like to acknowledge the contribution that has been made by Carl R. Rogers and Allen E. Ivey.

Attending behaviour is the way you use your body, particularly your head, eyes, face, and upper torso, to communicate to other people that you're paying attention and are interested in what they have to say.

Question-asking and information-gathering techniques are designed to get people talking and keep them talking, and to clarify what they've said.

'Reading back' is a paraphrasing-summarising technique you can use to prove to people you're listening and to make sure you've heard them correctly. It's the most difficult of the listening skills to master and put into practice. It's called 'reading back' because that's exactly what you do—'read back' in your own words what you heard the other person say. Reading back has the effect of making people feel understood and, often, building on or expanding on what they've already said. Along with the other two skills, reading back truly helps you achieve the goal of listening, which is helping another person think out loud.

Let's take a look at these listening skills in more detail.

Attending Behaviour

Psychologists have long recognised the tremendous importance that attention from others plays in our lives. Infants need almost constant attention, thriving on the tender touching and close physical presence of their mothers and fathers. Children, spouses and close friends require our undivided attention when they're troubled or upset. No one likes to talk to people who don't pay attention.

Even though much has been made of the importance of attention, until relatively recently little mention was made of the specific things that people do—or don't do—when they're 'attending' to one another. Attending, which is just a fancy way to refer to the process of paying attention to or showing interest in another person, is composed of these three simple elements:

1. making eye contact;
2. using good body language; and
3. minimising distractions.

Making Eye Contact

How often have you tried to talk to someone who wasn't looking directly at you? If not actually impossible, it's awfully disconcerting to try to communicate with someone who's not looking you in the eye. Yet, as important as it is, many people don't do it when they're listening.

Think of the times you've been at a party and somebody says, 'Oh, so that's what you do for a living. Tell me more about that.' Then, just as you're getting into your answer, the person begins looking about the room, nodding at other people, and waving at new arrivals. If you're like most people, this behaviour will stop you dead in your tracks. You think, 'Why on earth ask the question if you're not interested in the answer?' Making direct eye contact sends the message, 'I'm listening'. Not making eye contact says, 'I'm not listening' or worse, 'I don't care'.

Here are some important things to remember about making eye contact:

▶ Instead of rigidly looking into the other person's eyes, break contact periodically.

▶ Try to maintain direct eye contact about 70 to 80 per cent of the time. Much more than this makes people feel uncomfortable. For example, have you ever been to a mental institution? (Visited one, we mean!) Many mentally ill patients make 100 per cent eye contact and, when they 'lock in' on you, it can be pretty unsettling.

▶ When breaking eye contact, don't look all about the room or dart your eyes from side to side. Rapid eye movement suggests tension or anxiety and will make people less willing to tell you what's on their minds.

▶ Don't let your eyes give away or telegraph negative reactions. This can really cause problems. A good interview can be totally wrecked when you unconsciously roll your eyes to the sky after a comment you totally disagree with or find hard to believe.

Using Good Body Language

For years now, people have been talking about the subject of body language. Some writers say our body language reveals all kinds of things about our hidden conflicts and secret desires. That's carrying things a bit too far. To us, body language simply means the way you use your body—especially your face, arms, and upper torso—to let people know you're interested in what they have to say.

There are four important aspects of body language:

1. body positioning;
2. nodding;
3. using your facial muscles;
4. using your arms and upper body.

1. Body positioning. When listening, position your body so your head and upper torso are directly facing the other person. 'Aim' your body at the person. If you have to look over your shoulder or off to the side to see the person, then you're probably not doing it right. Avoid leaning way back in your chair, in the classic 'laid-back' position. Your main objective is to listen, not prepare for a nap.

2. Nodding. In addition to maintaining good eye contact, nod your head periodically to send the non-verbal message, 'Keep talking, I'm listening.' If you're not a natural nodder, it's pretty easy to learn. Just stand in front of a mirror and start talking to yourself. (Of course, you'll want to do this in the privacy of your home; otherwise people will think the pressure of the job is finally getting to you!)

As you look at yourself in the mirror, nod your head a couple of times every few seconds. It'll appear even more natural if you say something like 'Uh-huh' or 'I see' as you nod. When you feel comfortable, practise with family and friends. As they talk, experiment with nodding and not nodding for short periods of time. See if you can notice any difference in their level of involvement.

3. Using your facial muscles. Learning how to use your facial muscles when listening is very important. People with stony expressions or poker faces communicate boredom or lack of interest. In fact, expressionless people are often misinterpreted as not paying attention when they really are listening. People with expressive faces don't have that problem. Their faces come alive with interest. As a result, people find them much easier to talk to.

Here are a couple of things you can do to cultivate the use of your facial muscles:

▶ Pay attention to other expressive people and 'go to school' on them. If you really want to see the use of facial muscles done well, turn on your favourite TV chat show and watch the host interview a guest. While you're watching, occasionally turn down the volume so you can't hear any of the dialogue. Focus on the host; you'll often see a great example of good attending behaviour.

▶ Once again, stand in front of a mirror. Begin by exercising your facial muscles. Wrinkle your forehead. Purse your lips. Drop your jaw. Furrow and then raise your eyebrows. Wrinkle your nose. Widen your eyes. Clench your teeth. Now try to express the following emotions just by changing your facial expression: confusion, surprise, shock, agreement, enthusiasm, anger, deep interest.

4. Using your arms and upper body. In general, it's best to assume a relaxed (but not slouched) posture in which your torso is tilted slightly toward the speaker. For the most part, a body that's leaning backward communicates less interest and involvement than one that is leaning forward slightly.

It's also a good idea to avoid sitting with your arms folded. This is the classic 'closed' posture. It's no accident that football referees stand firmly planted with their arms folded tightly across their chests when they're being verbally besieged by an irate manager or player.

Instead of folding your arms, place them comfortably on the armrests of your chair or rest them naturally in your lap. When combined with direct eye contact and a slight tilting forward of the upper body, this is a very good listening posture.

Every now and then, you'll want to *really* communicate that you're listening to another person. Maybe they'll be having trouble saying something. Or perhaps they'll be unsure how receptive you are at that moment. In situations like these, assume an intensive listening posture. just lean forward even further and rest your elbows on your knees as you look directly at the other person.

In the illustration overleaf, compare the bad listening posture to the more effective ones.

Bad **Listening Posture**	**Good** **Listening Posture**	**Intensive** **Listening Posture**

Take a few minutes to practise these postures and imagine the effect each would have on an imaginary talker. Better yet, try them out on a co-worker, spouse, or close friend. Get their reactions. Remember, the key is to be relaxed and comfortable, but still attentive.

Minimising Distractions

Earlier in the book we talked about minimising distractions of an external nature when setting the stage for a performance improvement interview. It's also important to minimise the distracting effects of personal habits and mannerisms when you're trying to listen.

While some distractions are unavoidable, most are under your control. To give you an idea, examine this list of *guaranteed* distractions:

▶ maintaining an open door policy at all times;
▶ failing to tell your secretary to hold incoming telephone calls;
▶ using the time you're meeting with people to get other things done, such as cutting and filing your fingernails, cleaning your desk, or balancing your cheque book;
▶ keeping your eye on the clock to make certain you won't be late for your next appointment;
▶ relaxing and making yourself comfortable by sitting back and putting your feet up on the desk;
▶ keeping one ear tuned to the intercom, the PA system or that FM station you like so much.

If you want people to feel heard, you've got to concentrate on them. So close your door, ask that incoming calls be held, and get ready to focus your attention on the employee. Before the interview, clear your desk and your mind of things that will distract you from your purpose at this stage of the process—getting employees to talk about themselves and their work.

To get some practice with these three aspects of attending behaviour—making eye contact, using good body language, and minimising distraction—try the following exercise.

1. Select somebody to talk with. Tell the person you'd like some help with an experiment that'll take only a few minutes.
2. To begin, ask a thought-provoking, comprehensive question to get the person talking. For example: 'Tell me a little bit about what school was like for you. You know, your best and worst subjects, extracurricular activities you took part in, what your social life was like, the kinds of friends you had, the role your parents played, and that sort of thing.'
3. Once the person begins talking, really pay attention. Do all the things we talked about earlier. Make direct eye contact, lean forward slightly, nod your head occasionally, and say 'Uh-huh' or 'Oh yes' every so often.
4. After a minute or two, gradually begin to attend *poorly*. Lean back in your chair, glance around the room, fold your arms across your chest, become poker-faced and look at your watch. While you do this, notice the effect on the other person. Some will look confused and perplexed. Others will stop talking to ask what's going on. Some will start to stutter and stammer. Some may even get angry.
5. After about thirty seconds of bad attending, start attending well again. Then, after another minute or two, stop the experiment and get the other person's reaction to what happened. Then explain what you've been up to. A nice way to express your thanks is to teach the person all you know about attending behaviour.

Question-Asking and Information-Gathering Techniques

Good attending is necessary to be a good listener, but it's not sufficient to get another person talking fully and freely. A skilful listener also directs and guides the interview by asking questions, suggesting topics, clarifying things that aren't clear, encouraging people to delve more deeply into certain areas, and so on. In this section, we'll talk about seven different question-asking and information-gathering techniques:

1. the invitation to talk;
2. open-ended questions;
3. fact-seeking questions;
4. the comprehensive question;
5. thought-provoking questions;
6. probing for specificity;
7. using encouragers.

The Invitation to Talk

Sometimes the best way to get people talking is not by asking a question, but by inviting them to talk about a given subject. For example, you could say, 'I'd like to hear about the people you most admire in life', or 'Tell me about some of your pet hates'. Notice that both of these are statements, not questions.

The invitation to talk does exactly what it says: it invites people to talk openly and freely about a given subject. Here are some other examples:

'I'd like to hear about how things went for you while I was on holiday last week.'

'Tell me what you think of the new computer we had installed in the financial department.'

'I'd be interested in hearing your reactions to the school committee's meeting last night.'

'Tell me about your working relationship with Terry.'

The invitation to talk has several nice features:

▶ it focuses attention on a specific topic but gives people plenty of latitude for their responses;
▶ if you periodically use an invitation to talk, your employees will feel less like they're being grilled or interrogated than if you only ask questions;
▶ a good invitation to talk is an excellent way to get information without showing your hand and having the employee's response coloured by your views on the subject.

Here's some practice. In the space below, write an invitation to talk that you might use with one of your employees.

_____

_____

_____

_____

_____

_____

_____

If you had difficulty, refer to the examples provided earlier. This time try to formulate an invitation to talk by beginning with phrases such as 'I'd like to hear ...' or 'Tell me ...' They'll make it easier.

Open-Ended Questions

The easiest way to understand open-ended questions is to compare them to closed-ended questions, which call for a 'yes' or a 'no' answer.

Closed-ended questions	Open-ended questions
'Did things go OK while I was away last week?'	'How did things go while I was away last week?'
'Has Lee been getting along with the other workers lately?'	'How has Lee been getting along with the other workers lately?'
'Do you like your job?'	'What do you like most and least about your job?'
'Have you learned anything from this experience?'	'What have you learned from this experience?'
'Do you think that book is appropriate for this course?'	'What are your thoughts about the appropriateness of that book for this course?'

Closed-ended questions don't really ask people to 'think out loud' or think expansively about a topic. They're especially ineffective with employees who are shy or reluctant to talk openly with their bosses. Here's an example:

Supervisor: Well, Chris, you've been working here for two months now. Are you pleased with your decision to transfer here from the art department?

Employee: I certainly am, Gerry. I'm very pleased.

Supervisor: When you started, you said you were looking for a job with a lot more responsibility. Do you think you're getting that here?

Employee: Yes, indeed! I have a lot more responsibility here than in my job with the art department. A lot more.

Supervisor: That's good, Chris. I'm happy to hear that. How about your new co-workers? Have they been helpful to you?

Employee: Oh, yes, very helpful, Gerry. I really do appreciate all they've done.

Supervisor: Well, that's great. How about me? Is there anything I can do to make the transition any smoother for you?

Employee: (*Looking thoughtful*) No, I can't think of anything right now.

Supervisor: OK, but if you think of anything, just tell me. All right?

Employee: Yes, Gerry. Of course I will.

In this illustration, Chris didn't give Gerry much information at all. If anything, Chris was telling Gerry what he thought he wanted to hear, a common employee tactic when dealing with bosses. It might have gone very differently if Gerry had asked open-ended questions like these:

'You've been here two months now, Chris. How would you compare this job to your old job in the art department?'

'Chris, how would you assess this job in terms of your original goal of wanting a position with more responsibility?'

'What are some things I could have done—or could do now—to help you make the transition to this new job?'

It would also be possible to answer these questions with very short answers, but Chris is less likely to do so because they're being asked in an open-ended fashion. Another benefit of open-ended questions is that they make it much more difficult for employees to simply tell their bosses what they think their bosses want to hear.

In general, open-ended questions are good ways to start a flow of conversation because they call for an extended answer. They send a message that says: 'Go ahead, take all the time you want. I'm interested in what you have to say.'

Here's a little practice. In the left-hand column are a series of closed-ended questions. Turn each one into an open-ended question, writing your response in the right-hand column. Then, compare your answers to ours.

Closed ended questions	Open-ended questions
Did you enjoy your summer holiday?	_____ _____
Are you planning to take any night courses next term?'	_____ _____
Do you have any recommendations for improving our personnel policies?	_____ _____

Open-ended questions can differ widely in the amount of thinking they ask people to do. For example, look at the following transformations of the first question:

'How did you enjoy your summer holiday?"

'What did you do on your summer holiday?'

'What did you like most and least about your summer holiday?'

'How did this summer's holiday compare to the one you took last year?'

The first open-ended question doesn't really challenge the employee to do much thinking. A simple 'I really enjoyed it' or 'It was awful' would suffice. The other three questions call for progressively more thinking on the part of the employee. Look at how the rest of your open-ended questions compare with ours, especially in terms of how much they challenge the employee to do some thinking:

'What are your educational plans for next term and how do they relate to your long-term goals?'

'In your opinion, what changes should we make in our personnel policies to bring them more into line with what people want and need these days?'

Fact-seeking Questions

When you want to get specific factual information from employees, you can ask fact-seeking questions. Although they're often asked in an open-ended fashion, the focus is narrow and precise. Here are some examples:

'How many minority applicants did we get for that position?'

'What's the percentage of nylon in that new swimsuit line?'

'What were our gross sales for the third quarter?'

'Who wrote that classic book on time management?'

'When is the deadline for submitting that proposal?'

'What's the square footage of our property on Emory Street?'

'Where can we get an order of 5,000 filled on a twenty-four hour basis?'

There are two major reasons why supervisors ask employees fact-seeking questions:

1. to get information they don't have that employees can provide; and
2. to learn whether employees know what they should know. For example, a motor mechanic should be able to describe the principles of electronic ignition. A life insurance agent should be able to answer specific questions about the difference between whole life and term policies. A biology teacher should know about the latest research on recombinant DNA.

If employees don't have the answers to fact-seeking questions, it doesn't mean they should be reprimanded or punished. it simply means that some corrective action may be needed.

Fact-seeking questions can be asked at any time, in casual encounters or in formally scheduled interviews. When used in formal interviews, it's better to ask them later on, after the employee has had a chance to loosen up and get comfortable. Used too early or too frequently, they give the employee the feeling of being quizzed or interrogated.

Imagine you're about to sit down with one of your employees. What are some things you don't know but would like to learn more about? What are some things the employee should know, but may not? In the space below, write a couple of fact-seeking questions you might use in an interview. Compare them to the questions presented earlier.

1. _____

_____

_____

2. _____

_____

_____

_____

The Comprehensive Question

One of the best ways to introduce a topic and to get somebody talking about it is to ask a comprehensive question. * To ask a comprehensive question, you do two things:

1. you introduce the general topic you'd like the person to talk about, either with an invitation to talk or an open-ended question; and
2. you identify some of the specific things the person might focus on when answering, but you provide the opportunity to add anything else.

Here are two examples of comprehensive questions:

'Gerry, I'd like you to tell me, in general, how things are going work-wise. You might want to talk about the things you've been doing

---

*Special thanks to Richard Fear, whose 'comprehensive introductory question' in the context of selection interviews has stood us in good stead in many other situations.

lately, what you particularly like and don't like, any problems you've been having, and anything else you'd like to mention.'

'How did things go on your holiday, Sandra? I'd like to hear about where you went, and what you did. What were the high and low points, that sort of thing.'

A comprehensive question helps stimulate people's thinking because it gives them hints about what to include in their answer. This can be especially useful with people who don't talk very much or who are having trouble getting started because they feel nervous or uncomfortable.

Now try to formulate a comprehensive question. Remember the basic format:

Tell me about _____

You might want to mention _____

_____

_____ , and anything else you think is important.

Write your question below.

_____

_____

_____

_____

You may have had a little trouble coming up with a good comprehensive question. That's natural. You'll feel a little uncomfortable until you get used to them. One way to practise using a comprehensive question is with children. As every parent knows, the classic answer to the question, 'How did things go at school today?' is 'OK' or 'All right'. Try a comprehensive question instead:

'Joe, I'd like to hear about what happened at school today. You know, any new things you learned, what's going on with your friends, the most interesting and most boring things that happened, and anything else that stands out in your mind.'

You may be surprised at the results.

Thought-provoking Questions

As we said earlier, questions vary widely in the amount of thinking they ask people to do. Some questions require no thought at all; others can be provocative and challenging. Look at some of the types of questions we've already discussed. Closed-ended questions ('Did you take a holiday this year?') and fact-seeking questions ('How many weeks off did you take?') aren't particularly challenging. In fact, they often have an indifferent or perfunctory quality about them. Open-ended questions ('How did you enjoy your summer holiday?') are better, but they also vary quite a bit in how much they ask people to 'sink their teeth' into a topic and really chew on it for a while.

Comprehensive questions are also pretty thought-provoking. For example: 'Tell me about what you did for a holiday this year. I'd like to hear about where you went, the kinds of things you did, how it compared to past vacations, how it lived up to your original expectations, and anything else you'd like to add.'

As you talk with people, think about the types of questions you tend to ask. Ask yourself, 'In general, how challenging and thought-provoking are my questions? What can I do to improve them?'

If you want to ask more thoughtful and provocative questions, there's something even more important than the *type* of question you ask. It's the *topic* you ask people to talk about and the *attitude* you convey when asking the question. For our money, a question is guaranteed to be thought-provoking if it has to do with your *relationship* with another person and how that person views you in that relationship. For example, let's say you go up to your spouse or romantic partner tonight and say something like this:

'Darling, I've been thinking about our relationship lately and I'd like to try to improve it. I'd like you to tell me what I could do, as your romantic partner, to make our relationship more satisfying and less frustrating for you. And when you start to answer, I'm going to try to be the best listener I can be. I won't interrupt or get defensive if you say something I might disagree with. Take all the time you want. I really want to hear what you've got to say.'

After you administer the smelling salts (after all, this question isn't your typical question), we'd bet your 'significant other' will find this question pretty thought-provoking. All romantic partners would. It invites them to talk about a *topic* they'd really like to talk about, but only if they had some confidence you'd really like to hear what they've got to say on the subject.

The same thing applies to your relationships with the people who work for you. What if you said pretty much the same thing to one of your employees:

'Lee, I've been thinking about our working relationship lately and I'd like to try to improve it. I'd like you to tell me what I could do, as your boss, to make your job more satisfying and less frustrating for you. And when you start to answer, I'm going to try to be the best listener I can be. I won't interrupt or get defensive if you say something I might disagree with. Take all the time you want. I really want to hear what you've got to say.'

Probing for Specificity

It would be nice if people always communicated their ideas clearly and fully, but they don't. Sometimes they say things that are unclear or confusing. Sometimes they use too few words or a word or phrase you don't understand. When this happens, it's a good idea to probe for specificity.

For example, imagine your employee says, 'Well, you know Jim. He can be a little difficult at times.' Rather than assume you know what the person means, you can probe for specificity by asking one of the following questions:

'Difficult?'

'I'm not sure what you mean by "difficult". Could you expand a little on that?'

'How do you mean that?'

'Can you give me an example of how he can be difficult?'

Each of these examples conveys the message, 'You've said something I don't quite understand. It would help if you'd clarify it for me.'

Sometimes you don't have to say anything to probe for more information. Just pause for a moment.

There are two other important points to remember when getting an employee to clarify something you don't understand:

1. Don't do it at the expense of cutting off the flow of conversation. Especially at the beginning of the interview, it's better to let the

employee get warmed up by talking for a while than to interrupt to clarify something. You can always come back to it later.

2. Be careful to probe in a neutral, non-threatening tone of voice. The last thing you want to convey is impatience or annoyance at the employee's use of vague or fuzzy language.

Below are three employee remarks that need clarification. For each one write in how you might probe for specificity. After you've finished, compare your probes to the ones we would have used.

Employee: I think I could use a little more support around here.

You: _____

_____

_____

Employee: She's a hard worker, but she doesn't show very good judgement.

You: _____

_____

_____

Employee: Seems to me that you've got a lot to learn about supervising people.

You: _____

_____

_____

Here's how we would have responded:

'How do you mean that, Max? What could I do to be more supportive?'

'What are some things she's done that have shown poor judgement?'

'In what ways could I improve the way I supervise people?'

A good way to practise probes for specificity is to use them in your everyday conversations with people. You'll get much more detailed and specific information if you do.

Using 'Encouragers'

'Encouragers' are short signals that show you're interested in what people have to say. They do exactly what the word says—they 'encourage' people to talk freely and fully. They're especially helpful in the opening stages of a conversation, when people are having trouble getting started or seem a little unsure about what to say.

Encouragers fall into two categories, verbal and non-verbal. For example, let's say you've asked an employee: 'Well, Claire, how have things been going on your job?' and Claire responds, 'Uh ... quite well.'

These are some examples of verbal encouragers you could use to get Claire to expand on her answer:

'Quite well?'

'Uh-huh.'

'Tell me more, I'm really interested in how things are going for you.'

'When you say "quite well" ...' (*Pausing to allow employee to answer*)

'It's a hard question to answer just like that. Take some time to think about it.'

These are some examples of non-verbal encouragers you could use:

▶ nod your head a couple of times while maintaining direct eye contact;
▶ lean forward in your chair;
▶ raise your eyebrows a little.

Verbal and non-verbal encouragers are most effective when used together—for example, saying 'quite well?' while leaning forward a little and raising your eyebrows.

Encouragers gently prod employees to tell you in more depth what they're thinking and feeling. Encouragers are much more effective than what most bosses do when employees hesitate or give a brief answer to a question: the boss starts talking! Because silent periods in a conversation make people uncomfortable, it's very tempting to start talking to reduce the discomfort. However, when you succumb to the temptation of filling the silent periods with your words, you can't expect to find out much about the employee. And the employee will be even less likely to talk when you finish.

So far, we've covered two major listening skill areas: (a) attending behaviour and (b) question-asking and information gathering techniques. Now let's move on to the third and final listening skill area.

'Reading Back'

Whenever two human beings sit down to talk, misunderstanding occurs. Partly, this happens because the two parties have such very different perspectives. Person A sees things from his point of view and Person B sees things from her point of view. How people achieve understanding, despite their different perspectives, is the focus of this third major listening skill area, which we call 'reading back.'

If you want to prove to people that you really do understand what they're saying, we know of only one way to do it. When they finish talking, try to restate or 'capture' the essence of what you heard them say, in your own words. We call this technique 'reading back' because what you're doing is trying to read back your understanding of what the other person said.

Reading back is important for several reasons:

1. It's positive proof you're trying to listen. It's possible to fake good attending, but you can't fake reading back. When you try to read people back, they appreciate the effort you're making to stay on their wavelength. And to read people back accurately, you have to pay attention. If you switch off for a second, you won't be able to do it. Just knowing you're going to read people back focuses your attention like nothing else we know.

2. It prevents misunderstanding. Just because somebody tells you something doesn't mean you've heard it correctly. Maybe you misunderstood. Or maybe the person didn't really mean it the way it came out. Reading them back gives people a chance to correct any misunderstanding you might have formed of what they said, or what they meant.

3. It helps people 'think out loud'. Having your remarks read back by another person is very stimulating. When you hear your thoughts and ideas summarised in another person's words, you almost invariably find new thoughts and feelings emerging. Half-formed ideas begin to take shape and solutions will often begin to emerge for problems that have been bothering you. It's hard to describe it accurately and completely in a few words here; it's one of those things you have to experience to fully understand.

There are three ways to read people back. Even though we'll present them separately here, in practice they tend to run together. They are:

1. reflecting feeling;
2. paraphrasing; and
3. summarising.

Reflecting Feeling

Often it's not what people say but how they say it that counts. The emotion behind the message becomes much more important than the message itself. When you want to respond to the emotion rather than the content of an employee's remark, use the technique of reflecting feeling.

Reflecting feeling is a simple, two-part process:

1. Identify the feeling behind the other person's remark: confusion, anger, frustration, excitement, determination, or whatever.
2. Read back or 'reflect' the feeling back to the employee, beginning your response with words like: 'So, you're feeling ... or 'Sounds as though you're feeling ...'

When you do this you send an important message: 'I'm as interested in your feelings as I am in your thoughts and ideas.' Here are some examples:

Supervisor: Sally, I'd like to hear about any problems you've been having at work over the last several months.

Employee: (*Quickly and angrily*) Don't you think they ought to do something about the air conditioning where our desks are? It gets like an oven over there during the afternoon! They said they were going to fix that system weeks ago!

Supervisor: (*Calmly, non-defensively*) Sounds like the delay is really beginning to make you angry ...

Employee: (*Jumping in quickly*) It certainly is! It's just terrible.

Supervisor: How are you and Cheryl doing with the filing backlog?

Employee: Well, we work on it at least an hour every day. But a lot of the time it seems as though we're shovelling sand against the tide. Every day a new batch comes in to more than make up for what we did the day before.

Supervisor: So, it's frustrating . . . and discouraging.

Employee: Absolutely! And while we're on the subject . . .

In these examples the employees were expressing some distinct feelings even though they didn't come right out and say so. In both cases, the supervisor reflected these feelings back to the employee and didn't even mention the content of the employee's remarks. By using this technique, you'll get employees to talk further about things that are bothering them and you'll demonstrate your concern about their feelings. Solutions to problems (and that's where content comes into play) can be dealt with later, after important feelings have been brought to the surface and expressed.

Practise reflecting the employee's feelings in the following examples. Write your answers in the space below each remark, comparing your responses to ours after you've finished.

Employee: (*Raising his voice*) Why is it you're always asking me to be the flexible one, the one with all the sensitivity? What about her?

You: _____

_____

_____

_____

_____

Employee: My biggest problem is dealing with criticism. When people start telling me how to do my job, especially that lot from upstairs, I get really wound up. I know that exploding like a volcano is bad, and I've got to learn how to change that if I'm ever going to get anywhere here. I've got to stop being so incredibly thin-skinned!

You: _____

_____

_____

_____

_____

Here's how we would have responded:

'You're angry because it seems as though I'm being unfair.'

'It sounds as though you're really determined to bring your temper under control.'

As practice, try using this technique in as many different situations as you can. For example, when your child enthusiastically tells you about the last-second home team victory, try saying 'Gosh, that must have been really exciting' or 'So, you were really thrilled to pull it out in the final seconds'. Or when your spouse says 'How could you do that when I specifically asked you not to?' try to acknowledge the feeling by saying, 'You're really angry with me for not listening to you.'

Reflecting feeling is a listening skill that sometimes seems a little awkward. Or even silly. However, when it's used genuinely in the midst of an emotional conversation, it can be a very effective tool. It may be easy to caricature this valuable listening skill (we certainly do from time to time ourselves), but that doesn't take away from its effectiveness.

When you reflect people's feelings, especially when they're upset or feeling strong emotion, be prepared for a continued outpouring. That's fine. That's actually what you want. If you continue to draw them out further (continuing to reflect feelings, if necessary), they'll invariably wind down and begin to feel more understood.

In our opinion, it's a waste of time to try to talk to people when they're upset, angry or experiencing some other strong emotion—they just aren't in a receptive frame of mind. It's much better to listen to them by reading them back and, occasionally, reflecting their feelings. As we've said before, if you want people to listen to what you've got to say, you must be prepared to listen to them first.

Paraphrasing

Paraphrasing is similar to reflecting feeling because it involves reading back. However, while reflecting feeling concentrates on emotion, paraphrasing focuses primarily on content. When you paraphrase, you simply repeat in your own words the gist of what you understood the employee said. For example:

Employee: It's really hard to get things done in this place. The telephones ring, typewriters rattle, radios blare! Half the things I do I have to do over again just to make sure there are no mistakes.

Supervisor: So ... all the distractions are really affecting your productivity.

Sometimes you'll combine reflecting feeling and paraphrasing in the same read back. For example:

Supervisor: How's your new job going, John?

Employee: OK, I suppose, but my new boss is a bit stiff and formal ... and uncommunicative. He never sits down and tells us how we're doing. I'm not really sure what he thinks of my work, or how I'm doing, to speak frankly.

Supervisor: It sounds as though your boss never gives you any feedback, good or bad, and that makes you feel uneasy ... and maybe a little insecure.

Employee: Yes, I never quite put it in those words, but that's exactly how I feel, and ...

Often a good paraphrase will tie together an employee's remarks concisely through the use of a word or phrase that seems to fit perfectly. When this happens, employees will often brighten up and say things like 'Exactly!' or 'That's it!' And you'll know you've just hit the bull's eye.

Try to paraphrase the following remarks, comparing your responses to ours after you've finished.

Employee: The trouble with Tom is that everything has to be done *exactly* his way. He doesn't realise that we all have our own ideas and feelings about how things could be done. And it doesn't make any difference if the final product is perfect or not. If you don't do it exactly his way, it's not done right.

You: _____

_____

_____

_____

_____

_____

Employee: I'm just not sure what to make of those trainee ratings. Whenever they complete those rating forms, they always say 'very satisfied, very satisfied'. But when they talk among themselves, they're always complaining about how bad things are. Listening to them then, you'd think they hated the programme. I just don't know what to make of it.

You: _____

_____

_____

_____

_____

_____

This is how we would have responded:

'So the "right" way to do things is his way, and his way only, even though you see other ways to go about it.'

'I think what you're saying there is that it's hard to know what to believe when they say such different things in different situations.'

Summarising

Summarising is similar to paraphrasing, but it differs in the amount of information that is read back. A paraphrase is a rephrasing or restatement of the central message contained in one or two employee remarks. It basically says the same thing, but in different words. A summary highlights or recapitulates the main points made in a more lengthy exchange between supervisor and employee. It's a condensation of a good deal of information into several major points or themes. Its purposes are similar to paraphrasing and reflecting feeling:

- ▶ it proves you've heard what the employee has been saying;
- ▶ it gives the employee an opportunity to correct any misunderstanding on your part;
- ▶ it allows the employee to add anything else that wasn't mentioned previously.

Here's an example of how a supervisor might summarise a long series of statements made by an employee:

Supervisor: Chris, I'd like you to take a few minutes to describe the things you do particularly well in your job.

Employee: (*Looking thoughtful*) The things I do well. OK. (*Pause*) Of course, there are a lot of things I don't do so well, but here goes. A number of people have told me I have good word processing skills, especially because I type accurately and rapidly. And I guess I'd have to agree with them. I picked up typing really fast at school and it does come easily to me. (*Pause*) Let's see, I think I'm also pretty good on the telephone. You know, being polite and cheerful, taking good messages, that sort of thing. Bob Peters says I am good on the phone. And Betty Marshall has complimented me on more than one occasion about my good telephone skills. (*Pause*) Let's see ... oh yes, my shorthand's pretty good even though I don't use it much on this job. I remember I got the highest grade in shorthand class. But that was ages ago. (Laughing and pausing for a moment) Hmm ... one more thing. I almost always get my work done on time. I know that's true because you've mentioned that yourself ... and also because nobody ever has to remind me to get things done. That about does it. (*Pause*) I can't think of anything else.

Supervisor: Okay, Chris, I heard you say a number of things there. (*Pause*) You started off by mentioning that you were a good typist. (*Pause*) Then I think you mentioned that you have very good telephone answering skills, (*Pause*) and that your shorthand is good. And, finally, that you can usually be counted on to get your work done on time. (*Pausing and looking at employee*)

Employee: Yes, that's right. Oh, I just thought of one other thing ...

In addition to the purposes mentioned earlier, summarising can be helpful in several other ways:

▶ a good summary often sharpens a rambling, disconnected series of remarks by highlighting the main points in a clear, concise manner;

▶ just knowing that you're going to summarise a lengthy series of remarks provides excellent motivation to listen carefully to what's being said;

▶ summarising is especially helpful in winding up one major segment of the interview and making the transition to a new one.

All you have to do is conclude your summary with something like, 'Unless you've got something else to add, I'd like to move on to a new topic'.

When you read someone back—whether you're reflecting feeling, paraphrasing or summarising—do it slowly. Pause to give the person a chance to jump in with a new thought or an elaboration on an old one. If the person interrupts you in the middle of your read back, that's fine. Just go back into listening mode and be prepared to read back whatever the person wants to say. When you finish reading back the new items, go back to the original remarks and read that back. And remember: effective, skilful listening is done at a reflective, thoughtful pace, never in a hurried manner.

A Quick Summary

Listening skills can be broken down into three areas:

1. attending behaviour;
2. question-asking and information-gathering;
3. reading back.

Attending behaviour includes three techniques for paying attention and showing an interest in what employees are saying:

1. making eye contact;
2. using good body language;
3. minimising distractions.

Question-asking and information-gathering includes seven techniques for getting people to talk, keeping them talking, and clarifying what they've said:

1. the invitation to talk;
2. open-ended questions;
3. fact-seeking questions;
4. the comprehensive question;
5. thought-provoking questions;
6. probing for specificity;
7. using encouragers.

Reading back includes three techniques for proving that you're trying to listen and demonstrating that you've correctly heard what employees are saying:

1. reflecting feeling;
2. paraphrasing;
3. summarising.

In the next chapter we'll present a detailed illustration of how a supervisor combines these listening skills in a meeting with an employee. You'll have an opportunity to practise these skills in that chapter. But to become a really proficient listener, you'll also need to practise these skills on your own.

Chapter 9

Step Four: Find Out How Things Are Going

BEFORE WE took a break from the ten-step process to talk about listening skills, we covered the first three steps in the performance improvement process:

Step One: Analyse your employee's performance;
Step Two: Ask your employee to meet with you;
Step Three: Begin the performance improvement interview.

In Chapter 8 we introduced you to a series of listening skills to help you get employees to open up and to talk freely. These skills will come in very handy in Step Four of the process, finding out how things are going from the employee's perspective. Here's what this chapter includes:

▶ the reasons why it's important to find out how things are going with an employee;
▶ a walk-through example of a supervisor using good listening skills to find out how things are going with an employee;
▶ possible setbacks that can occur at this stage and strategies for dealing with them; and
▶ time out for practice and a self-evaluation on this part of the process.

Why It's Important to Find Out How Things Are Going

Let's get back to where you left off in the ten-step process. In Step Three you began the interview by doing a number of things to get the meeting off to a good start.

▶ You set the stage by minimising potential distractions and interruptions.

▶ You made the employee feel comfortable and welcome with a warm greeting and some casual conversation.

▶ You 'structured' the interview by mentioning the purpose of the meeting (to review the person's work performance) and previewing what was going to happen in the remainder of the session.

▶ You also talked briefly about how the two of you could get the most out of the session.

▶ You asked if the employee had any questions or concerns before moving on.

Now you're ready to find out how things are going with the employee. This means asking the employee to talk about two things:

1. how things are going in general at work; and
2. any problems the employee might be experiencing at work that you should know about.

There are several reasons why it's important to cover these points at this stage of the interview.

1. You signal to employees that you really do want to listen to what they've got to say. As we've said before, most bosses aren't very good listeners to their employees and, to be frank, some of them are absolutely terrible listeners. By asking employees about how things are going at work and about any problems they are having, you send a message that says, 'I want to hear what's going on. Your job and your concerns are important to me.' You're giving employees a chance to say what's on their minds—something that doesn't happen as often as it should between managers and employees.

2. You allow employees to vent some of their frustrations. We all need to let off a little steam now and then. Usually, however, we do it with our co-workers and not with our bosses. However, when bosses do give employees a chance to vent their frustrations, it's almost always good for morale. In performance improvement meetings it also helps clear the air early in the session so that the rest of the interview can proceed more smoothly.

3. You give employees a chance to talk about problems that you should know about. As a manager, you're limited in how much you can get around and how much of the overall operation you can see at any given time. By finding out what's going on from the employee's perspective, you're much more likely to identify problems early on, before they get out of hand. When employees do bring problems to you, don't respond by getting defensive or angry. And don't make the critical mistake of saying to employees, 'Don't bring me problems, bring me solutions.' This will guarantee you'll hear nothing at all.

4. By finding out how things are going with all the people you supervise, you begin to get a perspective on your work unit that most managers and supervisors never have. As a boss, you can only see things from your perspective, which can be pretty limited. By finding out how things are going from all the people who report to you, you'll begin to see things from your employees' point of view as well as your own. This will make you a much more effective manager of people. If you have any doubts about this, think back to supervisors you've had in the past. How many times did you wish they could see things from your perspective?

5. By listening now, you build employee receptivity for later on in the meeting. By asking these questions early in the interview, you're not simply gathering valuable information. You're also increasing the chances that the employee will listen to you later in the interview. We call this 'building receptivity'. By listening first, you make employees more receptive to what you have to say later, when you get to other important subjects, like what they can do to improve their work performance.

Walking through an Example

Here's an example of a boss finding out how things are going with an employee. Throughout the script we'll provide a commentary on points of special interest or techniques the supervisor is using. Read through the script ignoring these comments so you get a feel for the interaction. Then re-read it paying close attention to the comments.

Gerry: Well, Chris, now that we've covered the reasons why I asked to meet with you and what's going to happen here today, I'd like to ask you to step back and think about your job for a few minutes. (*Pausing to allow words to register with Chris*) Why don't you begin by telling me how things are going in general at work for you? After that, I'd like to hear about any problems you're having that you think I should be aware of. (*Pause*) As I said earlier, I want to be the best listener I can be while you're talking. I won't interrupt or get defensive if you say something I disagree with. I just want to hear what you have to say. [Notice how the supervisor invites the employee to 'think out loud' about how things are going. Also notice the supervisor's commitment to be a good listener. Have you ever had a boss say anything like this?]

Chris: Well, I think things are going pretty well. (*Pauses and says nothing for a second*)

Gerry: (*Nodding head and smiling slightly*) Uh-huh.

Chris: Uh, let's see . . . That's hard to answer all at once.

Gerry: (*Nodding and smiling*) Yes, it is. Take your time. Just think out loud. [Sometimes the employee will have a tough time getting started. Notice how the good use of verbal and non-verbal encouragers gets Chris going.]

Chris: (*Loosening up a little*) Let's see. Well, I'd have to say that things have been going pretty well for me here. I like it here much more than my last job. (*Pause*) The atmosphere's a lot more relaxed and the people here are very nice. You'd be amazed how many of them have come up and introduced themselves and asked if they could help in any way. Ahh ... (*Pausing*)

Gerry: (*Nodding*) Uh-huh.

Chris: Well, yes ... oh, uh ... the family health care benefits! Thank goodness for the benefits! (*Smiling broadly and pausing*)

Gerry: (*Smiling back*) It sounds as though you really appreciate the benefits. [This is just a short read back that reflects the feeling the employee is expressing.]

Chris: Do I! My son broke his leg—pretty badly, too. He was in the hospital for almost two weeks. I won't even tell you what the bill was, but the private insurance plan covered all of it. He's back to normal now, but he's likely to break another one soon, with all his running around. (*Stops and doesn't add any more*)

Gerry: (*After making sure Chris isn't going to say anything else*) That's great about your son. I'm really glad he's back to normal.

(*Pausing for a second*) Well, Chris, it sounds as if you're pretty pleased with things here. (*Pause*) You like this job much more than your previous one. (*Pause*) You appreciate the relaxed atmosphere, especially the friendliness and helpfulness of people. (*Pause*) And the benefits have been a great help, especially given the situation with your son ... (*Stops as Chris looks as if he wants to say something*) [A concise read back, done in a relaxed, reflective manner. Notice how it gets the employee to mention one more important item. It's common for read backs to stimulate additional thoughts like this. Also, it's fine if the employee interrupts a read back to add something or clarify a thought. That's one of the main reasons for doing them.]

Chris: Absolutely! And one more thing. I see an opportunity to advance here, which is very important for me ... and for my family. My last job was strictly dead end. Even though I liked the work and the company, there was nowhere for me to grow there.

Gerry: (*Pausing to make sure nothing else is coming*) OK, so one more thing on the plus side is the chance to advance here.

Chris: Exactly! That's very important to me. At least it's important to me now. (*Looks thoughtful*) Just a few years ago I lived as if there was no tomorrow. But not any more. (*Pause*) I suppose that's what getting married and having children does for a man?

Gerry: In other words, marriage and parenthood force people to mature quickly?

Chris: You said it! At least it did with me. (*Pausing for a moment*) I think that just about sums it up. I can't think of anything else.

Gerry: I've appreciated everything you've said so far. (*Pause*) Well, Chris, you've talked about a number of things you like. But no situation is perfect. I'd like to hear about anything you don't like or any problems you've been having at work. [See how the supervisor smoothly makes the transition from one topic to the next.]

Chris: Problems? Hmmm, I certainly can't think of anything major. (*Looking down and hesitating*) Ah ... well, maybe there are a couple of little things that've been bothering me. (*Looking a little uncomfortable*)

Gerry: (*Leaning forward slightly and nodding*) I'd like to hear about them.

After some initial hesitation, the supervisor's use of an encourager (combined with good attending behaviour) gets the employee talking. As a supervisor, Gerry is also sending an important message to Chris:

'It's OK to talk about problems to me.'

Chris: Well, for one thing, the work load gets pretty heavy sometimes. And, when it does, I have a little trouble keeping up. When the pressure is on, it seems as if all the managers act like their work is the most important to do. And right now, too! Some of them get pretty upset if they don't get what they want right away. (*Pause*)

Gerry: (*Nodding and looking intently, but not saying anything*)

Chris: It's very frustrating. And it makes me feel really under pressure, especially when I'm behind schedule and they all start asking about their own pet projects.

Gerry: Uh-huh (*Continuing to attend well*)

Chris: I really feel put on the line when that happens. Sometimes I feel so tense I just want to run away from the entire situation. (*Pause*) I don't quite know how to resolve it, but I'd really like to see the problem cleared up.

Gerry: (*Waiting to make sure Chris is finished*) I'm hearing several things there, Chris. At times, the work load gets pretty heavy and you have a hard time getting everything done. (*Pause*) Second, to make matters worse, it's during those extra-busy times you feel pressured by some of the shop managers to focus on just their special projects. (*Pause*) Finally, and maybe most important, you're saying that you're at your wit's end about how to resolve the problem. (*Looks to see if Chris wants to build on the read back*) [A good read back is done slowly and tentatively, with ample opportunity for the employee to break in with a related thought. Often, a good read back will lead employees to bring up 'touchy' subjects or other topics they are reluctant to mention.]

Chris: Yes, that about sums it up. (*Pause*) Well, there is ... uh ... (*Pause*) Well, while we're on the subject, there is ... ah ... well, it has to do with Terry. (*Pause*)

Gerry: (*Wrinkling forehead with quizzical expression*) Uh-huh?

Chris: I don't want to speak out of turn, but she can be difficult at times.

Gerry: When you say difficult, how do you mean that, Chris?

A probe for specificity often leads to very good information. Imagine how little information the supervisor would have received if the following statement were made instead: 'Yes, we do know how difficult Terry can be.'

Chris: Well, it's related to the work load problem. As you know, we're supposed to help each other out when the crunch comes. I mean, I'll ask her for some help but she'll say she's so busy doing her own work she doesn't have any extra time to help with mine. But she can somehow seem to find the time to chat for a half-hour on the phone while I'm breaking my neck to keep the managers off my back. I don't know, it just annoys me when other people don't pull their weight. You know?

Gerry: So ... you get pretty annoyed when she says she's too busy to help, but you see she really does have the time. (*Pause*) And that just compounds the time-pressure problem you mentioned earlier? [A good, brief read back that captures exactly what Chris was thinking and feeling. This time the supervisor gets clear confirmation that Chris feels heard.]

Chris: Yes! It really has been been bothering me. I wasn't going to say anything, but you got it out of me. (*Pause*)

Gerry: Well, I'm just glad we're talking about it. (*Waiting a moment to see if Chris has anything else to add before summarising everything he's been saying about problems*) Well, Chris, putting it all together, it sounds as if your main problems have to do with the occasionally heavy work load, (*Pause*) the pressure you feel when all the managers want their work done at once, (*Pause*) and Terry's unwillingness to help out when the crunch comes.

Chris: (*Nodding*) Right. And those really are problems! (*Smiling*) [Just identifying problems often makes employees feel better. It takes a load off their minds. Notice how the supervisor keeps to the game plan by deferring any talk about solutions until later in the interview.]

Gerry: You've identified some problems, Chris, but they sound like solvable problems to me. A little later I would like us to put our heads together to find some solutions. But now I'd like to move on to another subject. I'd like you to tell me what I could do, as your boss, to make your job here a little less frustrating and lot more satisfying. You may recall I asked you to think about that question when I asked you to meet with me the other day ...

At this point we'll leave the interview between Gerry and Chris, picking it up again in Chapter 10.

Practise Finding Out How Things Are Going

After reviewing the walk-through example at least once, practise handling this stage of the interview yourself. Find another supervisor or a close friend to help you, someone you feel comfortable with. Give the person as much information as you can about a real employee, someone you currently supervise. Tell your partner how you think the employee would behave in an interview and ask the person to play the employee's role as accurately as possible. Then go ahead and give it a try. Tape the interview, if possible. After you've finished, review the tape or recall your conversation carefully. Use these questions as a guide for self-evaluation.

▶ How did you come across? Relaxed, tense, loose, tight? Did you sound like a person you'd feel comfortable talking to? If you sounded a little stiff or gruff, you might want to practise softening your tone. If you tended to speak too fast or too slowly, practise varying your tempo by slowing down or speeding up. If you found yourself sounding a little bland, add a little enthusiasm to your voice by emphasising certain words or using the upper and lower registers of your voice.

▶ Did you follow the overall format of this approach? Did you begin by asking how things were going in general at work for the employee? After that, did you ask about any problems the person was experiencing that you should be aware of?

▶ How was your body language, especially your attending skills? Did you make and maintain direct eye contact, lean forward slightly as the person was talking, and hold down any distractions that might have got in the way?

▶ How would you assess your question-asking and information-gathering techniques? Did you start by asking a comprehensive, thought-provoking question that really invited the employee to think out loud? During the interview, did you use open-ended questions? Many people fall back into the bad habit of asking 'yes' or 'no' questions at this point. If this was true for you, practise asking questions that can't be answered with yes-no answers.

Ask questions like these:	Avoid questions like these:
'How do you feel about ...'	'Do you ...'
'What are your thoughts about ...'	'Is it ...'
'I'd like to hear what you have to say about ...'	'Can't you ...'
	'Wouldn't you ...'
'What do you think of ...'	'Have you ...'

What did you do to help the other person continue talking? Did you use verbal encouragers, such as 'Uh-huh,' 'I see,' 'Tell me more,' and 'Go on'? Did you use non-verbal encouragers, such as nodding your head, wrinkling your forehead, and, in general, using your facial muscles to communicate interest?

How effective were you at reading back what the employee said? For many managers and supervisors, it's common to conduct an entire interview and never use this valuable listening skill. If you didn't, this is an area where you need more practice. If you did, ask how good you were at 'capturing' what the other person was saying.

How well did you deal with silences in the conversation? If you had a tendency to fill in the gaps with your words, you may have to work on pausing during these moments of silence, even though it may make you a bit nervous. Practise counting silently to five (or even ten) after you ask a thought-provoking or open-ended question. You may be surprised at some of the thoughtful answers you'll get before you finish counting.

Overall, how involved and co-operative did the person become? How successful were you in building up the person's receptivity? Did your partner feel you were really interested and really listening? Or did it seem as if you were just going through the motions?

Possible Setbacks

When things go wrong at this stage of the interview, they tend to fall into three categories:

1. employees who make critical remarks about you or the perform-ance review process—and (in the process) who express anger, frustration or general dissatisfaction;
2. employees who refuse to go along with your game plan; and

3. employees who ramble on and on whenever someone gives them an opportunity to talk.

The Employee who Makes Critical Remarks

Let's say you asked your employee how things were going at work and you heard one of these replies:

'I don't quite know who's fault it is, but we just don't have much leadership around here. And I'm not the only one who feels that way.'

'Well, now that you mention it, we haven't been getting very good supervision around here.'

'Well, things would go a lot better if you supervisors would do your jobs better. There are a lot of problems in this place that you don't know anything about.'

'I tell you, some changes need to be made around here pretty soon or a lot of people are going to resign. And I'm not the only one who'll tell you that.'

'Well, I just don't think you've been a very good supervisor.'

Although it might be tempting, here are some things you should not do when an employee talks to you in this way:

▶ Don't get angry or respond in kind. That's playing right into the employee's hand and won't get you anywhere.
▶ Don't get defensive and start explaining your behaviour or citing mitigating circumstances.
▶ Don't lecture the employee about insubordination, behaving inappropriately, or saying things that are out of line. The employee probably won't listen anyway.
▶ Don't avoid responsibility by blaming problems on somebody else or factors beyond your control.

So, what *do* you do? Paradoxical as it may sound, drawing people out and getting them to talk even more is an effective way of dealing with angry, critical, and disparaging remarks. Bring all your listening skills—especially good attending skills and reading back—to bear on the problem. Here's an example, with our commentary:

Employee: (*Angrily*) I tell you, some changes need to be made around here pretty soon or a lot of people are going to resign. And I'm not the only one who'll tell you that!

Supervisor: (*Calmly and non-defensively*) I hear a lot of anger in your voice, Lee. (*Leaning forward slightly*) I'd like to hear more about how you're feeling. [Notice how the supervisor has ignored the content of the employee's remark and focused on the feeling of anger. Notice also the invitation to talk even more.]

Employee: (*Slightly startled*) Well ... as a matter of fact, I am pretty angry! I don't know whose fault it is, but we don't get much leadership around here. And I'm not the only one who thinks the quality of the supervision in this place leaves a lot to be desired!

Supervisor: (*Calmly once more*) Lee, it sounds as though your anger and frustration have a lot to do with the supervision you're getting ... or maybe that you're not getting. (*Pausing, looking at employee, pausing again*) I'm also wondering if a good deal of that frustration and anger isn't directed at me? (*Pause*)

The supervisor continues to read back, but now confronts the employee with a suggestion that the critical comments are probably directed at *her* and not some undefined group of supervisors.

Employee: Well, uh ... (*A little flustered*) I ... uh ... didn't mean anything about you personally. Well ... uh, that's not true either. It does have something to do with you. (*Pause*)

Supervisor: (*Pausing for a moment*) Go ahead, you can speak frankly with me. I'm not going to get angry with you for speaking candidly and honestly with me. Besides, I need the feedback. I really do. [Notice how the supervisor not only encourages the employee to speak frankly but 'models' how to go after feedback rather than fight it or defend against it.]

Employee: Well ... uh ... sometimes you have the tendency to ... uh ... to give me a lot of work to do without telling me why I should do it. (*Pause*) I don't know, sometimes it seems as though I waste a lot of my time doing things for no purpose at all.

Supervisor: (*Pause*) So, one of the things I could do is to explain the purpose of the work I assign to you ... give you a better idea of why I want it done and why it's important?

Employee: Yes. That would help a lot.

Supervisor: OK, what else could I do to be more helpful?

Employee: (*Much more relaxed*) Well, there are a couple of other things if you're sure you'd like to hear them. (*Smiling tentatively*) [Now they're really getting down to business.]

Supervisor: (*Smiling*) Yes, Lee, I'd like to hear them. Go ahead ...

In this example the supervisor made good use of listening skills—especially reading back—to deal with the employee's critical remarks. Imagine how the meeting would have gone if the supervisor hadn't been such a good listener and responded 'in kind' to the employee.

Practise Responding to Critical Remarks

For some practice, fill in the form on page 140. Try to use the technique of reading back to respond to the critical remarks. Then look at the next page and compare your responses to the ones we would have made.

Responding to Critical Remarks

After you read each critical remark, write down how you would respond to the employee.

1. *'When you said we were going to have a meeting to review my work I didn't realise it was just going to be another one of these little fireside chats we have every so often.'*

_____

_____

_____

_____

2. *'Why is it the employees are always having their work performance evaluated and not the supervisors? Can you answer that question?'*

_____

_____

_____

_____

3. *'Am I having any problems at work? You're absolutely right I'm having problems. I'm having problems just having to sit down here to talk with you about my work performance!'*

_____

_____

_____

_____

4. *'I think there are a lot of things you could do to become a better supervisor. The most important is to be more sensitive to the needs of your employees!'*

_____

_____

_____

_____

Responding to Critical Remarks

Compare your responses to the ones we'd have made in each of these situations:

1. *'When you said we were going to have a meeting to review my work, I didn't realise it was just going to be another one of these little fireside chats we have every so often.'*

We probably would've ignored the sarcastic tone and simply read her back, focusing on the underlying message. Saying something like, 'Carol, it sounds as if you see this as just another meeting between the two of us, and probably not a very important one either.' If the employee denied this and said, 'No, really I was just kidding', we'd probably persist and say, 'OK, but whatever you're feeling, I want to hear about it. I consider this a very important meeting. We won't be able to get much out of this unless we're open with one another.'

2. *'Why is it the employees are always having their work peformance evaluated and not the supervisors? Can you answer that question?'*

This is an excellent question, but it's also a statement of how the employee feels about one-way performance review meetings. As we've said before, a question is often just a statement in disguise. That's certainly true here, so we wouldn't have answered the question right away, not when the employee's receptivity was so low. We would've said, 'Let me see if I've heard you correctly first. I think you're saying that this seems like an unfair situation because the feedback only goes one way.' Then we'd continue to draw the employee out until the person was ready to hear what we had to say.

3. *'Am I having any problems at work? You're absolutly right I'm having problems. I'm having problems just having to sit down here to talk with you about my work performance!'*

We probably would have started off by calmly saying, 'Bill, you sound pretty angry about having to sit down and talk with me about your work.' If that failed to move things forward, we might have probed for specificity by saying, 'You said it was a real problem to have to sit down here to talk with me about your work performance. What is it that makes it a problem for you? I'd like to hear what you have to say.'

4. *'I think there are a lot of things you could do to become a better supervisor. The most important is to be more sensitive to the needs of your employees!'*

We probably would have read this back, but we could have also probed for specificity, saying, 'Tell me, Jack, how could I be more sensitive to the needs of the employees here? And to your needs in particular?' We'd try to draw the person out until we heard some concrete and specific advice, as opposed to the general admonition to be 'more sensitive'. After the person finished, we'd try to capture it all in a summary read back.

The Employee who Refuses to Go Along with Your Game Plan

Although it happens rarely, sometimes employees can sabotage the interview by stubbornly refusing to go along with your game plan. When this happens, the interview is at a precarious stage. Here, we'd suggest a technique we call 'Stop, Look and Listen' to get the interview back on track. It's a simple three-part process in which you:

1. *stop* the interaction as soon as the discussion becomes argumentative or unproductive;
2. *look* squarely at the problem by describing it succinctly and objectively to the employee;
3. *listen* for suggestions you both can live with for resolving the problem.

For example, let's say you've asked an employee to describe any problems he might be having at work. After listening to a couple of problems, and actually drawing the employee out in some detail, you say:

Supervisor: Okay, Jason, I think I've got a pretty good idea about some of the problems you're experiencing at work. I'd like to defer talking about solutions to those problems until a bit later and move on to a new topic now. What—

Employee: (*Interrupting*) What do you mean 'defer talking about solutions' until later? What's the sense of identifying problems if you don't want to talk about solutions to them?

Supervisor: (*Calmly, after pausing to make sure employee has nothing further to say*) Jason, it sounds as though you're feeling frustrated and irritated about moving to a new subject before talking about solutions.

Employee: You're quite right I'm feeling frustrated. I mean, it just doesn't make sense to me. Do you understand what I'm saying?

Supervisor: I think so. (*Pause*) You're saying you want to talk about solutions right now, not after we've discussed other topics.

Employee: (*More calmly now*) Exactly. That's exactly what I'm saying.

Supervisor: I also think talking about solutions is important. And I had planned to spend a lot of time later in the interview to do just that—after we'd talked about some other things, such as your suggestions for how I could make your job more satisfying and a thorough review of your work performance.

Employee: (*Firmly*) Well, I still think it's important to talk about solutions while the problems are fresh in our minds and not after we've cooled off.

Supervisor: (*Using 'stop, look and listen' technique*) Jason, let's step back from this just for a minute to try to get a fresh perspective. It seems we disagree about how to proceed. You'd like to discuss solutions to some of the problems you identified, while I'd like to talk about solutions after we've covered some other topics. I'd like to find a way out of this that we can both live with. What suggestions do you have for how we might proceed at this point?

Employee: (*Thoughtfully*) Hmm ... I don't really know. (*Smiling and in a joking tone*) We can always do it my way. (*Both laugh*) Hmm ... something we both can live with. Well, we can maybe spend a few minutes talking about solutions now. Then, if it looks as though we're not going to come up with any solutions quickly, we can talk about it later in the meeting.

Supervisor: (*Leaning forward*) Good suggestion. How about if we spend ten minutes now talking about some potential solutions? If, after that time, we don't ...

When using the 'stop, look and listen' technique, it's very important to come up with 'win—win' solutions, solutions both people can live with. Too often in disagreements, people see things from a win-lose perspective. However, with a little resourcefulness and a willingness to compromise, you can usually find solutions that will move things forward and that will be acceptable to both parties. Over the years, we've noticed that some of the best 'win—win' solutions have come from employees.

Let's review what we've discussed so far about possible setbacks. To deal more effectively with employees who make angry, critical, and disparaging remarks or who refuse to go along with your game plan:

▶ don't lose control of the interview by getting defensive, becoming angry, or biting back;

▶ focus on the employee's feelings rather than the content of the remarks—you'll generally get to the heart of the matter more quickly;

▶ encourage the person to talk *even more* by reading back and probing for specificity;

▶ if necessary, use the 'stop, look and listen' technique. Stop the unproductive interaction, look at the problem the two of you are facing, and listen for a 'win—win' solution.

The Employee who Talks Too Much

Now let's look at the employee who talks a lot—the person who tends to go on and on, especially in the presence of a good listener. Here are some techniques that seem to work pretty well with these long-winded types:

1. Hold down your use of verbal and non-verbal encouragers. Don't nod so much, reduce the number of 'uh-huhs', and cut back a little on direct eye contact. Don't resort to bad attending though. You don't have to completely discourage the person; you just don't want to be *too* encouraging.

2. Get a quick sign-off to your read back and then move on quickly to a new topic. After a long-winded response, briefly summarise what the person said, look for a sign that the person agrees with your read back, and then move on to another topic quickly, before the person launches into another monologue. This will convey that you're listening, but that the message could have been delivered more concisely. However, make certain the person 'signs off' on your read back before going on. The person will usually let you know with a nod or some other non-verbal indicator.

3. If you don't get a reasonably direct answer to a question, ignore what the person said and repeat the question. This is called the 'broken record' technique, for obvious reasons. You don't want to use it too often, but sometimes it's helpful.

4. Try the reflecting feeling technique. When you read back what you think the person is trying to express, concentrate on the underlying feelings rather than the content of the person's remarks. Many times long-winded people will use a lot of words to avoid expressing their feelings more directly. Reflecting these feelings in a read back can help cut through a lot of the verbiage.

5. Set some time limits on the interview and remind the person of these time limitations during the course of the meeting. This technique often communicates to the employee that long-winded answers will only eat up some valuable time.

6. When the employee does give concise answers, make positive and rewarding comments. Psychologists call it 'Rewarding the desired behaviour'. Saying something like 'Nicely put!' or 'That was a very clear and concise answer' helps get an employee to reply briefly.

Here are a few examples of supervisors using some of these approaches:

Employee: (*Responding to a question about how things are going*) Oh, pretty well, I suppose. I'd have to say the thing I like most about working here is the convenient location. You know, the Underground station is close to my house and near here. (*Employee continues to talk about this subject, while supervisor maintains eye contact, but reduces frequency of nodding and facial expressions*) Uh ... oh ... things have really improved since Bill was hired. You have no idea the effect it's had on lightening the work load and brightening up the morale around here. Why just the other day several of us were talking ...

Supervisor: (*Listening for several more minutes, then breaking in when the employee stops for a second to catch a breath*) OK, so what I hear you saying is that things are going pretty well. (*Quick pause*) You seem especially happy about how easy it is to get to and from work and you're pleased with how things have gone since we hired that new person to lighten the work load.

Employee: Yes, exactly. (*Looking as if he may be ready to build on previous remark*)

Supervisor: (*Quickly jumping in*) OK, good. Now, let me get your ideas on another subject. Tell me, what ...

Supervisor: You said earlier that you felt the new human resources manager we hired was not very trustworthy. I'm not sure what you meant by trustworthy. Tell me a little more about that.

Employee: Oh, she's all right. You know, she really does some things very well. Why just the other day ... (*Continuing for several minutes about her good points*)

Supervisor: (*Briefly summarising and then repeating original question*) So those are some examples of what she does well. Now earlier you said she wasn't very trustworthy. How did you mean that?

Supervisor: Pat, how do you feel about the new assignment you got last week?

Employee: You know, that's going to be a lot of work. For one thing... (*Explaining for several minutes about how much work will be involved*) Now that's not to mention all of the other responsibilities I currently have. For example ... (*Enumerating current* *responsibilities in more detail than is necessary)*

Supervisor: (*As employee pauses*) Pat, it sounds as though you feel pretty frustrated with the assignment and also maybe a little annoyed that we didn't consider your current responsibilities when we made the assignment?

Employee: (*Slightly taken aback*) Uh ... yes! That's exactly how I feel!

Supervisor: (*Responding quickly*) I can understand that, Pat. And I want you to know that you don't have to beat around the bush with me. I want to know how you're feeling. The more direct you are with me the better.

Practise responding to a Talkative Employee

Ready for a little practise? Again, if you've got a tape recorder and someone to practise with, you'll get more out of this than if you just use your imagination.

Let's say you ask the employee, 'I'd like to hear your thoughts on the new quality control procedures' and you get the following response: 'Well I'm not really sure. But the thing is, I'm more concerned about the inventory problems we've got. Why just yesterday ... (*Going off on a tangent that has nothing to do with your question*)

How would you respond? Write your answer in the space below and compare your response to ours.

Employee: Why just yesterday ...

You: _____

_____

_____

In a situation like this, we suggest you briefly acknowledge the answer and then repeat the original question. We'd say something like, 'So those are your thoughts about the inventory problems. What's your opinion of the new quality control procedures?'

A Quick Summary

Finding out how things are going means asking the employee to talk about two basic things:

1. how things are going in general at work; and
2. any problems the employee might be experiencing at work.

After walking through an example of a supervisor conducting this part of the interview, you had an opportunity to practise it and give yourself some feedback. Finally, you learned some techniques for dealing with problems that may crop up at this stage of the process: the employee who makes critical remarks, the employee who refuses to go along with your game plan, and the employee who talks a lot.

In the next chapter you'll continue in listening mode, as you ask the employee the question, 'What can I do to make your job less frustrating and more satisfying?'

Chapter 10

Step Five: Ask Your Employee 'The Question'

ABOUT SEVEN years ago, we put on a seminar on 'People Problems and How To Resolve Them' at the annual convention of a major trade association. In the audience there were around 350 people, about 98 per cent of them men. We were talking about listening skills, and had just begun the subject of 'Asking Thought-Provoking Questions.' The members of the audience seemed very interested and were quietly and respectfully listening to everything we had to say.

At some point, we looked out into the audience and offered our opinion that most husbands weren't particularly good listeners to their wives. Judging from the head-nodding in the audience, everybody agreed with us on that point. To drive the point home, we urged the men in the audience to go home and ask their spouses, 'What could I do, as your husband, to make our marriage more satisfying and less frustrating for you?' Even though the audience had agreed with our assertion that husbands weren't such hot listeners, they didn't take to this suggestion well at all. To our surprise, the audience exploded with a chorus of objections. From all around the room, we heard things like:

'Are you joking?'

'There is no way I would do that!'

'What? Do you think I'm crazy?'

'No way! That'd just open up Pandora's box!'

'Absolutely not! I'm not asking for trouble!'

We were surprised. We'd heard objections to some of our recommendations before, but never quite so dramatic as this (even though much of what we were hearing was good-natured and tongue-in-cheek). After the commotion died down, several members of the audience dubbed this thought-provoking question, 'The Question', and that's how we referred to it for the rest of the session. By the end of the seminar, most of the group still had reservations about asking it, but several said they'd give it a try.

We pretty much forgot about the session until two weeks later, when one of the people who attended the seminar phoned Mardy Grothe to report on what happened when he asked his wife 'The Question'. This is a reconstruction of that telephone call (even though it's not his real name, we'll call the gentleman Bill here):

Mardy: (*Picking up phone*) Hello.

Bill: Hello, Mardy, this is Bill Williams. You don't know me, but I attended your seminar a few weeks ago. I just wanted to tell you how much I enjoyed it. It was very stimulating. I especially liked the way you and Peter played off each other.

Mardy: (*Obviously pleased*) Well that's terrific, Bill. Thanks for calling. I really appreciate your call. Even though we often get positive comments after a session, it's pretty rare for someone to call several weeks later.

Bill: Well, Mardy, I just had to call to tell you what happened to me. (*Pause*) You know, my wife and I drove down to the convention from our home. After all, it's only a six-hour drive, so we thought it would be a nice little holiday for the two of us.

Mardy: That's nice. (*Wondering where this is going*)

Bill: Anyway, after the convention ended, we were driving out of the hotel car park, heading for home. So I thought to myself, 'Maybe this would be a good time to ask her "The Question."' So I did.

Mardy: (*Happy to hear this*) Why Bill, that's terrific ...

Bill: (*Quickly jumping in*) ... Mardy, she talked for six hours!!!

Mardy: Oh, really ... (*Afraid maybe he had opened up Pandora's Box*)

Bill: ... And, let me tell you, Mardy, that was the single best thing I've done in the thirty-five years we've been married. She told me things I'd never heard before. (*Pausing for a moment*)

Mardy: (*Relieved, but not letting on*) That's great, Bill. Just great!

Bill: Now, I'm not going to get a personality transplant or anything, but I want you to know that I've started to do just a few of the things she suggested. (*Pause*) And the quality of our relationship has already gone up several notches. Thank you!

Mardy: Bill, I'm so happy you called ...

The conversation lasted only a few more minutes. Ever since then, we've referred to the question, 'What can I do to make our relationship more satisfying and less frustrating for you?' as 'The Question'. End of story.

We're now at Step Five of the performance improvement process, where we'd like you to ask your employee 'The Question'. In your case, though, the wording gets changed slightly. When a boss asks 'The Question' it goes like this: 'What can I do, as your boss, to make your job less frustrating and a lot more satisfying?'

In this chapter, we'll:

▶ discuss some reasons you won't want to ask 'The Question';
▶ offer our thoughts on why it's important to ask it anyway;
▶ pick up the example from the last chapter where Gerry, the supervisor, asks Chris, the employee, 'The Question'; and
▶ discuss some possible pitfalls and setbacks at this stage of the process.

Let's start by talking about some reservations you might have about doing what we're suggesting.

Why You Don't Want to Ask 'The Question'

Even though we think it's very important to ask this question, you probably won't want to, for several reasons, as follows.

1. It's threatening to ask for feedback. This question, just because of the way it's framed, invites a certain amount of criticism. And, as some wag once said, 'Criticism is hard to take, especially when it comes from friends, family, co-workers, and strangers.' In our view, criticism is hard to take, even when (or perhaps *especially* when) it's good for us.

While it may be a good idea for bosses to ask their employees a question like this, how many of us always do what's good for us, especially when the thing we should do is either hard or scary to do?

So, if you have some reservations about asking the question, that's natural. You're a human being; you're supposed to have feelings like that.

2. You'll probably expect the worst. Just like the husbands in our audience, you're probably going to expect the worst. You may think: 'The employee's just going to make all kinds of unreasonable demands I'm not going to be able to meet. And then where will I be? Probably a lot worse off than I am now. Better *not* to ask the question in the first place.'

Before you get carried away, though, ask yourself: 'What would I say if *my* boss asked me a question like this?' Close your eyes and think about it for a moment. What would your boss have to do to make your job more satisfying and less frustrating? Be a better listener? Be better at giving you helpful feedback? Not be such so grumpy when he arrives in the morning? To be better at following up on what she said she would do? Think about it. Is what you want so extreme and unreasonable? Probably not. The same applies to what your employees want of you.

3. You may think the employee should ask *you* the question, not vice versa. This reservation is a bit more subtle, but it's just as powerful. It was best expressed by a manager in one of our seminars, who said: 'Wait a minute! This chap works for me, not vice versa. I'm paying him a good salary. I'm giving him an opportunity to make a good living. He should be asking *me* a question like that, not the other way around. It just seems the wrong way round to me!'

If the thought of asking employees 'The Question' grinds you the wrong way, you probably have a lot of company.

4. It's something that's not commonly done. Have you ever had a boss who asked you a question like this? How many times have you asked a question like this of your employees? How many times have your colleagues asked a question like this of their employees? If you're like most people, the answer to all three of these questions is, 'Never'. Not having had it done to you, and not seeing it done around you, it becomes a little more understandable why you don't do it.

5. The professional literature doesn't advise it. We've read dozens of books over the years on performance review meetings and performance appraisal systems. In the classical approach, the focus is on the employee and the employee's performance. In fact, even though a few performance evaluation systems recommend that employees rate their bosses too, we don't recall reading one book where it's recommended that bosses look their employees right in the eye and ask a question like this.

This lack of interest in directly soliciting feedback from employees is also true of the best-selling business books. In Kenneth Blanchard's book, *The One-Minute Manager*, for example, there is not even a hint that the boss might want to *get* some feedback from employees. Lee Iacocca doesn't suggest it in his book. Even Tom Peters and Robert Waterman, in their book *In Search of Excellence*, don't recommend it (although we've got to believe they'd support it if they were asked). No wonder bosses don't do it and feel so unsure about the wisdom of doing it.

These are just a few reasons why you probably have reservations about asking your employees this question. But we think you should ask it anyway. Here's why.

Why It's Important to Ask 'The Question'

There are a number of reasons why it's a good idea to ask 'The Question':

1. Employees love it. They may be a little shocked when you ask it. They may even be suspicious. One supervisor told us a very interesting story. After asking his employee the question, the employee looked sceptically at him, then looked suspiciously all around the room, and finally said, 'Are we on *Candid Camera* or something?' Whatever their initial reaction, though, our experience has shown that employees love it when they're asked this question. They love it so much, it's often hard for them to believe it's really happened.

2. It's an excellent way to get feedback on how you're doing as a boss. All the management textbooks say it: bosses are insulated from feedback. All this means is that employees don't tell their bosses how they really feel about them as managers of people. When you think about it, why should they? Most of them would just get into a lot of trouble if they did. So they end up saying more or less what they think their bosses want to hear. (Samuel Goldwyn, the colourful movie mogul, once said it best when he barked out, 'I don't want any

Yes-men around me! I want people to tell me the truth, even if it costs their jobs!')

However, just asking the question doesn't necessarily mean employees will open up and give you direct and candid feedback. That's where good listening skills come into play. But we guarantee you this: If you ask the question and do a good job of listening, you'll hear things you've never heard before from employees about how they see you as a boss and what you could do to become a better manager.

3. When you ask the question of a number of different employees, you'll begin to hear some common themes. If one employee says you always seem to give short shrift to the positive and accentuate the negative, that's one thing. Maybe you're just dealing with an overly sensitive employee. But when you hear the same thing from a second, and then a third employee, perhaps you'd better start paying attention to what you're hearing.

4. It's a great way to step out of your shoes and see yourself from another perspective. The famous Scottish poet, Robert Burns, talked about the importance of being able 'to see ourselves as others see us'. If you want to grow as a person, it's very important to try to see how you look from the perspective of other people. It's helpful just to think about a question like, 'What would it be like to work for me?' But when you ask 'The Question' of employees you begin to actually find out.

5. It's a helpful antidote to the problem of self-deception. Most of us, whether we admit it or not, see ourselves in a slightly more positive light than others do, especially the people we live with and work with. These people are the true experts on us. Yes, they see the good points. But they see the warts and pimples as well. And, it's good to hear about that side of our personalities every now and then.

6. It can be the 'key' that unlocks the door to improved performance. As we have said already, sometimes your employee's poor work performance is related to *your* performance as a manager. For example, if your employees are losing respect for you because you won't confront a problem employee who's making *their* lives miserable, it'll show up in their motivation to do a good job. Or, if employees resent you because you're always looking over their shoulders and pointing out the mistakes they're making, and never telling them what they're doing right, that may hurt their performance as well. If you can find out what you're doing that's 'irritating' employees, and then correct it, the impact on employee performance is often dramatic.

7. It lays the groundwork for a performance agreement between the two of you.   Before you ask somebody to do something for you—whether it's an employee, a spouse or romantic partner, or a teenage child—we think you ought to be prepared to ask another important question as well: 'What can I do for you?' In Latin, the expression for this is *quid pro quo*, which means 'something for something'. Here's how that expression applies to the situation you're in with the employee. You want the employee to improve, to change in some important ways. That's why you're reading this book. We understand that. But if you think about it for a moment, you'll realise the employee probably wants a few things from you as well. Asking 'The Question' at this stage of the interview opens the door for a 'you-do-something-for-me-and-I'll-do-something-for-you' type of performance agreement, which you'll be getting to later in the meeting. Remember the key principle here: if you do something the employee wants and needs from you, you'll greatly increase the chances the employee will do what you want.

8. It's the right thing to do.   This may sound a little moralistic, but we're going to say it anyway. Remember: 'Do unto others as you'd like to have done unto you'? Ask yourself if you'd like your boss to ask you a question like this (we've never yet heard a person say 'no'). If you would, ask your employees. We call this 'The Golden Rule of Management'.

In fact, if after reading this section, you decide you don't want to ask this question of your employees, we'd like you to walk towards the nearest mirror, look into it, and ask yourself, 'What kind of person are we dealing with here?'

We hope we haven't come on *too* strong in stressing how important it is to ask this question of employees. However, we see it as potentially the single most important step of the performance improvement process.

How to Ask 'The Question'

Let's return to the meeting between Gerry and Chris. In the last chapter, we left them as they were finishing discussing some problems Chris was having on the job. Gerry was making a transition from that subject to this new topic.

Gerry: You've identified some problems, Chris, but they sound like solvable problems to me. A little later I'd like us to put our heads together to look for some solutions. But now I'd like to move on to another subject. I'd like you to tell me what I could do, as your boss, to make your job here a little less frustrating and lot more satisfying. You may recall I asked you to think about that question when I asked you to meet with me the other day.

Chris: Yes I do! (*Smiling broadly*) I've never had a supervisor ask me anything like that before, so it rather took me aback, to say the least. We even discussed it over the dinner table that night when I got home.

Gerry: (*Briefly reading back*) So ... you were surprised at the question?

Chris: Yes, but pleasantly surprised. I even mentioned it to some of my friends at the club this past weekend. They couldn't believe it either. (*Pause*) Anyway, I've been giving it a good deal of thought.

Gerry: (*Leaning forward*) Good! I'd like to hear what you've got to say.

Chris: Well, we've already talked about two things you could help me with, the time-pressure problem with the managers and the problem with Terry. If you could help solve those problems, that would definitely make my job less frustrating. (*Pausing for a moment*) [This is fairly common. In the previous step you asked the employee to tell you about any work problems. For many employees, helping resolve the problems they mentioned earlier will be greatly appreciated, and they'll bring them up again here.]

Gerry: (*Nodding*) Uh-huh.

Chris: Besides that, probably my biggest complaint is that I don't really know where I stand with you. I mean, you're always saying things are fine and all that. But I know I'm not perfect, and I think maybe you're ... oh ... holding back on negative things. (*Hesitating briefly*) So I'd like you to tell me what I'm doing wrong, too. I don't want you to feel you've got to handle me with kid gloves just because I'm the new boy here. (*Pausing and looking a little uneasy*) I don't know. I'm not sure how clear that was. You know what I'm trying to get across here? (*Pausing, looking directly at Gerry*) [It's also quite common for employees to think they've been unclear, even when they've been crystal clear. This is especially common when they're giving feedback to their bosses or mentioning other 'touchy' subjects.]

Gerry: What you're saying sounds pretty clear to me. Let's see if I heard you correctly. (*Pause*) You're saying you don't want me to pussyfoot around with you just because you're new here. And if I've got some complaints about how you're doing your job, you'd like to hear that, too, not just general comments about how things are going fine or OK. [You can always tell when your read back is right on target.]

Chris: Right! That's exactly what I was trying to say. (*Pause*) That was a big problem in my last job. My boss was one of those 'nice guy' types who never gave me any constructive criticism. All he ever said was, 'You're doing really well'. I don't want someone to beat me over the head, but I certainly want a boss who'll challenge me and help me grow. You know what I mean?

Gerry: That is, how will you be able to improve if you don't know what you're doing wrong?

Chris: Exactly. (*Pausing to think for a moment*) Hmmm, what else? Well, another thing is ... uh ... I'd really like to know more about what everybody does around here. I mean, I know Bill Sutton is the business manager and Frank Smith is the purchasing agent, but I don't know what they really do or why they do it. (*Pausing*)

Gerry: (*Waiting for a moment to see if Chris is going to add anything*) You mean you'd like to have a somewhat better idea of what other people, like Frank and Bill, do in the company. How they fit into the grand scheme of things?

Chris: Yes. I think it would help me to understand the big picture better, so to speak.

Gerry: (*Pausing*) OK, what else?

Chris: You know, I can't think of anything else! Here's the first time ever a boss asks me a question like that, and I can only think of a couple of things to say. (*Both laugh*) But, in all honesty, I can't think of anything else right now. [The employee appears to be very comfortable. Receptivity is going up and up.]

Gerry: (*Smiling*) Well, it's not as though this is your last chance.

If you think of something else later on, I'd like to hear about it.

Chris: OK, I'll do that.

Gerry: (*Slowly and reflectively*) Well, Chris, based on everything you've said so far, it sounds as though I could do several things to make life more satisfying and less frustrating for you here. (*Pause*) The first is to try to help solve the time-pressure problem, with all the managers wanting you to work on their 'pet' projects at the same time. (*Pause*) The second is to try to help solve the Terry co-operation problem. (*Pause*) The third is to be better at telling you what I think you're doing wrong on the job or where I think you could improve. (*Pause*) And the fourth is to help you learn about what other people in the company, like Bill and Frank, are doing. (*Looking directly at Chris*) [A good summary read back of everything Chris has said so far—from the previous step as well as this one about things Gerry could do to make his job more satisfying and less frustrating.]

Chris: I think that sums it up nicely.

Gerry: Excellent. We'll be coming back to these points a little later in the meeting, when we talk about where we go from here. (*Shifting to next topic*) But now let's move on to a discussion of your work performance. Why don't we begin with you ...

With receptivity as high as it is, the supervisor now feels comfortable moving to a discussion of the employee's work performance.

The meeting Gerry had with Chris went without a hitch, but they don't always go so smoothly. Let's take a look at some potential setbacks.

Potential Pitfalls

There are a couple of problems you might run into at this stage of the process. They are:

▶ the employee who doesn't want to answer 'The Question';
▶ the employee who really unloads on you;
▶ the employee who requests things that are out of your control.

We'll discuss each one briefly, along with a few suggestions about what you can do to to cope with the problem.

The Employee Who Doesn't Want to Answer 'The Question'

Sometimes employees won't take you up on your invitation to think about what you could do to make their jobs more satisfying and less frustrating. Despite your prodding, they may say something like: 'No, honestly, I can't think of anything you could do for me' or 'I'd rather not mention anything, if you don't mind'.

There are several reasons why employees might do this:

1. They're afraid of getting burned.   It's risky to give bosses candid and direct feedback. Many employees feel their jobs are at stake. Besides, maybe they've been burned in the past by a boss they spoke frankly to. Or maybe they're afraid you'll try to get back at them if they say something you don't like.

2. They don't think you mean it.   If employees doubt your sincerity, don't expect to hear too much of anything. They've got to believe you genuinely want to hear what's on their minds to run the risk of giving you feedback.

3. They think it's wrong to criticise a boss.   Their numbers may be dwindling, but, yes, there are still some employees like this around. They don't think it's right to say anything negative or critical to bosses and other authority figures.

4. They're extremely shy or reticent.   Very shy or bashful employees may have something to say, but they're going to say it when *they're* ready, not when you want them to. Remember, though, that nothing will get them ready faster than high quality listening on your part.

5. They're afraid to bring up a very 'touchy' subject. Sometimes bosses do things that *really* bother employees (like taking drugs, having affairs with employees, or engaging in unethical or illegal business practices). When this is the case, most employees will say nothing at all in response to 'The Question'. As one employee told us, 'If I'm not going to talk about what's really bothering me, I'd rather not come up with a selection of made-up ideas just to answer the question.'

Here are some thoughts about how to handle employees who don't answer—or don't want to answer—the question:

▶ Try to find out what's causing the blockage. Use your listening skills. Maybe you'll find out it's because of a supervisor in the past, or something you yourself have said or done. Try saying something like:

> 'I'm a little surprised you have nothing to say, Pat. After all, I'm far from a perfect boss. Can you help me out a little here and tell me why you don't want to answer the question?'

▶ Press for an answer, but don't be pushy. You can say something like:

> 'I can understand your being a little hesitant, but I'd really like to hear what you've got to say. I'm not going to hold it against you if you say anything critical. And I won't know how to make your job more satisfying if I don't get some help from you. Why don't you give it a try.'

▶ If the employee persists, accept it, but leave the door open for the future. You can say:

> 'All right. But I want you to know that, when you're ready, I'm going to be all ears to what you've got to say. Maybe it'll be later in this session, or maybe it'll be in our next meeting. Whenever it is, I want to hear it.'

The Employee Really Unloads on You

Although it rarely happens, sometimes an employee will get very emotional or upset and say something that's very critical of you. Maybe the employee has been holding something in for a while and, now that the flood gates are open, it comes out in torrents. So remember, if you're going to ask the question, you've got to be prepared to hear some things you're *not* going to like ... and with some employees you may even hear some real anger or vitriol.

A few years ago, the crew of *Saturday Night Live* captured this phenomenon in a humorous way. The scene is late at night on a huge ship in the middle of the ocean. On the bridge is the admiral and his young lieutenant, played by Steve Martin. They're all alone. Finally, the admiral looks over at his lieutenant and says in a somewhat arrogant, imperious manner: 'Well, lieutenant, it's late in the evening and no one else is around. You can speak frankly to me now about how the ship is being run.'

Surprised by this unusual request, Martin says, 'R-Really sir?' and then adds sheepishly, 'Y-you want me to speak f-frankly?'

'Yes, lieutenant,' the admiral replies confidently. 'I want to hear exactly what's on your mind.'

In his classic Martinesque manner, the young lieutenant then looks over at the admiral and says, 'Well, I think you're DIS-GUSTING!!! You're the worst excuse for an admiral I've ever seen!!'

We doubt if anything like this will happen to you. In fact, the vast majority of employees will be pretty reticent. But, every now and then, one of them will get carried away. When this happens, you'll probably be a little dumb-struck. You might even end up feeling something like this:

'OK, stop right there! You've over-stepped your bounds. This isn't feedback you're giving me, this is insubordination.'

Well, maybe it is. But we doubt it. And yes, maybe the employee did go a little overboard and say things that were a little extreme or a little unfair. But remember: the employee only did what you asked, which was to speak candidly and forthrightly. Now what are you going to do? Are you going to punish the person for doing what you requested?

So be prepared. It may happen. But not so often that you won't want to take the risk. When it does happen, here are some things you might want to do.

▶ Stay in listening mode, as hard as it is to do. If you can, read back what the person is saying, trying hard to reflect the employee's feelings. Sometimes a simple, 'So you're feeling pretty angry at me for having done that' is all you'll need to say. Remember, though, if you choose to do a read back, expect the person to build on it and talk even more.

▶ When the employee finishes, acknowledge the employee in some appropriate way, but don't respond by overreacting in return, lecturing, or getting defensive as you try to explain your actions.

▶ You might simply say you're sorry he feels the way he does, adding that you're glad he told you what was on his mind.

▶ Assure the employee you won't be vindictive. You might say, 'Even though it hurt to hear what you said, I'm not going to hold it against you in any way.'

The basic message you want to send is this: 'I'm a big enough person that I can take an attack on me without getting defensive, losing my cool and responding in kind, or trying to get back in some underhanded way.'

The Employee Requests Things that Are Out of Your Control

Sometimes, employees will ask for things—like a change in corporate policy—that you have no control over. Maybe the employee will have a big problem with the holiday leave policy. Or a major disagreement over some personnel benefit. Or a huge argument with some company rule or regulation. What do you do when this happens?

Your natural tendency, if you're like most bosses, will be to explain, or possibly even defend, the company's policy. And maybe even point out a few things the employee doesn't know—but maybe should know—about the situation. This is not very effective. Here's another alternative.

▶ Start by listening to the employee. Whether you agree or disagree, find out exactly how the employee feels about the matter.

▶ When the employee finishes, offer your view. If you agree, say so. But don't do it in a complaining, 'you-and-me-against-the-rest-of-the-world' manner. Tell the employee what you've done, or what you plan to do, to try to change the policy or remedy the situation.

▶ If you disagree with the employee, say so. But don't do it in a condescending, 'I'm-right-and-you're-wrong' manner. When you're offering your view, try to avoid lecturing or attacking the employee. Don't forget to 'stop talking and start listening' if you notice the employee's receptivity dropping.

▶ Think about what you and the employee can do to remedy the situation, whether the two of you agree or not. Suggest some things the employee could do (such as a letter to the CEO, a meeting with the personnel manager, or a formal complaint to the company's grievance committee). Tell the employee that, even though you don't share her view, you'll bring her complaint to the attention of the appropriate people in the company; assure her you'll do your best to make sure her opinions are represented in any future company discussions on the subject. The message you want to send is: 'Even if I disagree with you, you have the right to express your views here. I'm going to speak for you—and others who may share your view—in my meetings with those higher up in the firm.'

This concludes our discussion of how to ask your employees 'The Question'. In the next chapter, you'll move to the heart of the interview, getting employees to analyse their work performance.

Chapter 11

Step Six: Get Your Employee to Do a Self-Analysis

UP TO this point we've covered the first five steps of the performance improvement process:

Step One: Analyse your employee's performance;
Step Two: Ask your employee to meet with you;
Step Three: Begin the interview;
Step Four: Find out how things are going;
Step Five: Ask your employee 'The Question'.

Now we're ready to move into a more sensitive area—a discussion of the employee's actual work performance. Before your pulse rate goes up, however, remember that we're talking about a constructive discussion, a discussion that's designed to help the employee improve and grow in the job. This doesn't mean you can always avoid a situation in which an employee will get defensive or touchy. But the approach we recommend here and in the next step will help keep negative reactions to a minimum.

Why Your Employee's Self-Analysis Is Important

The best way to begin a discussion of an employee's work performance is to get the employee to talk about it before you do. Let's take a look at several reasons why it makes sense to get employees to do an analysis of their job performance:

1. Employees will appreciate it.   It's rare when a person who plays a significant role in our lives—whether it's a boss, spouse, parent, or friend—asks us to think about the things we do well and the areas where we'd like to improve. But when they do, it's an undeniable expression of interest in us and it almost always makes us feel good about the other person.

2. You'll see things from another perspective. No matter how *you* view your employee's performance, you can be sure of one thing: your employee's view will differ from yours in some important respects. Perhaps she'll identify some strengths you weren't aware of. Or maybe he'll mention some areas where he'd like to improve that you hadn't thought of. If you don't ask the employee to do a self-analysis, you'll learn nothing. And if you offer your view first, the employee's analysis will be influenced by what you've said.

3. It'll tell you something about the employee.   How an employee handles this task will give you some valuable information about the employee. Some will come prepared with a typewritten list, while others will appear totally unprepared. Some of your best employees will say they can't think of anything they do really well, but they can think of lots of areas where they could improve. Some of your marginal employees will find lots of strong points and very few areas needing improvement. Whatever happens, asking employees to do a self-analysis will tell you things about them you might not have known otherwise.

4. It involves employees in the process.   One of your goals as a manager is to make your employees active participants in an overall performance improvement process. You've already begun to involve them by finding out how things are going and asking 'The Question'. Now, having employees analyse their work performance is a good way to keep them involved. And when they feel a part of the process, they'll be willing to invest more time and effort into eventually improving their job performance.

5. You get a much clearer picture of how your view compares with the employee's view. This will be important later in the interview when you negotiate a performance agreement with the employee—that is, when the two of you try to reach an agreement on what you'll both be doing in the future. The more the two of you agree on the specific areas where the employee needs to improve, the smoother this negotiation will go. However, even if you initially disagree about what needs to be worked on, a good understanding of how you differ will help when you try to hammer out a performance agreement later.

6. You often get valuable new information about employee strengths and areas needing improvement. You may be surprised when employees are able to document strengths you weren't even aware of. You may also be pleasantly surprised when employees identify some area where they'd really like to improve that you hadn't thought of, like technical writing, public speaking, or time management. By supporting their desire for improvement in these areas, you may make employees more willing to work on other areas as well.

How to Get Employees to Do a Self-Analysis

Step Six in the performance improvement process is as simple and straightforward as the previous five. Its purpose is to help employees:

▶ identify several areas where they think they're performing effectively, citing at least one concrete example in each area; and

▶ identify several areas where they think they could improve, citing some specific things they could do to actually show improvement in each area.

What you're trying to do at this stage is help employees do some careful, analytical thinking about their job performance. To get an employee to do this:

1. make some kind of transition statement from the previous step to let your employee know you're moving to a new topic—the employee's work performance;
2. explain exactly what it is you'd like the employee to do—to start by describing some things she thinks she does particularly well at work and to finish by describing some areas where she thinks she could stand to improve;
3. actively listen (with special emphasis on good attending and reading back) until you're satisfied the person has given you the kind of detailed information you're looking for.

To show how this is done, let's listen in on a performance improvement interview between Clara Boothby, a forty-eight-year-old head nurse of the paediatric ward in a suburban hospital, and Moira Meskill, a paediatric nurse in her first job after college:

> **Clara:** Moira, I think I have a pretty good idea now about how things are going for you at work and some of the problem areas I can help clear up. I also appreciated your thoughts about what I could do to make your job here more satisfying and less frustrating. (*Pause*) Now I'd like to move on to a new subject— your work performance. When we set this meeting up last week, I believe I asked you to do some thinking about how you think you're doing in your job ...

The supervisor starts off with a transition statement that makes a nice link between the old and new subjects. Now notice how Clara explains to Moira what she would like her to talk about.

> **Clara:** ... I'd like you to start by telling me several things you think you do particularly well at work. And for each of the things you mention, maybe you could cite a specific example or two. (*Pause*)
> **Moira:** OK. (*But looking a little puzzled*)
> **Clara:** For instance, let's say my boss asked me to do a self-analysis. And let's say that one of the things I thought I was pretty good at was written communication. To give her an example, I might say, 'I think I write clear memos that get right to the point, and a number of people in the department and throughout the hospital have actually told me they never have any trouble understanding what I've written.' See what I mean?
> **Moira:** OK, I think I see what you mean.
> **Clara:** All right, why don't you give it a try.

Notice how Clara makes heavy use of the listening skills we discussed earlier. Also notice that she's very careful to avoid making judgements or evaluations of what Moira is saying, even though she may disagree. Doing this would make Moira's receptivity and spirit of co-operation drop rapidly.

> **Moira:** Well, as you know, this is my first real nursing job, and I'm still learning a lot about what I'm good at and ... what I'm not so good at. (*Pause*) But even though it sounds like I'm blowing

my own trumpet, I'd have to say there are some things I am pretty good at. (*Reaching for a notepad*) I actually wrote some of them down as I was getting ready for this meeting.

Clara: (*Nodding and leaning forward slightly*) Oh, yes.

Moira: Well, for one, I think I relate well to children. I think maybe that comes from being the oldest child in a family of five children. I was always wiping somebody's nose or changing somebody's nappy when I was growing up! (*Both laugh*) I also think I'm flexible. You know, able to absorb the punches and adapt to new situations without any trouble. (*Pause*) I also think I'm good at responding quickly and calmly in an emergency, you know, without losing my head. (*Pause, looking thoughtful*) I suppose that's about it.

Clara: All right, Moira, I heard you mention three things. (*At a slow, thoughtful pace*) One, relating well to the children. (*Pause*) Two, being flexible. (*Pause*) And three, responding well in emergency situations. (*Pause*)

Moira: Exactly! (*Tentatively*) And there's one more thing I didn't have on my list that I've just thought of. [When you read someone back and she responds by saying 'exactly' or 'precisely' it's proof positive you're really on another person's wavelength. Also, it's common for people to mention one more thing, something they haven't thought of before, after they've heard their thoughts and ideas summarised. Here, Moira 'builds on' Clara's read back.]

Clara: Go ahead, Moira. I'd like to hear it.

Moira: Well, I suppose it has to do with relating well to the parents of the children as well as to the children themselves. You know, answering their questions, paying attention to their feelings. That sort of thing.

Clara: (*Pausing to make sure employee is finished*) OK, so another thing you feel you're good at is responding to parents' questions and concerns.

Moira: Right. Exactly. (*Adding nothing*)

Clara: (*Pause*) OK, Moira, let's take the first thing you mentioned, relating well to children. I think it'd be helpful if you described that a little more specifically. For example, in what ways are you good at relating to children? What are some of the things you actually do that lead you to view this as one of your strong points? [Good probes for specificity here, which not only ask for more detailed information, they communicate genuine interest in the employee.]

Moira: Well, that's a good question. (*Pausing*) Let's see. I think it's because I try to communicate with the children on their level ...

Clara: Uh-huh.

Moira: ... You know, I try to use the kinds of words they use. I try to explain medical terms in their language, in words they can understand. (*Pause*)

Clara: OK. Anything else? [This is a nice use of an 'encourager'. When followed by a pause and an attentive expression, it almost always gets employees to talk more.]

Moira: Another thing is ... well, so many children are so fearful when they come here. They're sick or injured, away from home for the first time, and in a strange and scary place. I try to take the fear out of the situation by becoming a friend to them.

Clara: Oh yes?

Moira: You know, I play little games with them, tell them stories and jokes to make them laugh, say goodbye when I'm going off duty. (*Pausing*) I also try to get them to tell me about their lives back home; things about their brothers and sisters, their parents, their pets. (*Stops, looks thoughtful, but adds nothing more*)

Clara: (*Pausing to make sure Moira is finished*) I'm hearing two major themes there, Moira. (*Pause*) One is trying to relate to the children by communicating with them at their level and the second is trying to reduce their fear by becoming a kind of hospital friend. (*Pause*)

Moira: Yes, that's it exactly. I think things like that are so important. (*Pausing, adding nothing*)

Clara: (*Nodding and smiling slightly*) OK, Moira, let's move on now to the second thing you said you were good at—being flexible. How do you mean that exactly? Once again, what do you *do* in terms of observable behaviour that makes you flexible?

Having covered the first area, Clara now moves on to the second area, where she'll try to find out what Moira actually does that makes her conclude this is one of her strong points. After that, she'll move on to the third area Moira identified—responding well in emergencies. Let's pick up their interview as they begin to discuss this area.

Clara: I think I've got a pretty good idea of what you mean by being flexible, Moira. Now let's move on to the third point you mentioned earlier, responding quickly in emergencies. How do you mean that exactly?

Moira: (*Pause*) Well, um, I mean that I'm good at keeping my head in a tense or critical situation. I think I've always been that way. You know, I don't get all in a panic like some people do.

Clara: You're able to keep your cool, so to speak?

Moira: Yes, that's a good way of putting it. (*Pause*) You remember the King child? How could we ever forget all the scares she gave everybody around here! (*Pause*) Anyway, I'll never forget that night when Katie discovered she had stopped breathing. She yelled out for me and I dropped everything. When I got there, I could see she was all plugged up with mucus, so I suctioned it out right away. Then I gave her a couple of seconds of oxygen to get her breathing normally again. I was operating completely on adrenalin. I wasn't nervous or scared during the entire episode. But afterwards ...

After discussing this and the final area where Moira thinks she's performing effectively, Clara does a summary read back of everything that's been mentioned so far. She does this for two reasons. One, to make sure she heard everything as Moira intended. And, two, to see if there's anything else Moira would like to add. Then she makes a transition statement and asks Moira how she thinks she could improve her work performance.

Clara: OK, Moira, I think you did a nice job of explaining how you're performing effectively at work. Now let's move to the other side of the coin. (*Pause*) I'd like you to talk about areas where you think you could improve your work performance. You know, those areas where you aren't performing as effectively as you might be. I'd also like you to think about some of the specific things you'd actually have to do to show you had improved in each area. (*Pause*) For example, one of the areas where I'd like to improve is handling conflicts between nurses and other hospital staff. One thing I know I could do to improve in that area is to sit down with both parties together rather than one at a time, which is what I have a tendency to do. OK?

Notice that Clara gives a complete explanation of what she wants the employee to do, in spite of the fact that Moira is probably catching on by now. At this point, Clara will shift back into listening mode, just as she was doing earlier.

Moira: I think I see what you mean. But don't you think you're in a better position to tell me where I need to improve? I mean you're familiar with my work now. (*Pause*)

Clara: Yes, I do think I'm in a good position to talk about some ways you could improve. But for now, I'd like to get some of your thoughts. I'll add my suggestions later. [This is a judgement call. Clara could have simply read Moira back, which might have yielded some important information about why she wanted Clara to go first. Instead, she puts the responsibility back on Moira's shoulders and Moira accepts it. If she hadn't, Clara would've used her listening skills to resolve the problem.]

Moira: OK, That sounds fair enough. (*Pause*) Let's see. (*Thinking out loud*) Areas where I could stand to improve. (*Pause*) Well, uh, the biggest thing—and I know you'll agree with this because you've reminded me of it often enough—has to do with the nursing care plans. I definitely think I need to be more conscientious about writing up nursing care plans when I finish my shift. (*Pause, looking thoughtful*)

Clara: Uh-huh.

Moira: Oh yes, another thing has to do with being better about getting here on time, especially when I'm working the day shift. (*Smiling*) Getting going in the morning has always been a problem for me ... and it's starting to show up here, too. How's that for starters?

Clara: Good. (*Pause*) So ... two areas where you think you could improve are being more conscientious about writing up nursing care plans and being better about getting to work on time. (*Pause*)

Moira: Yes, and ... and another thing I can think of has to do with being more interested in my professional growth and development.

Clara: (*With a quizzical expression*) Oh, yes?.

Moira: You know, attending workshops and seminars to improve my nursing skills. I haven't done anything in that area this past year. I suppose I've been away from school long enough now that the idea of being back in a classroom doesn't sound so bad any more. (*Smiling*)

Clara: (*Smiling and pausing for a moment*) OK, so the third area, then, has to do with improving your nursing skills through some kind of in-service training. (*Pause*) Anything else?

Moira: No, I can't think of anything right now.

Up to this point Clara has got Moira to identify three general areas where she'd like to improve her job performance. Now, Clara will help Moira think about what she'll have to do specifically to improve in each area.

> **Clara:** Moira, let's start with the first area you mentioned, being more conscientious about writing up nursing care plans. What are some things you'd have to do to satisfy yourself that you had actually improved your performance there?
>
> **Moira:** Hmmm ... that's a tough one. (*Pause*) Well, for one thing, I'd just have to spend more time working on them. One problem is that I put them off until the last minute. I usually end up scribbling my notes, so they can be hard for incoming nurses to read. (*Pause*) Oh, another thing is that, because I'm rushing, I sometimes forget to write down important information, like medication I gave or a request a patient made. I haven't done that very often, but I have to confess I have done it when I was rushing.
>
> **Clara:** OK. (*Pause*) So to improve in this area you'd have to take the time to write notes that are legible and also complete. [We applaud Clara's patience here. Having heard Moira confess to sometimes not writing down important information, it would have been tempting to jump in with an opinion or a lecture—perhaps even a reprimand—about that. However, that would've simply forced the interview off track as they focused on that one area. Better to come back to it later, when both of them are trying to come up with a performance agreement they'll carry with them into the future.]
>
> **Moira:** Right, if they were legible and complete I would definitely say I had improved in this area. And so would a few other people who have to read them. (*Smiling*)
>
> **Clara:** (*Smiling*) Including me! (*Both laugh*) All right, Moira, a little later, we'll talk about that goal even more specifically. But now let's turn to the second area where you thought you could stand some improvement—getting to work on time. What do you think you'd have to do to convince yourself you had improved in that area?
>
> **Moira:** (*Smiling*) That's easy! Just get to work on time.
>
> **Clara:** OK. But I wonder if you could be a little more specific than that. For example, if you got to work on time every day for the next five days, would you say you had achieved your goal?
>
> **Moira:** Oh ... I see what you mean. (*Pause*) Uh ... I suppose now

I arrive a few minutes late about twice a week. Hmmm. I'd say that if I cut that down to being late only once a month, I'd have achieved that goal ...

We'll leave the interview at this point. However, we think you'll agree that Clara has done a fine job of getting Moira to do a thoughtful self-analysis.

A Quick Section Summary

Getting employees to do a self-analysis means two things; first, getting them to identify some areas where they think they're performing effectively and, second, some areas where they think they could stand some improvement. To complete this step, you do the following three things:

1. Make a transition statement from the previous topic. For example, 'OK, John, now that I have a sense about what I could do to make your job less frustrating and more satisfying, let's turn to a new topic—your work performance.'
2. Explain precisely what you want the employee to talk about. For example, 'Why don't you begin by talking about the things you do well in your job, mentioning some concrete examples and specific illustrations along the way. When you finish describing things on the plus side, turn your attention to the other side of the coin. Mention some things you think you could do to improve your performance, once again being as specific as you can.'
3. Use your listening skills—especially attending, probing for specificity and reading back—to help the employee do a complete and thorough self-analysis.

Possible Setbacks

It's fairly easy to get your employees actively involved in this part of the interview. We've found that most people actually enjoy taking a thoughtful look at their own performance.

However, there are a couple of potential trouble spots. Both have to do with situations in which the employee's analysis is very different

from the one you'd make. More specifically:
1. an employee think she is strong in precisely an area where you think she needs improvement;
2. an employee identifies areas needing improvement that are very different from areas you think he needs to work on.

Disagreements About Areas of Strength

Let's take the first situation, where employees think they're performing well in an area where you think they need a lot of improvement.

Imagine that you're a manufacturing plant general manager and you're conducting a performance improvement interview with one of the plant supervisors who reports directly to you. You've explained that you'd like him to describe areas where he thinks he's performing effectively on the job. In your opinion, you feel the areas that need improvement include motivating the employees who report to him, meeting production deadlines, and using better judgement in making decisions. The employee starts his self-analysis by saying as follows.

> **Employee:** OK ... let me think about that for a second.
> **You:** (*Nodding*) Fine, take your time.
> **Employee:** (*Pause*) Well, I think I get along pretty well with my people and keep them motivated. And I get a lot of production out of them. (*Pause*) I think I'm also a pretty good decision maker. (*Pause*) And I think I'm pretty good at getting the work out on time.

You're surprised. The employee says he's pretty good in the three areas where you, quite frankly, think he needs a lot of improvement. In the space below, write down how you would respond to the employee at this point. Once you've filled in your response, compare it with ours.

> **Employee:** (*Pause*) Well, I think I get along pretty well with my people and keep them motivated. And I get a lot of production out of them. (*Pause*) I think I'm also a pretty good decision maker. (*Pause*) And I think I'm pretty good at getting the work out on time.

You: _____

_____

_____

_____

_____

No, the correct response is not, 'You've got to be kidding!' or 'Are you out of your mind?' even though that's what you might be thinking. If we were you, we'd respond with that old standby, a read back:

> **You:** I heard three things there, John. It sounds as though you feel you're pretty good at dealing with your employees, (*Pause*) meeting production deadlines, (*Pause*) and making decisions (*Done slowly and thoughtfully*).
>
> **Employee:** Yes, I'd say those are the things I'm pretty good at. (*Pauses, adds nothing more*)
>
> **You:** (*Very calmly, without letting on that you disagree*) OK. Let's take the first area you mentioned, motivating your people. Why don't you give me some examples of things you're doing effectively in that area?
>
> **Employee:** OK. (*Pausing to think*) Well, one thing I can think of right away is the production records notebook I keep. I review it every week with each one of my machinists. (*Pauses, adds nothing*)
>
> **You:** (*Leaning forward slightly*) That sounds interesting. Tell me more.
>
> **Employee:** Well it works like this ...

It was probably tempting for you to say something like: 'Now wait just a minute! I think we're pretty far apart in our thinking about what you do well on the job and what you don't. I mean, how can you say you're good at motivating your people when all I hear are complaints from them? And how can you ...'

However, saying something like this would have had a very negative effect on the employee's receptivity and level of co-operation. And it almost certainly would have forced you into a protracted and unproductive argument. By using your listening skills instead—in particular, the skill of reading back—you gain several advantages:

1. You get a much more detailed picture of why an employee thinks he's good in these particular areas. It may be, in this example, that 'motivating his people' means something very different to your foreman than it means to you. This is potentially important information about how he sees his job, which you can find out only by actively listening to him.

2. By asking for specific examples, you may well learn some things you didn't know the employee was doing. For instance, in this example you may not have known your foreman was keeping a production notebook, or how he was using the notebook in meetings with his machinists. Based on this new information, you might even decide to revise your analysis of the employee's performance.

3. You'll keep the employee's receptivity high. At this point in the interview, it pays to keep the employee talking. Given that this kind of self-analysis is motivating to most employees, the last thing you want to do is interrupt, inject your own opinions, and disparage the employee's view. That will just destroy all the hard work you've done so far to build up the person's receptivity. Be patient when you have a different opinion. You'll have a chance to present your analysis of the employee's performance in the next step of the process.

Disagreements About Areas in Need of Improvement

Now let's consider the second potential trouble spot—where the employee mentions areas needing improvement that are very different from the areas you had in mind. What do you do in a case like that?

Our advice here is exactly the same as in the first situation—listen to what the employee has to say. At this stage your job is not to talk, it's to listen. Your goal should be to learn as much as you can about:

▶ the areas where the employee would like to improve;
▶ why the employee feels it's important to improve in these areas;
▶ the specific things the employee would have to do to demonstrate improved performance.

Active, effective listening is the best way to get this kind of information. Even if you strongly disagree with an employee's self-analysis, this is not the place to offer your opinions. Your opportunity to do that comes in the next step, when you present your analysis of the employee's performance.

Chapter 12

Get Your Message Across: Presenting Ideas Effectively

UP TO this point in the interview you've been primarily in a listening mode—asking questions, drawing the employee out, probing for further information, and making sure you heard things correctly. Except for the first few minutes of the interview, when you 'structured' the meeting, the employee has done almost all the talking.

Now it's time to shift gears. You're about to present your analysis of the employee's performance. Instead of listening to the employee's ideas, you'll be presenting your own. The purpose of this chapter is to help you do this as effectively as possible. It will show you how to:

▶ hear yourself as others hear you (maybe for the first time);
▶ 'attend' to people when you talk to them by using your eyes, arms, and the rest of your body as tools to help get your message across;
▶ avoid 'the fuzzies' by speaking clearly and not using confusing or ambiguous language;
▶ avoid emotionally loaded expressions that lower an employee's receptivity;
▶ stop talking and start listening when the employee's receptivity dips;
▶ pay attention to pace and timing while you talk;
▶ preview, deliver and summarise your messages.

Why Presentation Skills Are So Important

Think for a moment about some bosses you've known who were pretty bad at communicating their ideas to other people, particularly to their employees. Think about *how* they communicate their ideas to other people and *why* you think they present their ideas so poorly. What is it about their 'presentation skills' that makes them so bad? What do they *do* that confuses, distracts, or turns people off? Try to be as precise and descriptive as you can, recording your answers in the space below:

_____

_____

_____

_____

_____

_____

_____

_____

_____

Here's a sampling of complaints we've heard from employees about the poor presentation skills of their supervisors.

'I had this boss who would never look at me when she was talking. She was rather timid and would always look down or slightly away from me when she talked. Because she didn't look me straight in the eye, I didn't really trust her. And I never really gave her ideas much weight.'

'The supervisor I'm thinking about was always trying to impress people with his knowledge and expertise. If there was a choice between a one syllable word and a four syllable word, you know which one he'd choose. Half the time we couldn't understand him and the other half we were so turned off we didn't pay any attention to what he said.'

'I had this supervisor who had longish brown hair. Every time she started talking, she would run her fingers through her hair, starting close to her scalp and slowly going all the way to the end. At times it was very distracting. I'd just watch her play with her hair and not hear a word she was saying.'

'I had a supervisor once who talked very slo-o-owly and in a real monotone. He always talked the same way, too, whether he was excited or bored. He put me to sleep whenever he opened his mouth.'

'I once worked for a young woman who was fresh out of college. She had this particularly irritating habit of saying "you know" after every two or three words. It was "you know this" and "you know that." She was quite intelligent, but she came across as uneducated and almost inarticulate.'

'I used to work for a guy we called 'rubbish mouth' because he never said anything nice. He was a verbally abusive person and often called people names, like "stupid", "bitchy", or "asinine". You can imagine how much we listened to his suggestions.'

Just as good listening skills have an important effect on employee receptivity, so do good presentation skills. Lack of skill in either area will reduce how open and receptive other people are to what you've got to say. To get a person ready to listen to what you have to say, you have to first listen skilfully. To keep a person listening, however, you've got to present your ideas and thoughts effectively.

Hear Yourself as Others Hear You

Many people don't know how they sound to others, much less how well they present their ideas. And when people do hear their voices for the first time, they're often surprised at the difference between how they sound to others and how they sound to themselves. This is true even for people who've heard themselves on tape many times. A participant in one of our workshops recently told us: 'I dictate all my correspondence, so I'm used to hearing my voice. But I always thought I sounded that way because I was using a cheap tape recorder!'

To get an idea of how you sound to other people, tape yourself talking naturally to someone. Find a friend or co-worker who'll listen attentively as you talk. If you can't find someone, go it alone. Just pretend you're talking to someone. The goal is to come up with a recording of your typical speaking style.

When you've finished, replay the whole tape without pausing or stopping to analyse it. Don't be surprised if your initial reaction is a little negative. Many people don't like the way their voices sound the first time they hear themselves. Then listen to the tape once more. This time try not to evaluate it; just become familiar with your voice and your speaking style. Use the following questions as a guide.

▶ Listen to the tempo of your voice. How quickly or slowly do you speak? Does your voice speed up and slow down or does it always travel at about the same speed? How does your voice reflect changes in your level of excitement or enthusiasm?

▶ What do you like most about your voice? What makes it an interesting or entertaining voice? In what ways would you change your voice to improve it? How could you become even more easy or pleasant to listen to?

▶ What distracting mannerisms do you have that get in the way? Do you have bad verbal habits, such as saying 'You know' or 'Ok' or 'um' much too often?

▶ How well do you articulate your words? Are the words crisp and clear when you speak or do you tend to slur or run them together?

▶ How about your volume? Do you tend to speak so softly that people have to lean forward just to hear you? Or do you bowl them over with your loudness?

▶ What do other people have to say about your voice or speaking style? Ask them for their reaction to the tape. What do they think you do well? What do they think you need to change to improve?

▶ How much do you use the upper and lower registers of your voice? Is your voice high or low? Nasal or throaty? How does your voice change when you become serious? When you become happy or friendly?

Attend to People When You Talk to Them

In Chapter 8 we talked about the importance of attending behaviour when you're listening and trying to get other people to open up. As important as attending is when you're listening, it's probably even more important when you're talking.

To review, attending means paying attention to and showing interest in another person. It has three components:

1. making eye contact;
2. using good body language; and
3. minimising distractions.

Making Eye Contact

We've noticed an interesting thing about eye contact. Some people are very good at looking people directly in the eye when they're listening. But when they start talking, they break direct eye contact. They look up, down, and all around. It's almost as if they are literally searching for the exact words to express their next thought. This can be very distracting for the listener. Plus, it often leads to the assumption that the talker is nervous, uncertain, or lacks confidence.

When you're talking to people, make a conscious effort to look them directly in the eye. Rather than stare at them, break eye contact periodically so you're looking at them directly 70 to 80 per cent of the time. The best time to break eye contact is when you're making a transition from one topic to another or when you're thinking about what to say next. These natural breaks are expected. But don't make them too frequent or too prolonged, or you'll lose your listener's attention.

Using Good Body Language

You don't just talk with your voice. You also use your body, particularly your face, arms, and hands. Too often, though, bad body language gets in the way. For example, no matter how eloquent you are or how much sense you make, you aren't likely to get your message across very well if you:

▶ don't face the person you're talking to directly;
▶ look down at the floor or up at the ceiling when speaking;
▶ talk with an expressionless stony face;

▶ slouch or lean way back in your chair;
▶ don't use any hand or arm gestures.

Here are some ideas on how you can use body language to improve your presentation style:

1. 'Aim' your body and eyes directly at the listener.   Try to position your head, shoulders and torso directly towards your listener. Try to imagine a direct line between your eyes and the other person's eyes. Some people have the habit of tilting their heads upwards when they speak, so they literally look down their noses at the listener. Others have a tendency to tilt their heads down and look up when they're talking, as if they were speaking over those half-circle reading glasses. Remember to face the person directly.

2. Use your facial muscles.   Your face, especially around your mouth and eyes, is filled with a rich array of muscles. Use them when you speak:

▶ smile;
▶ wrinkle your forehead;
▶ widen your eyes;
▶ clench your teeth;
▶ raise your eyebrows.

Using these techniques will not only make you more interesting to listen to, but you'll also be more persuasive because you'll be expressing how you feel about your message as you're sending it.

3. Lean forward slightly.   In addition to facing the listener and making direct eye contact, tilt your upper torso slightly towards people when you're speaking to them. Don't slouch. Get into a comfortable position, with your body directly facing the listener and leaning forward slightly.

4. Use gestures.   Gesturing simply means using your arms and hands to express yourself better and give the listener a clearer picture of what you're saying. It's very helpful when you want to emphasise something (for example, hold up two fingers and say, 'I want you to remember just two points'). And it brings life and vitality to scenes and situations you're trying to describe.

Below is a brief anecdote. As you read through it, imagine how a stiff, uninteresting person would say it. Then imagine how one of your more animated, expressive friends might tell it. Then try it yourself. Stand in front of a mirror and describe the scene out loud, first underplaying and then exaggerating the use of gestures:

> 'I was jogging along the other day and I happened to come across these two interesting-looking chaps. One was built like a Sumo wrestler—very short, very round, with a protruding stomach that looked like a huge beach ball. He was bald on top, but he had this very curly hair that stuck out all around his head. The other chap was about six feet two and thin as a rake. They were both talking nineteen to the dozen, laughing and talking and using a lot of arm and hand gestures. They were completely absorbed in their conversation and totally oblivious to anything or anybody around them. I just smiled to myself and kept jogging along.'

To summarise, you'll improve your presentation style if you use good body language, particularly if you:

▶ directly face people you're talking to;
▶ use your facial muscles;
▶ lean your upper body forward slightly;
▶ use gestures when you speak.

Minimising Distractions

Minimising distractions is as important to good presenting as it is to good listening. In addition to the distractions we mentioned in Chapter 8, others to avoid include:

▶ the overuse of phrases such as 'you know', 'right', 'OK' and 'like';
▶ the frequent repetition of stock phrases such as 'to reiterate', 'ipso facto', 'albeit', and 'if I might be so bold';
▶ the use of the same example again and again;
▶ distracting mannerisms such as running your fingers through your hair, stroking your beard, using a toothpick, and twirling a strand of hair around your finger.

Listeners often pay so much attention to these distracting behaviours that they completely tune out the person who's talking. We know a man who has the habit of closing his eyes and placing his thumb and index finger on his temples when he's listening to people. If that weren't bad enough, he does the same thing when he's *talking* to people, which is even worse. One of his employees said, 'Who can listen to him? It's like watching someone with a perpetual migraine.'

If you have any distracting habits and mannerisms, you probably aren't aware of them. That's part of the problem; they're real blind spots. So, periodically listening to yourself on audiotape (or, even better, seeing yourself on videotape) will help. It's also a good idea to ask for feedback from people you feel comfortable with and whose judgement you trust. In either case, you'll become more aware of how you come across to people and the effect your habits and mannerisms have on them.

To summarise, good attending behaviour is as important when you're presenting as when you're listening. Maintain direct eye contact, use good body language and minimise distraction.

Avoid the 'Fuzzies'

Bosses are always giving feedback to employees and telling them how to do their jobs. But often the suggestions they make aren't all that helpful. For example, here are some typical comments managers and supervisors might make to their employees:

'You should take more pride in your work.'
'I'd like you to improve the credibility of your sales pitch.'
'I think you should adopt a more professional orientation.'
'You need to work on being more decisive.'
'You're going to have to improve your attitude.'

What's wrong with these statements? Well, if you examine them carefully, you'll notice they're too general and non-specific. None of them describes precisely how supervisors want their employees to behave or what they want them to do differently. Each statement contains an abstract concept, like 'pride' or 'credibility'. Robert Mager, in his book *Goal Analysis*, calls concepts like these 'fuzzies'.

Fuzzies are words that sound good but don't say very much. They're limited in their helpfulness because they don't describe what employees need to *do* in any specific way. And if employees aren't clear about what their bosses want them to do, they're not very likely to do it.

The best way to avoid a case of the fuzzies is to use action words rather than abstractions. Action words clearly describe the specific behaviour you'd like to see an employee demonstrate. So, whenever you find yourself about to use an abstract word, ask yourself the question, 'What will the person actually have to do, in terms of observable behaviour, to convince me he's done what I've asked?' Lets say you want an employee to have a better attitude. When you ask the question, 'What will the person have to *do* to demonstrate an improved attitude?' you might come up with the following list of observable behaviours:

▶ he'll ask for additional work when he's completed tasks already assigned;

▶ she'll ask me to explain company policy when she disagrees with it;

▶ he'll speak to me directly about complaints instead of to co-workers;

▶ she'll speak more positively about her job, her co-workers, or the company;

▶ he'll disagree with me without raising his voice and interrupting me;

▶ she'll greet me and co-workers with a smile in the morning when she arrives.

Here's a little practice. Imagine that you want the receptionist in your office to be more friendly and courteous to people when they walk into your office. This is another real fuzzy. Ask yourself the question, 'What will the employee have to do to show more friendly and courteous behaviour?' Answer the question in the space below and then compare your ideas to ours.

What will the receptionist have to do to show more friendly and courteous behaviour?

The receptionist will have to: _____

_____

_____

_____

_____

_____

Here's how we answered the question:

The receptionist will have to:

▶ make direct eye contact and smile at visitors when they enter;

▶ use the names of people when addressing them;

▶ ask 'How can I help you?' when people approach the desk;

▶ say 'Please make yourself comfortable', or an equivalent, when
▶ asking people to wait in the reception area;
▶ engage in friendly conversation with people while they're waiting;
▶ ask visitors if they have any questions the receptionist can answer
  while they're waiting;
▶ make positive comments about the dress or appearance of
  visitors.

Avoid Emotionally Loaded Expressions

Emotionally loaded expressions are words, phrases, or remarks that
cause employees to feel resentful, hurt, or angry. They fall into three
categories:

1. Criticisms that include potentially insulting words:

'Bill you're just too fussy.'
'If you weren't such a hothead, we could resolve this dispute.'
'That was a stupid thing to say.'

2. Loaded questions that put employees on the defensive:

'Is that the best you can do?'
'Do you really think you can gain his co-operation by threatening
him?'
'Come on! Do you really expect me to believe a story like that?'

3. Absolute statements or exaggerations:

'You always take ten minutes longer for lunch than anybody else.'
'It was the most ridiculous thing you could possibly have said.'
'You always blame your mistakes on everybody but yourself. As
far as you're concerned, you never make a mistake!'

Even though it's tempting to resort to them when you're struggling
with another person, try to avoid using emotionally loaded expressions. They cause hurt and confusion, turn people off, severely
diminish receptivity, and usually lead to some kind of not-so-positive
response in reply. Some employees won't respond openly to them,
but will try to get back at you in an indirect or subtle way, like

complaining about you behind your back or not showing a lot of enthusiasm for your suggestions. Others will be more direct. They'll remind you that you're not perfect and start pointing out areas where you need improvement. Or they'll get flustered and defensive and explain the mitigating circumstances that led them to act the way they did. Whatever their reaction, once you inadvertently blurt out an emotionally loaded expression, you can forget about getting much involvement or co-operation from employees for at least a while, and possibly for a very long time.

Emotionally loaded expressions are tempting to use, especially when you're feeling angry, annoyed or frustrated over what an employee has done. But try to avoid them. They'll only make things worse. Below you have a chance to practise analysing emotionally loaded expressions.

Emotionally Loaded Expressions

In the following list of phrases, there are five emotionally loaded expressions and five helpful comments. Put a ✗ next to the emotionally loaded expressions. Then compare your answers to ours.

_____ 1. 'I'd like you to come and tell me when you have no more assigned work to do.'

_____ 2. 'I think you'd be a lot better off if you weren't so thin-skinned.'

_____ 3. 'That was rather a silly remark, wasn't it?'

_____ 4. 'I'd like you to spend more time on planning and less on double-checking the expense accounts.'

_____ 5. 'Before you decide yours is the best way, I'd like you to listen to my idea.'

_____ 6. 'What were you trying to prove in there anyway?'

_____ 7. 'What are some other ways you might be able to reach the same objective?'

_____ 8. 'You're never at your work station when I need to talk to you.'

_____ 9. 'Why do you always do that when the boss comes round?"

_____ 10. 'What did that buyer say or do that made you so angry?"

Answers and Discussion

      1. This is a specific, reasonable request.

X   2. Most people don't like to be called thin-skinned.

X   3. Being called silly is insulting.

      4. Same as 1.

      5. Same as 1.

X   6. A hostile question.

      7. A helpful, open-ended question.

X   8. An absolute, unhelpful statement.

X   9. A 'double whammy': an absolute statement combined with a question that puts the employee on the defensive.

      10. Probing for specificity gives the employee an opportunity to explain things without becoming defensive.

Be Prepared to Stop Talking and Start Listening at Any Time

Sometimes an employee's willingness to listen to you—what we call receptivity—drops very quickly. Maybe it's because you used an emotionally loaded expression. Perhaps you used a 'fuzzy' that confused the person. Or maybe you said something the employee flatly disagreed with. Whatever the reason, it's usually pretty easy to see a decline in receptivity. For example, your employee may:

▶   look confused;
▶   start to argue with you;
▶   look away;
▶   show an expression of disagreement;
▶   shake his head back and forth;
▶   look startled or taken aback;
▶   furrow her eyebrows;
▶   raise his eyes to the ceiling;

- ► begin to interrupt;
- ► fold her arms firmly across her chest;
- ► lean way back in the chair;
- ► hold out his hand to signal 'stop'; or
- ► look as though she's dying to say something.

Whenever you see an employee's level of receptivity drop like this, our advice is simple: Stop talking and start listening. If you keep on talking, the person won't listen anyway because his receptivity has plummeted. And talking to somebody who's not listening is a big waste of time.

Here's an example. The supervisor, an office manager, is meeting with the company receptionist to discuss work performance. At this point in the interview the office manager is offering her analysis of the receptionist's performance.

> **Supervisor:** Well, I think one of the areas where you could improve is the way you handle visitors when they walk in the door. I think you could be friendlier and more courteous to them ...
>
> **Employee:** (*Sitting up straight and interrupting*) What?!!

Obviously, the employee's receptivity has plummeted. In this situation, it would be very easy for the supervisor to press the issue and continue talking, perhaps by documenting what she meant by friendlier and more courteous treatment. This temptation would be especially strong if she were well prepared for the meeting. But she doesn't do this. Notice how easily she shifts from presenting mode to listening mode.

> **Supervisor:** (*Pausing for just a moment, and then calmly*) You seem pretty surprised by my comment, Sandra. (*Pause*)
>
> **Employee:** (*Very animated*) Surprised is right! I can't believe you could say that! I think getting along with people has always been one of my strong points. [Realising the employee's receptivity is still pretty low, the supervisor stays in listening mode and uses another read back.]
>
> **Supervisor:** So it's especially surprising—and maybe confusing— to hear that I'd like you to improve in an area you see as one of your strengths? (*Pause*)
>
> **Employee:** (*More calmly*) Yes, it is surprising. I mean ... well I know everybody has some room for improvement, no matter how good they are. And I suppose that applies to me, too. But I was pretty

surprised when you mentioned it. [The employee's receptivity is going up, but it's still not high. One more read back should do the trick. Patient, skilful listening is the only way we know to bring up receptivity.]

Supervisor: Well, Sandra, I think there you're saying that all people can stand to improve in some ways, even though at first they may be a little surprised at the suggestion.

Employee: Yes, that's it exactly. (*Leaning forward*) Now I'm wondering what you meant earlier. [Now the supervisor has a receptive audience.]

Supervisor: Well, first of all, I agree with you that getting along with people is one of your best points. (*Pause*) For one thing, you've got a great smile, and it just makes people feel good when you smile at them. For another, you have a very warm and sensitive voice, which can have a calming and soothing effect on people, especially when they're upset. But there are also some things I think you could do to improve how you deal with visitors. But before I mention them, I want to be sure we've fully discussed your reaction when I first raised the subject. (*Pause*)

Notice how the supervisor moves gradually back into presenting mode, beginning by mentioning some of the natural strengths of the employee. Notice also how the supervisor checks with the employee to make sure there are no lingering feelings that will get in the way.

Employee: (*Smiling*) No, I think I got it all out of my system. I really would like to hear your suggestions.

Supervisor: (*Smiling and leaning forward*) Good. OK, to begin ...

Employee receptivity can drop rapidly, but it usually takes some time to build it back up. The only way to bring it up is by patient, skilful listening, as the supervisor did here. Once it's been brought up, continue with what you want to say. However, always be ready to stop talking and start listening again if receptivity goes back down.

Pay Attention to Pace and Timing

Public speakers and comedians pay very close attention to pace and timing when they talk. Managers and supervisors should too. You'll have a much better chance of getting your message across if you pay attention to these simple principles:

- ▶ pause after your main points;
- ▶ vary your speaking style—avoid sameness; and
- ▶ don't interrupt the other person when you want to talk.

Pause After Your Main Points

Pausing when you're talking to another person is helpful for several reasons:

1. It gives your main points a chance to sink in.   The brain, like any other computer, takes a moment to 'process' new information. By pausing, you give your employee a moment to digest what you've said before moving on to your next point.

2. You give people an opportunity to let you know they're still with you or that you're losing them.   It's during pauses that you'll notice expressions of sustained interest or detect dips in employee receptivity.

3. It ensures that you don't monopolise the conversation. When you pause, you send a message that goes something like this: 'If you've got an important reaction to what I'm saying, go ahead and jump right in.'

Notice how this supervisor uses pauses effectively.

Supervisor: After thinking a lot about your work performance, Gerry, I think there are two major areas where you could stand some improvement (*Pause*)

Employee: (*Looking attentively*) Uh-huh.

Supervisor: The first thing I'd like to do is offer my suggestions in both areas and get your reactions to them. (*Pause*)

Employee: (*Nodding*) OK, that sounds fair enough to me.

Supervisor: Good. After that, I'd like us to compare my idea to the ideas you came up with earlier about how you thought you could improve. (*Pause*) The goal will be for us to reach some agreement on what makes the most sense for us to work on in the next four to six weeks. (*Pause*)

Employee: (*Nodding*) All right.

Supervisor: And, finally, I'd like the two of us to identify what I'm going to be doing in the next month or so to help you improve in those areas we agree on. (*Pause*)

Employee: (*Smiling*) Sounds fine to me.

Supervisor: (*Leaning forward slightly*) I'm looking forward to doing whatever I can to help you do your job better and also get more satisfaction out of working here. (*Pause*) OK, Gerry, the first thing ...

Varying Your Speaking Style

There are at least two ways you can vary your speaking style to make it more interesting.

1. Try to make the speed of your voice reflect what you're saying and feeling. When you're enthusiastic or excited, speed it up a little. When you're serious or sober, slow it down. Make important points slowly. You can do this by pausing or by simply saying things more slowly and deliberately.

2. Use the upper and lower registers of your voice. A person in one of our seminars called it hitting the high notes and the low notes. It's related to voice tempo, but it goes well beyond that. For example, when you're really serious and want people to remember what you're saying, speak with a deeper voice and more slowly. When you're excited or happy, bring your voice up a bit and speak more quickly.

Don't Interrupt the Other Person

The tendency to interrupt is understandable, especially when people say things you flatly disagree with or find hard to accept. You may even feel the urge to interrupt when you agree with people. For example, someone says something that stimulates your thinking and you want to offer your reaction before you forget it. But whether you agree or disagree, interrupting is nothing more than a bad habit. Here are several reasons why it's worth a little effort on your part to give it up:

1. It's bad from an information-gathering perspective. Interrupting cuts people off before they've had a chance to finish their remarks. And if employees aren't talking, you're not getting the kind of information you need to function effectively as a manager.

2. It colours people's remarks. Employees are very attuned to the 'sensitive points' of their bosses—they quickly learn what gets them excited or upset or angry. So they feed you what they think you want to hear, not what they really think.

3. It's annoying and irritating. You don't like being interrupted and neither do your employees. However, since bosses have so much more power than employees, many of them interrupt whenever they feel like it, no matter how rude it is. The long-term effects on employee morale can be serious.

4. It leads to lowered receptivity. We've said it before and we'll say it again here: people who feel you aren't interested in listening to them aren't going to be very interested in listening to you.

To review, you can make your presentation style more effective if you:

1. pause after your main points;
2. vary your speaking style; and
3. don't interrupt.

Tell Them What You're Going to Tell Them And What You've Told Them

Public speakers often begin their talks with a preview of what they're going to say and end their talks with a summary of what they've said.

This is popularly known as:

▶ tell them what you're going to tell them;
▶ tell them; and
▶ tell them what you've told them.

This technique is also a good one to use when you're meeting with employees. By giving employees a preview of what's coming, you give them a chance to get on your wavelength before you get to the heart of your message. By summarising what you said after you say it, you reinforce the major points you want remembered. It's a useful model in many types of speaking situations.

Here's an example of a supervisor using this technique:

Supervisor: I've been thinking a lot about your work performance lately, Terry, and I've come to the conclusion that there are three major areas where you're really doing well.

Employee: Uh-huh.

Supervisor: (*Leaning forward*) I'd like to begin by briefly mentioning all three strong points and then, after that, I'd like to cover each one in detail. (*Pause*)

Employee: (*Nodding*) OK. That sounds fine to me.

Supervisor: Well, the first thing that really jumps out when I think of your strong points is your skill in writing and editing copy. You're better at that than almost anybody I know. (*Pause*)

Employee: (*Slightly embarrassed*) Thanks.

Supervisor: A second major strength is your ability to spot younger talent. You've been the first person to identify some people who've become valuable assets to the organisation. (*Pause*)

Employee: Well, it's actually pretty easy to recognise real talent when it's staring you in the face.

Supervisor: Easy for you, perhaps. But not so easy for me and an awful lot of other people.

Employee: (*Smiling*) OK.

Supervisor: The third major area where I think you're doing a really good job is bringing in new business. If all my people were as effective as you were in that area, I'd be managing director by now!

Employee: (*Smiling broadly*) I was hoping you'd mention that. As you know, I've been pretty happy with myself in that area, too.

Supervisor: I know you have, and for good reason too. Now to get back to that first area ...

Now that all three areas have been previewed ('Tell them what you're going to tell them'), the supervisor will cover each one in detail ('Tell them'). After the supervisor and employee fully discuss what the employee is doing well, the supervisor closes this part of the interview by summarising what they've talked about, using the technique of 'Tell them what you've told them.'

Supervisor: OK, Terry, before we move on, let's take a quick look at what we've just discussed. As I see it, there are three major areas where you're performing very effectively. The first is writing and editing copy. The second is identifying new talent in the company. And the third is bringing in new business. I'm really pleased with your performance in all of those areas.

Employee: (*Beaming*) Thanks. It makes me feel good that you've noticed my strong points and didn't just focus on my weaker areas.

'Telling them what you've told them' after you've made a presentation is a valuable technique for several reasons:

1. It helps people remember the major points. Sometimes so many things are discussed in so much detail that people focus on the trivial things and fail to recall the important points. The old expression about not seeing the forest for the trees describes this tendency well. Summarising the main points helps people remember the important things.

2. It helps a conversation flow more smoothly. Summarising a segment of conversation is a nice bridge for making a transition to the next topic. For example, in the preceding illustration, it would have been very easy for the supervisor to make a transition by saying, 'Now I'd like to move on to some areas where I think you could stand some improvement.'

3. It's a good re-emphasis tool. Sometimes, important points deserve to be restated. Summarising is a good way to send the message: 'These are some important points we've just covered and I'd like to repeat them for emphasis.'

A Quick Summary

In this chapter, we've suggested a number of ways you can improve the way you present your ideas to other people. We've talked about the importance of hearing yourself as others do and argued that attending is as much a presenting skill as a listening skill. We've suggested some ways you can speak more clearly to employees by being specific and avoiding fuzzy language. We've talked about the dangers of using emotionally loaded expressions and stressed how important it is to stop talking and start listening whenever you notice a dip in receptivity. After discussing some aspects of pace and timing, we introduced you to a public speaking technique called 'Tell them what you're going to tell them (and tell them what you've told them)'. Now you're in a good position to move on to Chapter 13, where you'll finally get to present your analysis of the employee's performance.

Chapter 13

Step Seven: Present Your Analysis of Your Employee's Performance

LET'S QUICKLY review what we've covered so far in our ten-step performance improvement process.

▶ In Step One you *analyse your employee's job performance.* You identify several things the employee does well, citing concrete examples of each. You also identify several areas where the employee could stand some improvement, along with a specific statement of what the employee would have to do to actually demonstrate improved performance in each area.

▶ In Step Two you *ask your employee to meet with you.* You briefly explain the purpose of the meeting, how you plan to prepare for it, and how you'd like the employee to prepare for it.

▶ Step Three is the point at which you actually *begin the performance improvement interview.* You arrange to meet in a quiet, private place. From the outset, you try to make the employee feel comfortable and welcome. Then you 'structure' the meeting by fully explaining the purpose of the meeting, what's going to happen during the session, and what the two of you can do to get the most out of the meeting.

▶ In Step Four you *find out how things are going* in general in his job for the employee and learn about any problems he's encountering that you ought to be aware of.

▶ In Step Five you *ask your employee 'The Question'* about what you can do, as her boss, to make her job more satisfying and less frustrating in the future.

▶ In Step Six you *get your employee to do a self-analysis* of his own job performance, in much the way you analysed his performance in Step One of the process.

Now you're at Step Seven, the very heart of the interview. This is what your patient planning, explaining and listening have been leading up to. Now you have an opportunity to present your ideas and suggestions, at a time when the employee is likely to be most receptive to hearing them.

The procedure you'll follow in Step Seven should sound familiar by now. You're going to present your analysis of the employee's work performance—the analysis you prepared in Step One—in the same way as the employee did in the previous step, starting with the positive and finishing with the areas needing improvement.

Specifically, during this stage of the process, you're going to do two major things:

1. identify several areas where you think the employee is performing effectively and provide a couple of concrete examples in each of these areas;
2. identify several areas where you think the employee could stand to improve his performance and identify specifically what he might do in each area to demonstrate that his performance has, in fact, improved.

Your goals here are fairly clear. First, you want to give your employees the benefit of your thinking about their performance. Because of your position, you can be considered a bit of an 'expert witness' and you've got some things to say that can be very helpful to your employees. Second, by presenting a thorough analysis, you'll be meeting a very important employee need—the need for candid, helpful feedback. In our view, all people crave feedback and there's no reason to believe your employees are any different. Finally, your eventual aim is to reach as much agreement as possible about the areas where both you and your employee see a need for improvement over the next weeks and months. Once again, you'll want to be as specific as you can be—avoiding the 'fuzzies'—when you think about future changes.

How to Present Your Analysis

Before you begin this stage of the interview, it may be a good idea to review Chapter 12 for various tips on how to present your ideas effectively. In addition to those techniques, here are a few other points to keep in mind when you present your analysis.

1. Use your performance analysis form, which we introduced in Step One, as a guide.   (We've repeated it on the following page for you.) The form, if you fill it in conscientiously, represents your best thinking on what your employees are doing well and the areas where you think they need to improve. It can serve as an excellent outline for presenting your ideas and suggestions.

2. Start with the positive.   Most bosses don't give their employees much, if any, positive feedback. If they do, it's often in the form, 'You're doing a good job, but ...' followed by a list of things the employee needs to work on.

It's very important to point out the things employees are doing effectively. For one thing, it's a way of reinforcing or rewarding the kind of on-the-job behaviour you want to see. It also sends an important message to employees: 'When I notice something good, I'm going to mention it. I'm not just going to focus on the negative.'
If you've tried your damnedest and simply can't come up with anything positive to say about an employee's performance, that's something to pay attention to. It may mean you're much more critical and negative than you thought. Or it might mean rethinking whether it's worth your time and energy to try to help the employee improve.

3. Try to establish as much agreement as you can between your analysis and the employee's analysis.   It may seem pretty obvious, but the more you and your employees can agree on the areas where they're performing effectively and the areas where they need to improve, the more motivated they're going to be to actually improve their performance. We're not suggesting that you pretend to agree with employees as a way to manipulate or 'con' them into changing. On the other hand, it just makes good sense to emphasise, early in your presentation, the areas where the two of you agree.

4. Always be ready to shift from talking to listening.   We

Performance Analysis Form

What is Your Employee Doing Well?	In What Ways Could He/She Improve?

1. _____
Example: _____
_____
_____
_____

Example: _____
_____
_____
_____
_____

1. _____
Specifically, the person will have to:
_____
_____
_____

_____
_____
_____
_____

2. _____
Example: _____
_____
_____
_____

Example: _____
_____
_____
_____
_____

2. _____
Specifically, the person will have to:
_____
_____
_____

_____
_____
_____
_____

3. _____
Example: _____
_____
_____
_____

Example: _____
_____
_____
_____
_____

3. _____
Specifically, the person will have to:
_____
_____
_____

_____
_____
_____
_____

4. _____
Example: _____
_____
_____
_____

Example: _____
_____
_____
_____

4. _____
Specifically, the person will have to:
_____
_____
_____

_____
_____
_____

talked about the importance of being able to make this kind of shift in Chapter 12, but it bears repeating. The critical thing to remember is this: just because your employee's receptivity to your ideas and suggestions is very high at one point, there's no guarantee it's going to stay high. Keeping your employee's receptivity up is a little like trying to walk on a balancing beam. You can be moving along just fine one moment and find yourself sitting on the ground the next. As soon as you sense that the employee's receptivity has dropped (the signals are usually clear), go back into an active listening mode. That's the best and easiest way to get back on the beam.

5. Get your employee's reaction to your analysis after you've presented it. As you present your analysis, carefully monitor the employee's reactions for signs of agreement or any drop in receptivity. Then, after you've gone all the way through it, get the employee's reactions to your analysis. This will give the employee an opportunity to express any strong reactions that may have been held back while you were talking. It will also give the employee a chance to think out loud and to digest what you said. Finally, it will give you an opportunity to make sure your message got across.

Walking Through an Example

Each employee is unique, so we can't cover all the bases—all the different kinds of reactions and how to respond to them—with one example. However, we've tried to strike a balance by choosing a hypothetical employee who is far from being an all-round star performer, but who definitely has some strengths. As you'll see, she also has some pretty typical reactions to portions of her boss's analysis, especially the parts she doesn't agree with. Let us introduce you, then, to Lisa, a salesperson, and her sales manager, Tom.

Tom Heyman and Lisa Straban both work for a large industrial furniture manufacturer. Tom, who's forty-seven years old, is a regional sales manager and supervises ten salespeople, including Lisa. Lisa is twenty-six years old, has had considerable sales experience for a person her age, and is the first female salesperson on Tom's sales team. They've been working together now for about nine months. Tom believes Lisa has very strong potential as a salesperson, but, at this point, still has a lot to learn. Lisa seems to like and respect Tom, but she's the kind of person who's reluctant to accept anybody's advice until she sees the results really work out there 'in the real world'. This performance review is a brand new experience for Lisa and a relatively new one for Tom.

When asked to do a self-analysis earlier in the interview, Lisa talked about three areas where she thought she was performing effectively and three areas where she thought she could stand some improvement. She thought her strongest point was making sales presentations. When asked to be more specific, she said she thought her sales presentations were well-prepared, that she made good use of graphics, and that her presentations were interesting because she used a lot of of arm and hand gestures and occasionally told jokes to lighten things up. She said her other two strong points were managing her time effectively and following up on prospects.

In terms of areas where she could stand to improve, Lisa said that the most important one was 'closing' more sales. Specifically, she said she'd like to improve her closing rate for large orders from 30 per cent to 40 per cent and that she'd like to decrease the closing period from an average of six weeks to an average of thirty days. The other two areas where she said she could stand to improve were doing a better job of getting interviews with prospects and being better at developing leads, especially leads to new markets.

Let's listen in on the meeting. We'll comment on how Tom is handling some of the issues and problems that crop up at this stage of the interview.

Tom: (*Nodding and then pausing for several seconds before speaking*) Anything else you want to add?

Lisa: No, Tom, I think that pretty much covers it.

Tom: Fine. Well, Lisa, I think that was a very complete and thoughtful analysis of your job performance. You really seemed to get into it.

Lisa: (*Smiling and obviously pleased*) Yes, I did, didn't I?

Tom: Now, I'd like to take a crack at it.

Lisa: Uh-oh. (*Smiling broadly*) Here it comes!

Tom: (*Pausing for just a moment*) You're a little concerned about what I have to say? [Can you identify the listening skill Tom just used? Why did he use it?]

Lisa: Yes ... well as this seems to be going, I think I am. It isn't the easiest thing to have somebody give you feedback on how you're doing your job—especially when it comes from your boss. I'm sure even you may feel a few jitters when your boss sits down with you to review your performance.

Tom: (*Nodding*) So, maybe it's natural for any employee—you, me, whoever—to feel a little anxious when they're doing what we're doing today.

Lisa: Yes, precisely. But even though I have to confess to feeling a little apprehensive, I'm ready to proceed. With no further delays. (*Smiling and leaning forward slightly*) [Tom's good listening skills have helped to 'clear the air'. If he hadn't surfaced this mild—and predictable—anxiety of Lisa's, it might have been an unnecessary distraction for the rest of the interview.]

Tom: (*Smiling*) OK, on with the show. (*Pause*) Earlier, I asked you to start with the areas where you think you're performing effectively. I'd like to do the same thing.

Lisa: (*Smiling*) OK. Good place to start.

Tom: Lisa one of the areas where you felt you were performing effectively was making sales presentations. I'm in full agreement with that. Two of our more demanding customers have told me independently that you make excellent sales presentations. And they're generally pretty choosy about the way they hand out compliments.

Lisa: (*Smiling and looking a little embarrassed*) That's nice to hear.

Tom: Yes, it is nice to hear. (*Pause*) Another thing, you may not know it, but our training department has asked me if they could use you as an instructor in a new sales training video they're developing.

Lisa: (*A little surprised*) No, I didn't know that.

Tom: I wanted to save it for this meeting. And I'd like to talk about it more a little later. [Given the somewhat negative reputation of performance appraisal interviews among employees, sometimes it's useful to 'save' something good, as Tom does here, for a session like this.]

Lisa: (*Obviously pleased*) Great!

Tom: (*Pausing as he makes transition to new area*) Another area where you thought you were pretty strong is following up on prospects. Again, I'm in full agreement.

Lisa: (*Nodding*)

Tom: At least three of our customers have told me they never would have considered our line if it hadn't been for your persistence in following up on them.

Lisa: (*Smiling*) I hope they weren't saying I was a pain in the neck.

Tom: (*Chuckling*) No, not at all. I think they were actually quite appreciative. (*Pause*) Along those same lines, I know we wouldn't have got the Greybar account if you hadn't been so doggedly persistent in following up on them.

Lisa: (*Laughing and holding up her thumb and forefinger about a centimetre apart*) Yes, but I must say I came about that far from giving up on them.

Tom: (*Chuckling*) But you didn't, and we got the account.

Notice that Tom, in discussing the areas where he thinks Lisa is performing effectively, has chosen to lead off with the two areas where he and Lisa are in solid agreement. So far, this has had the effect of keeping Lisa's receptivity very high. Now Tom is about to embark on some areas where there doesn't appear to be much agreement between them. Let's see how he handles this potential problem.

Tom: Lisa, now I'd like to talk about some additional areas where I think you're performing effectively—areas you didn't mention.

Lisa: (*Smiling and leaning forward a little*) OK.

Notice what Tom does not do here. He doesn't mention that he disagrees with Lisa about her time management skills. Since Tom sees time management as an area where Lisa needs to improve, he won't bring it up until he's finished talking about all the areas where he thinks Lisa is performing effectively.

Tom: Well, for one thing, I think you're a pretty good morale booster around this place.

Lisa: (*Looking genuinely surprised*) What? I wouldn't have believed you'd say such a thing about me!

Tom: (*Pausing before reading back*) It sounds as though that one came as a bit of a surprise to you?

What's happening here? Tom is in the process of telling Lisa he thinks she's a good morale booster in the sales department. He expects Lisa to react very positively to this message, but her reaction appears to be more confused than pleased. Being a skilful listener, Tom doesn't try to clarify what he means. Instead, he stops talking and shifts to a listening mode. This will give Lisa an opportunity to talk about what's confusing her. If Tom continued to talk, Lisa might not hear a word. Why? Because she'd still be trying to figure out what Tom meant by 'morale booster'.

Lisa: (*Both smiling and scowling at the same time*) Yes. I'm not sure I like the sound of that.

Tom: (*Nodding and leaning forward slightly*) Uh-huh.

Lisa: Well, I suppose all I could think of when you said morale booster were those rah-rah cheerleader types. You know what I mean. All good looks and no brains. And always on the sidelines, cheering somebody else on!

Tom: (*Pausing briefly*) So, the idea of being a 'morale booster' has rather a negative connotation for you.

Lisa: (*Nodding her head*) Yes, but somehow I don't think that's what you had in mind, was it?

Tom: (*Smiling*) No, that's not what I had in mind.

Lisa: (*Smiling*) Good. So what *did* you mean when you said I was a good morale booster? [Receptivity is back up, as a result of Tom's good listening.]

Tom: (*Pausing and looking up at the ceiling for a few seconds before speaking*) Well ... what I meant by morale booster was that a lot of the things you do around here have a sort of motivating, inspirational effect on the other people in the department.

Lisa: (*Looking a little puzzled but really paying attention*)

Tom: Let me be a little more specific. (*Pause*) Ever since we've been working together I've noticed that you're always trying to help out the salespeople in other territories. You share techniques with them that you've found successful. You give them leads you've obtained from your own customers and prospects. You know, that sort of thing.

Lisa: (*Smiling and nodding*) Yes, I do try to do those things. But I wouldn't call that morale boosting. I just call that being helpful.

Tom: (*Smiling and nodding*) I agree. I think 'helpful' is a much better way to characterise what you do. But it also has a positive effect on morale, which is great. (*Pause*) Let me give you another example. Several of the girls in the office have also told me how helpful you've been—

Lisa: (*Interrupting*) Tom, I don't want you to misunderstand this, but don't you think it's a little inappropriate to refer to the women in the office as 'girls'? [Another drop in Lisa's receptivity, this time because Tom has inadvertently used an emotionally loaded expression—referring to adult women as girls. Notice that her question to Tom is not really a question, but a statement in disguise. Let's see how he handles this one.]

Tom: (*Pausing and then softly*) Lisa, it sounds as though you're a little ... offended, or maybe irritated, by my use of that word?

Lisa: (*Quickly*) Yes, I am, Tom. That's exactly how I feel. (*Pause*) I have to listen to my customers talk that way all the time. And I always cringe when they do. But I don't say anything because I think it just wouldn't be appropriate in that kind of situation. However, when you use that expression, I really feel I've got to say something about it.

Tom: (*Pausing to make sure she's finished*) So, it's something you feel strongly about and you don't want to bite your tongue, like you do in a sales situation. (*Pause*)

Lisa: Yes, that's it exactly. (*Pause*) Don't get me wrong, Tom. I don't want to come across as an angry, strident feminist, but I see myself as a woman, not a girl. Just as you see yourself as a man and not a boy. And the same goes for the women who work in the office. I know you don't mean any disrespect by it, but I'd really prefer it if you wouldn't use that expression any more.

Tom: Lisa, thanks for telling me how you feel. And straightening me out. As you know, it's an old habit. But I'll try very hard to refer to the ... women in the office as women from now on.

Tom handles this drop in receptivity by being a good listener. If he had chosen to discuss or, worse, debate the point, the entire interview might have been sidetracked or completely derailed. Whatever his personal view on this matter outside this interview, he chooses here to respect Lisa's feelings. Imagine how differently the interview might have gone if Tom had said something like, 'Don't be so sensitive! I didn't mean anything by it.'

Tom: OK, let me move on now to another area where I think you're performing effectively. In fact, it's an area where you ...

Tom will now talk about the final area where he sees Lisa performing effectively, developing leads. As before, he'll use concrete examples to make his points. When he's finished talking about this area, he'll summarise briefly the four major areas he's mentioned and ask if Lisa would like to add anything. Then he'll make a transition statement and begin to identify some of the areas where he thinks Lisa could improve. Let's pick up the interview at that point.

Tom: OK, let's move on now to some of the areas where I think you could improve. (*Pause*)

Lisa: (*Nodding*) OK.

Tom: Based on observing your performance lately, Lisa, and thinking quite a bit about it, I'd say there are four areas where you could stand to improve. (*Pause*)

Lisa: (*Looking attentive*) Uh-huh.

Tom: The first thing I'd like to do is explain my thinking in each area and get your reactions to what I've said. [Notice Tom's use of the 'Tell them what you're going to tell them' technique here.]

Lisa: (*Nodding*) OK.

Tom: Then I'd like to talk about how these areas tie into the areas you said you'd like to improve in. (*Pause*) And finally, I'd like us to reach some agreement on what it makes most sense for you to be working on to improve your performance over the next couple of months. (*Pause*)

Lisa: OK.

Tom: And after that, I'd like us to agree on what I can do, as your supervisor, to help you improve and also make your job more satisfying. (*Pause*)

Lisa: Sounds good.

At the very beginning of the interview, Tom gave Lisa a preview of what was going to happen in the session. But since this is such a critical and sensitive stage, Tom has chosen to repeat the preview, going into a little bit more depth than he did at the beginning. This should help to remind Lisa of the big picture—that the overall purpose of the interview is not to criticise Lisa's performance but for the two of them to work together to improve it.

Tom: All right. One of the areas where I think you could improve—and I think it ties in with your wanting to achieve a greater closing percentage—is in handling the objections that prospects frequently raise to our product line.

Lisa: (*Wrinkling forehead as Tom talks*) Handling objections? (*Pausing for a moment*) I think I have to disagree with that, Tom. I think I'm actually pretty good at handling objections.

Tom: (*Leaning forward*) So you're a bit surprised, then, that I'd identify that as an area where you could improve. (*Pause*) [Lisa's receptivity has dropped sharply here. What would happen if Tom tried to explain himself rather than listen to what she has to say?]

Lisa: Yes, I am surprised. I mean that's an area I think I'm really strong in. In fact, I even keep a notebook on objections so I can always be coming up with better arguments to counter them.

Tom: (*Still listening attentively*) Uh-huh.

Lisa: (*Starting to wind down a little*) Uh ... (*Now smiling*) ... maybe I should let you tell me what you meant.

Tom: (*Smiling*) OK, but you really did seem surprised, maybe even a little stung, when I said you needed to improve in an area that you think you're doing very well in.

Lisa: (*Smiling*) Yes, that's pretty much how I felt. But maybe I responded a little quickly there. What exactly did you mean? [Now Lisa's receptivity seems to be back up, so Tom will take a crack at clarifying what he meant.]

Tom: First of all, let me say I agree with you that your arguments for the objections that prospects raise are really quite good.

Lisa: (*Looking even more curious and leaning forward slightly*) How's that?

Tom: Well, when a prospect offers an objection to a product, such as saying it's too expensive or it's not compatible with their other furniture, I do think it's awfully tempting to come back with an argument for why the prospect is wrong.

Lisa: (*Nodding*) Absolutely. I agree.

Tom: But I think the best thing to do when prospects offer objections is to get more information before offering your arguments. (*Pause*) What I mean is, it's better to draw the prospects out and get them talking about their objections in detail. (*Pause*) I know it's paradoxical, but sometimes they'll talk themselves right out of their objections. But even when they don't, they'll usually be more willing to listen to your arguments if you listen to their objections first.

Lisa: (*Looking thoughtful*) Hmm ... that is something to think about.

Tom: It sounds as though you're willing to consider that as a possible strategy for handling objections?

Lisa: (*Still looking very thoughtful*) Yes ...

Tom: I'll tell you what. Why don't we come back to this a little later and move on now to another area? (*Pause*)

Lisa: (*Nodding*) Fine.

Tom seems to have got Lisa interested, if not completely convinced, in a new strategy for dealing with prospect objections. Rather than push for full commitment on this issue immediately, Tom has decided to let her think about it for a while. We've found that an 'incubation' period like this often has a positive effect when trying to get people to see things in a new way.

Tom: OK, a second area where I'd like to see some improvement is in meeting reporting deadlines. (*Pause*)

Lisa: (*Shaking her head and smiling*) I just knew those damn reports were going to creep into this conversation somehow.

Tom: (*Smiling*) I suppose this is the time, isn't it?

Lisa: (*Smiling, raising her palms to the ceiling, and shrugging*) Tom, what can I tell you? I hate those reports, and you know it. I think they're a big waste of time. I'll admit it. I'm guilty. But I just wish we could do away with them altogether.

Tom: (*Pause*) It sounds as if you really find the reports unpleasant, that they're almost an obstacle to getting more important things done? [The old standby, reading back.]

Lisa: (*Sighing*) Exactly. That's exactly how I feel. But what do *you* have to say on the subject? Maybe I'm just not seeing the big picture here. [Receptivity's back up.]

Tom: Well, Lisa, I must say I don't totally disagree with you. I'm not that keen on paperwork either. On the other hand, if those reports don't get in on time, it causes me and the people I work for a lot of problems. (*Pause*) And even though it may seem that nobody ever looks at those reports, they're actually quite helpful to our management information systems people.

Lisa: (*Nodding*) Yes, I'm sure that's true.

Tom: I think I have a pretty good idea how you feel about the reports, Lisa. And you seem to be pretty much aware of the problems I have when the reports don't get handed in on time. What thoughts do you have about resolving this situation? [Here Tom has put the responsibility for a solution on Lisa by asking an open-ended question]

Lisa: (*Firmly*) Tom, I'll make a commitment to you right now to get those reports in on time, all the time.

Tom: (*Smiling*) Lisa, I'm glad to hear you say that. (*Pause*) A little later on I'd like us to talk about some things I can do to make the whole reporting process at least a little easier for you.

Just a word or two here on technique. Notice that Tom has chosen to take the tack of getting at least partial commitment from Lisa on each area of improvement without going into specific detail on exactly what she'll be doing to improve. As you'll see, Tom's strategy will be to come back to each area a little later for this kind of specific commitment. This is not the only way to do it, however. You might choose to complete one area before moving on to the next. We'd recommend that you experiment before you firmly adopt any one strategy. Let's jump ahead now to the final area where Tom thinks Lisa can improve—the area of time management. Remember, this is an area Lisa identified as one of her strengths.

> **Tom:** OK, why don't we move on to the last area where I think you could stand to improve—time management. (*Pause*)
>
> **Lisa:** Well, as I said, Tom, this is an area where I think I'm pretty good. (*Real coolness in her voice*) But I'd like to hear what you have to say. [At this point it seems as if Lisa is almost challenging Tom to show her how she could improve in the area of time management.]
>
> **Tom:** Well, Lisa, maybe at this point it would be helpful if you reviewed for both of us the specific ways you think you're good at time management. Then I could give you my thoughts on the subject and maybe offer some additional things you could do that might make you even more effective. How does that sound?

Tom realised he didn't have a very good audience for what he wanted to say. So, he decides to try to get Lisa talking in order to build up her receptivity. Notice also that he's never disagreed with Lisa's contention that she's good at time management. Rather, Tom has simply said that he'd like to make some suggestions that would help make her even more effective in this area.

> **Lisa:** (*Softening up a little*) OK, well, let's see. As I said, I work pretty fast and get a lot of things done in a fairly short period of time.
>
> **Tom:** (*Nodding*) Uh-huh.
>
> **Lisa:** I think I'm pretty well organised. You know, I can always lay my hands on whatever I want because I have good filing and record-keeping systems.
>
> **Tom:** Yes, you certainly do.
>
> **Lisa:** Um ... I think I'm pretty good at delegating tasks to other people in the department who can probably do them better and faster than I can.
>
> **Tom:** (*Nodding*) Uh-huh.
>
> **Lisa:** Hmm ... I guess that about covers it. OK, (*Smiling just a little*) I'd like to hear your suggestions, Tom. [Receptivity seems pretty high here. A good time for Tom to try to get a few points about

time management across to Lisa.]

Tom: OK, I think that review was very helpful. (*Pause*) I think the three areas you mentioned—working fast, being organised, and delegating tasks—are all important aspects of time management. And I agree that you're good at all three. (*Pause*)

Lisa: (*Nodding*) That's good. But, then what are you suggesting?

Tom: I'd say the only major suggestion I'd make for improving your time management skills is in setting priorities. (*Pause*)

Lisa: (*Leaning forward and looking very attentive*) Yes?

Tom: Let me be more specific. Why don't I tell you exactly how I do it just to see what you think.

Lisa: (*Still looking attentive*) OK.

Tom: First thing Monday morning I take a pad and write down all the tasks I'd like to accomplish by Friday at 5 p.m.

Lisa: (*Smiling*) I bet that's a pretty long list.

Tom: Then I make an assumption. (*Pause*) I assume that doing only about 20 per cent of those tasks will account for about 80 per cent of the value of completing all the tasks on the list. (*Pause*)

Lisa: (*Looking thoughtful*) Oh, yes. I think that's called the 80/20 rule, isn't it?

Tom: Right. Once I've identified those key tasks, I try to devote almost all my energy for the rest of the week getting them done. If none of the other tasks gets done, I don't worry about it.

Lisa: (*Still looking thoughtful and nodding*)

Tom: OK, so that's my weekly 'to do' list. I make up a similar daily 'to do' list the first thing every morning.

Lisa: (*Nodding*) Hmm. I like that. Yes ... I like that. (*Pause*) I think it's probably a lot better than what I do now, which is having about a hundred of those 'Post-It' notes plastered all over my office and my flat. I even have some on the dashboard of my car. (*Both laugh*)

Tom: (*Pausing as laughter subsides*) Well, this might be a *little* more systematic than that! (*Pause*) But seriously, Lisa, if you'd be willing to adopt those two habits, I think you'd find yourself making even more effective use of your time than you do now.

Lisa: I think you're right. I'll try it.

Let's take a look at the progress Tom has made so far. After reviewing what he thinks are Lisa's strong points, Tom has presented his ideas and suggestions on the areas where he thinks she could improve. In the process, he's had to handle several dips in Lisa's receptivity, but she now appears to be ready to agree to make some changes in each of the four areas. Now Tom's job is to help Lisa make some specific commitments in each of these areas.

> **Tom:** Well, Lisa, that pretty much covers the four areas I felt you could improve in. (*Pause*) Now it seems to me that our task is to try to agree on the specific things you'll be doing in each area over the next several months. (*Pause*)
>
> **Lisa:** (*Nodding*) OK. Makes sense to me.
>
> **Tom:** (*Smiling*) I know I don't even have to say this, but I think the specific things you'll be working on should include your own ideas and suggestions as well as mine.
>
> **Lisa:** (*Chuckling*) No, you didn't have to tell me that, Tom.
>
> **Tom:** (*Still smiling*) Good. OK, Lisa, why don't you take a few minutes to talk about the specific things you'd like to concentrate on over the next several weeks and months, given all the things we've talked about so far ...

At this stage of the interview you're striving for a certain amount of agreement between you and the employee on: (a) the major areas where the employee will be attempting to improve job performance over the next several months, and (b) the specific evidence both of you would accept as proof the employee had actually made significant improvement in each area.

So far, Tom and Lisa both have achieved pretty good agreement on the general areas where Lisa will be working to improve her performance. As we leave them at this point, they're beginning to get specific about the tasks Lisa will actually complete to satisfy both of them that her performance has, in fact, improved.

Getting down to specifics, as Tom and Lisa are about to do, is roughly the dividing line between this step, presenting your analysis of the employee's performance, and the next step, negotiating the performance agreement. So we'll leave Tom and Lisa here and get back to them in the next chapter.

A Quick Section Summary

Before turning our attention to some possible setbacks, let's quickly review some of the most important points to keep in mind during this stage of the interview.

1. Remember that the performance analysis form is your

basic guide through this stage of the interview.   It's a reminder to you of the areas where you think your employee is performing effectively and the areas where you'd like to see performance improved.

2. Start with the positive.   Before you offer your ideas and suggestions on the areas you think employees can improve, tell them in specific terms what you think they're doing well.   We can't stress this point enough.

3. Try to establish as much agreement as you can between the employee's analysis and your own.   This will give the employee a sense that the two of you are working as a team.

4. Always be ready to shift from a presenting mode to a listening mode to keep your employee's receptivity up.   Remember how many times Tom had to do this to maintain Lisa's involvement in the performance improvement process.

5. Get your employee's reactions to your analysis after you've presented it.   Give your employee a chance to think out loud about what you've said.   It will also give you an opportunity to make certain your employee has understood what you've said.

Possible Setbacks

At the beginning of this chapter we said that the listening skills you've learned will help get you out of trouble if things start to go wrong. Throughout the example interview, Tom was able to keep Lisa's involvement and receptivity fairly high simply by reading Lisa back and letting her talk when she was bothered by, or disagreed with, something Tom said.

However, even though the interview with Lisa was not all plain sailing for Tom, Lisa didn't cause Tom any major difficulties. Unfortunately, some employees can be a bit more troublesome.

In the last section of the chapter, we've anticipated some of the more difficult situations you might find yourself in when you try to make some performance-related suggestions or observations.   After you read through each situation, imagine how you might handle it.   If you feel more adventurous, ask another person to help you role play the situation, or write down your response on a sheet of paper.

After you've responded to each situation, you'll have an opportunity to compare your responses to ours. Our answers certainly aren't the only effective ways to handle these situations, but practical experience has taught us that they work very well.

Situation 1: Touching a Nerve

Have you ever been in a dentist's chair after your dentist has been drilling for a while and then starts to clean out the cavity with a water nozzle? When that cold water hits an exposed nerve, you just about jump out of the chair, up through the ceiling.

Sometimes when you're talking to employees about how they can improve their performance, you get a similar reaction. You're calmly explaining something to the employee, and wham, the person comes back with a very strong response that startles you. Here's an example.

> **Supervisor:** Good. All right, Pat, let me move on to another area. I think another thing you could do to improve your overall performance is to take a more active part in our weekly staff meetings. I think—
>
> **Employee:** (*Interrupting and throwing hands up in the air*) Oh that's ridiculous! Really ridiculous! All I can say is I have a completely different opinion on that matter from you! (*Folding arms across chest and leaning back*)

Imagine you were the supervisor and had provoked this reaction.

How would you handle the situation?

We approach the situation with these thoughts:

▶ the issue of participating more actively in staff meetings is obviously a sensitive one for Pat;

▶ the supervisor is unlikely to get anywhere until he responds to Pat's very strong feelings;

▶ once Pat has had an opportunity to express these feelings, the supervisor will be in a position to get specific information on why this is such a sensitive issue and what the two of them can do to resolve the problem.

For example:

Employee: (*Interrupting and throwing hands up in the air*) Oh that's ridiculous! Really ridiculous! All I can say is I have a completely different opinion on that matter from you! (*Folding arms across chest and leaning back*)

Supervisor: (*Calmly and softly, after pausing to make sure Pat is finished*) You sound pretty angry, Pat. (*Pause*) And it sounds as if you see the situation from a very different perspective. [A nice read back.]

Employee: Absolutely right I do! (*Leaning forward*) I'd just like to remind you of something! I used to speak up all the time at staff meetings, if you remember. But I'm definitely not going to do that any more!

Supervisor: (*Remaining calm*) So something happened, maybe something I did, to change your mind?

Employee: (*A little more softly now*) Yes. [By staying in the listening mode, the supervisor should start to get more specific information.]

Supervisor: (*Nodding*) Tell me, Pat. I'd like to know.

Employee: I'll tell you exactly what happened. Every time I said something at a staff meeting, you'd follow up whatever I said with, 'I think what Pat is trying to say is ...' (*Pause*) It was really annoying. I don't know, I felt you didn't have any confidence in me. It was as though you had to act as a translator for me.

Supervisor: (*Nodding*) So because I had this annoying habit of trying to 'translate' for you, you decided to just shut up completely.

Employee: (*Now visibly calmer*) Yes that about sums it up. I probably should've said something, but I didn't. Until now.

Supervisor: Well, Pat, I'm glad you did. (*Pause*) I'm really sorry I did that. I honestly wasn't aware of it, but I want to make sure I stop doing it completely in the future.

Employee: (*Smiling a little*) That would be great.

Supervisor: You've got a deal. OK, so if I agree to ...

Situation 2: Giving Ground Grudgingly

Every now and then you'll run into an employee who goes along with your suggestions, but does so in a reluctant, half-hearted fashion. For example, in response to a suggestion you make on how performance could be improved, the employee might blandly respond by:

▶ nodding slowly with a blank expression;

▶ saying, 'Yes, OK, that would be all right';
▶ turning both palms upwards and saying 'Why not?';
▶ saying, 'OK, whatever you say, boss'.

Let's say you're in the middle of a meeting with an employee and have been getting these kinds of half-hearted responses to your suggestions for the last ten minutes. What would you do to build up the employee's obviously low level of receptivity to your suggestions?

There are two basic strategies we'd recommend when you're getting half-hearted, grudging responses to your suggestions for improvement:

1. reading back; and
2. using the stop-look-and-listen technique.

You can use the reading back technique whenever you get a lukewarm reaction from an employee to your suggestions. For example, let's say you suggest that an employee's written communication skills could be improved by writing briefer and more concise memos. In response, the employee says, 'Yes, I suppose that's a good idea' in a half-hearted tone of voice. You might respond by saying:

'you don't seem very enthusiastic about my suggestion.'
'it doesn't seem as if you're completely sold on that idea.'
'you're not sure that's something you really want to do?'

This strategy often works because (a) it accurately captures the verbal and non-verbal messages the employee has been sending and (b) it puts the responsibility on the employee's shoulders to respond in some way. Sometimes, employees will deny being half-hearted or unenthusiastic, but you'll immediately see an improved attitude and a greater spirit of co-operation. Sometimes, the employee will open up and tell you very directly why your idea doesn't seem to be a very good one.

But this strategy doesn't always work. Sometimes the employee will continue to insist, but still in a half-hearted tone of voice, that your suggestion is a good one to follow. And you'll be left with the feeling that something is still being held back from you.

In this situation we recommend using the stop-look-and-listen technique:

1. *stop* the interaction as soon as you notice the discussion is becoming unproductive;

2. *look* squarely at the problem by describing it succinctly and objectively; and

3. *listen* for suggestions that you both can live with for resolving the problem.

Here's an example of a supervisor using this technique with an employee who doesn't seem to be really interested in any suggestions for improvement.

> **Employee:** (*Nodding half-heartedly to the latest suggestion the supervisor has made*)
>
> **Supervisor:** (*Slowly and in a non-punitive tone*) I've noticed that you don't seem to be very enthusiastic about any of the suggestions I've made in the last few minutes. (*Pause*) Several times you've shrugged your shoulders or said, 'Yes, I suppose that's OK,' and that sort of thing.
>
> **Employee:** (*Not saying anything but looking a little more attentive*)
>
> **Supervisor:** When you react that way to my suggestions, I feel a little confused and frustrated—I feel we're not really making any progress here.

The supervisor has decided to stop the unproductive interaction, describe the problem as objectively as possible, and disclose his feelings about the interaction to the employee.

> **Employee:** (*Still looking attentive but not saying anything*)
>
> **Supervisor:** I'd like to turn this situation round. What ideas and suggestions do you have for how we can make this a more productive session for both of us?

Now the supervisor will listen to the employee's suggestions for dealing with the problem. Responsibility for making the session more positive has been put squarely on the employee's shoulders.

> **Employee:** (*Hesitating somewhat*) Well ... I see what you're saying ... but, well, there is something that has been bothering me.
>
> **Supervisor:** (*Nodding and leaning forward slightly*) I'd like to hear about it.
>
> **Employee:** (*Starting to build up a little steam*) Well, I must say, I don't feel too wonderful about listening to your suggestions for how I can improve after I told you about that big problem we've got in inventory control and you didn't make any commitment

to do anything about it. Do you understand what I'm saying?

Supervisor: Well, let's see. (*Slowly*) I think you're saying you got the problem off your chest by telling me about it, but now you feel I'm not really doing anything to help solve the problem?

Employee: (*Nodding*) Yes, that's it. And that's why I'm not feeling all that co-operative now. (*Pausing, adding nothing*)

Supervisor: (*Thinking for a second*) OK, I can appreciate that. (*Pause*) How about if we set up a specific time later this week to discuss that problem ... in depth? (*Pause*) If we agree to do that, would you agree to get more involved in what we're talking about right now?

Employee: (*Nodding vigorously*) I think so. You've got yourself a bargain.

Supervisor: Good. How about Thursday ...?

Notice that the employee didn't come up with any suggestions for how to improve the situation. However, by finding out why the employee wasn't being very responsive, the supervisor was able to suggest a way for both of them to get what they wanted.

Situation 3: Getting Caught in an Argument

Every now and then, even an experienced, skilful supervisor will get into an argument with an employee when discussing the subject of job performance. For example, let's say you find yourself in the same bind as the supervisor below:

Supervisor: All right, Ron. Let's move on to another area where I think you could stand to improve your performance. It has to do with meeting reporting deadlines. For instance just the other day—

Employee: (*Interrupting*) Oh, come on! I almost always get my reports in on time. Besides, I'm a lot better about it than anybody else in the department. And nobody reads those wretched reports anyway.

Supervisor: (*Wrinkling his forehead and shaking his head*) Now wait a minute, Ron. Let's take a realistic look at this. I know for a fact that six of your last ten monthly reports have been at least a week late. And if you think nobody—

Employee: (*Interrupting*) I'm sorry. That's just not true. Now maybe one or two—

Supervisor: (*Interrupting and losing patience*) Now you hold on, Ron. I've got some figures Terry has been keeping ...

Well, here you are. You had no intention of getting into an argument with the employee, but now you're right in the middle of one. How would you get out of this situation? After you've thought about your response, see what we'd do to extricate ourselves from an argument like this.

Unfortunately, arguments are like a lot of situations in life—once you get into them, it's hard to get out of them. And when you do get into a good one, your autonomic nervous system—pulse, blood pressure, and adrenalin—usually goes into high gear. For a short while, your ability to think flexibly and openly is short-circuited and it's difficult to do anything but continue to push your own point of view.

In spite of this, however, we think you have two options:

1. stop talking and start listening;
2. take a break.

The first option is easier said than done, but we think it's almost always worth a try. The trick here—and it's not easy—is to force yourself to stop countering everything the employee says and go back into listening mode. Here's an example:

Supervisor: (*Interrupting*) Now hold on, Ron. I've got some figures Terry has been keeping—
Employee: (*Interrupting*) I don't care about any figures that Terry has been keeping ...
Supervisor: (*About to interrupt but catching himself*)
Employee: ... I keep my own records. I know when my reports are late, and I know when they're on time.
Supervisor: (*Nodding and assuming a more relaxed expression on his face*) OK. Go on.
Employee: (*Slowing down just a bit*) I mean, this is something we've disagreed on for a long time. And I just don't think you're aware of how hard I try to get those reports in on time, in spite of all the other things I have to do. (*Calmly now*) You know what I mean?
Supervisor: I think so. (*Patiently and calmly*) I'm hearing several things. (*Pause*) One, you're saying the records you keep indicate that your reports have been getting in on time, regardless of what

Terry says. (*Pause*) Two, I think you're saying I don't appreciate where these reports fit into the bigger picture of your whole job.

Employee: You've got it. (*Softening some more*) Now I realise you have a responsibility also to ...

In this example, the supervisor really had to exercise some self-restraint to stop interrupting and to start listening to the employee. As hard as it was to do this, however, it appeared to get some results. The employee's tone was beginning to soften, and receptivity was slowly on the rise.

We'd like to believe that this 'stop talking and start listening' technique is always the best way to get out of an argument, but we're painfully aware that sometimes it doesn't work. As hard as you try, you just can't muster the will to listen to the employee. The impulse to rebut, counter and find holes in the employee's argument is just too strong.

When you're so upset or annoyed you just can't do what it takes to listen to the employee, we recommend the second option—take a break. By this, we mean taking an intermission from the interview so both you and the employee will have an opportunity to cool off a bit and get a little perspective on what's going on.

Here are a couple of things to remember when you suggest to the employee that you both ought to take a break from the interview.

▶ Make your suggestions softly but firmly. If the employee is a forceful person and seems intent on winning the argument, you may run into a little resistance. Just be persistent. You may have to repeat your suggestion several times before the employee agrees to a cooling-off period.

▶ Try to make the break long enough for the two of you to clear your heads, but short enough so you can get back to the interview while it's still reasonably fresh in your minds. A break of half an hour to an hour is probably ideal. If this isn't possible because of other commitments, then you ought to resume the interview as early as possible the next day.

In this chapter we've gone into quite a bit of detail on how to present your analysis of the employee's performance. Along the way, we've talked about a number of specific ways to keep the employee's receptivity up while you're offering your thoughts and suggestions. We also discussed a number of potential setbacks, and how to handle them. In the next chapter we'll discuss the climax of the interview—negotiating a performance agreement between you and the employee.

Chapter 14

Step Eight: Negotiate the Performance Agreement

IN TERMS of the overall performance improvement process, let's review what you've done so far:

- ▶ in Step One you analysed your employee's job performance;
- ▶ in Step Two you asked your employee to meet with you;
- ▶ in Step Three you began the performance improvement interview;
- ▶ in Step Four you found out how things were going in general at work and about any problems the employee was experiencing.
- ▶ in Step Five you asked what you could do to make the employee's job more satisfying and less frustrating;
- ▶ in Step Six you asked the employee to do a self-analysis, focusing first on strong points and then on areas needing improvement;
- ▶ in Step Seven you presented your analysis of the employee's performance, first identifying things the employee does well and then specifying areas where the employee needs to improve.

You're now at Step Eight, in many ways the climax of the interview. This is the part of the process you've been building up to from the very beginning. Your goal at this stage is to come up with a handwritten agreement between you and the employee on:

- ▶ specific tasks the employee is going to work on during the next four to six weeks to improve his work performance.
- ▶ specific tasks you're going to work on during this same period to: (a) help the employee improve her work performance and (b) make her job less frustrating and more satisfying.

To give you an idea of what you're up to in this step of the process, we'll eventually pick up Lisa and Tom where we left them in Step Seven and we'll listen in as they negotiate a performance agreement.

Here's an overview of what we'll cover in this chapter:

▶ important points to keep in mind about the content and style of a performance agreement;

▶ the negotiating strategy for arriving at a performance agreement that both you and the employee can live with; and

▶ an example of a supervisor (Tom) and employee (Lisa) actually negotiating a performance agreement.

In the last chapter we noted that the dividing line between presenting your analysis of the employee's performance and 'negotiating the performance agreement' is not sharply defined. With a little practice the two steps should merge so comfortably and fluidly that it's hard to tell where one ends and the other begins.

Some Important Points to Keep in Mind

Before we talk about performance agreements and how to negotiate them, let's take a look at the situation you're in with a typical employee. If you're like most bosses, you're probably satisfied with some aspects of the employee's performance, but you'd also like the employee to change in some important ways. That's fine. But ask yourself this question: 'Why *should* the employee change?' Should the employee change simply because you're the boss and that's what you want? It would be nice if it were that easy, but unfortunately it isn't. (It's the same with other people in our lives, like spouses and children. We may want them to change, but they're not going to do it simply because we want them too.)

If you want an employee (or anyone else, for that matter) to change, you've got to be prepared to answer the question, 'What's in it for me?' When you ask this question, the answer usually has a lot to do with *you*. That is, it has to do with who you are as a boss and how well (or maybe how badly) you've been meeting some important needs of the employee. For example, if your employee has a strong need to be treated courteously and respectfully, but you're an overreacting type of boss who frequently rants and raves all around the office, guess what your employee probably wants from you? Or, if your employee has a strong need for decisive, 'take-charge' leadership, but you're an avoiding, 'nice guy' type of boss who sweeps pressing personnel and organisational problems under the rug, guess what your employee probably wants from you?

Our message is really quite simple: if you can do something the employee wants and needs from you, you'll greatly increase the chances that the employee will do something you want. So, if you want improved work performance, be prepared to give the employee something in return, the *quid pro quo*, or 'something for something'. This concept is at the heart of what it takes to form a performance agreement.

If you're like most bosses, though, you're probably much clearer about what you want from your employees than what your employees want from you. That's the reason we added Step Five (asking your employee 'The Question') to the performance improvement process. Once again, we'll stress how important it is to ask employees that question: 'What can I do, as your boss, to make your job here more satisfying and less frustrating?' The answers—if you do a good job of drawing the employee out—should give you all the information you need to decide what things you need to work on in a performance agreement with an employee.

This notion of 'something for something' is probably the most important thing to remember as you approach the challenge of negotiating a performance agreement. However, there are four additional things to keep in mind :

1. keep the negotiating process and the language of the agreement informal, even though it's in writing;
2. make sure the agreement has something of value in it for both you and the employee;
3. limit the performance agreement to high-priority tasks;
4. be specific in writing out what both you and the employee are actually going to be doing in the future.

Let's talk about each of these points in a bit more detail.

Put It in Writing, But Keep It Informal

As time passes—even after a few days—it's very easy to forget a task you and the employee agreed verbally, no matter how clearly stated.

That's why it's important to put the performance agreement in writing. A written agreement not only provides a document you can refer back to, but the act of writing things down helps people remember things. We've also noticed that people tend to be more committed to doing things when they actually write them down.

On the other hand, putting something in writing has a tendency to make people a little nervous. For this reason, you should make the agreement as informal as you can. Here are some suggestions.

▶ Write the agreement by hand on a blank sheet of paper. Don't type it. Just draw a line right down the middle of the sheet. On top of the left-hand column, write, 'What (the employee's name) is going to work on.' On the top of the other side, write, 'What (your name) is going to work on'.

▶ Avoid using anything that even vaguely resembles a printed form. The document should be created during the session, not before it.

▶ Even though you may be tempted, don't use the expression, 'performance contract'. That'll really make people nervous.

▶ Assure the employee that the performance agreement is for the sole use of the two of you and that copies won't be sent to the personnel department or any other organisation officials.

▶ Don't be afraid to cross out items in the agreement if you need to. This will make it look less imposing and more informal.

Make Sure There's Something in It for Both of You

The performance agreement should have significance and value to both of you. If either one of you sees the agreement as being lopsided in favour of the other person, it's a safe bet that the person who's getting the short end of the stick won't live up to his or her part of the bargain, at least not fully.

How to form a performance agreement with something in it for both of you will become clearer as you read through the chapter. At this point, though, keep in mind that the agreement ought to include:

▶ some tasks for the employee to work on based on the individual's analysis of his own performance, especially the areas where he feels he could stand to improve;

▶ some tasks for the employee to work on based on your analysis of her performance and the areas where you think she could stand to improve;

▶ some things you can do that will assist and support the employee with the tasks he'll be working on; and

▶ some tasks for you to work on based on what the employee told you when you asked her 'What can I do, as your boss, to make your job here less frustrating and more satisfying?'

Stick to High-Priority Tasks

If we've learned anything about helping people change their behaviour and improve their performance, it's this: don't bite off more than you can chew! So, when you're forming your agreement, stick to high priority tasks and try to set realistic, achievable goals.

In our experience, you and your employee will have a tendency to want to do too much. This is understandable, even laudable. But it's not good. If you try to do too much, you may end up accomplishing very little or giving up altogether. And you'll be worse off than you were before you began the whole performance improvement process.

Although it may be difficult, try to limit the performance agreement only to those tasks that you and the employee think are a high priority. If you find it too difficult to limit the agreement to only a few tasks, then go ahead and put down a more extensive list of things for both of you to *get started on*, with the understanding that *it'll take some time* to accomplish all the tasks.

Be Specific

This is just a reminder to avoid the use of fuzzies and to use clear, precise language in writing out the tasks in the performance agreement. Here are some examples.

Instead of saying:
John will be more courteous to customers.
It would be better to say:
When customers come to him with a problem, John will smile at them, speak in a friendly tone of voice, read back his understanding of their problem, and ask how he can help.

Instead of saying:
Sally will work on her written communications skills.
It would be better to say:
Sally will enrol in a company-sponsored business writing course and involve Jane (her supervisor) in giving her feedback on homework assignments.

Instead of saying:
Terry will work on improving the credibility of his sales presentations.

It would be better to say:
When making sales presentations, Terry will talk about how the product meets the special needs of the customer, use documents and technical data when making a 'pitch', and stop his presentation to listen whenever the customer voices a question or concern.

The Negotiating Strategy

Here's the basic strategy we recommend for the negotiating process:

1. Begin by asking what the employee would like to work on. Let's assume you presented your analysis of the employee's performance and that there's been at least a reasonable receptivity to your ideas. A good way to begin the negotiating process is simply to ask what tasks the employee would like to work on over the next several weeks to improve his work performance. While the employee is talking, it's OK to take a few notes. But, as we've said before, don't let your note-taking detract from your active interest in what the employee is saying. Use your listening skills to help the employee 'think out loud' about what tasks she needs to work on in the weeks and months ahead.

2. Make additional suggestions, if necessary, about what you'd like the employee to work on. After you find out what the employee would like to work on, you may very well hear answers that include all the areas where you'd like to see the employee improve. That's a nice situation to be in, because all you have to do is agree with the employee. But if the employee overlooks some areas, now's the time for you to suggest additional tasks. Just make sure you build on the employee's thoughts when you offer your suggestions. For example, you might say, 'OK, Kevin, those are some very good candidates for tasks you could work on. I have a couple of suggestions I'd like to put on the table as well.'

As we said earlier, the list of tasks you're going to come up with is probably going to be too long. Some of the tasks will have to be eliminated to keep the list manageable and to avoid overburdening the employee.

Here's another thing to bear in mind at this stage. At this point in the interview, it's especially important to keep the employee's receptivity up. So, unless you feel very strongly about it, avoid suggesting additional tasks the employee strongly resisted earlier in the interview. Here the old adage, 'Discretion is the better part of valour,' is very relevant. This is not to suggest that you completely forget about some of the more controversial tasks; it simply may be better to defer them to a follow-up meeting, after you've developed a little momentum as a result of this first session.

3. Strike a bargain.   After you and the employee have talked about what the employee could potentially work on, the two of you should try to agree on the specific tasks that will be actually written up in the 'What (the employee) is going to work on' section of the performance agreement.

Here are a few reminders.

▶ Stick to priorities. Only tasks that are really important to either or both of you should be written down.
▶ Be specific. The more clearly you state the tasks the employee is going to work on, the greater the chances are that the person will actually do them.
▶ Muster your listening skills. You'll need them.
▶ Be patient. Sometimes good bargains take a while to work out.

4. Ask the employee for suggestions about what you should work on.   After you and the employee decide on the specific tasks the person is going to work on, it's time to focus on what you can do. This means two things. First, it means finding out what you can do to assist in carrying out the tasks the employee has agreed to. A good way to do this is simply to ask, 'What can I do to help you with any of these tasks?' Usually, employees will come up with a number of helpful suggestions. The second thing, though, is probably even more important. Simply ask the employee to think back to earlier in the interview when you asked the question, 'What ideas do you have for how I can make your job less frustrating and more satisfying?' Based on the employee's answer, ask for suggestions about specific things you could do. Once again, use your listening skills to draw the person out fully and completely.

5. Make additional suggestions, if necessary, on things you could work on to help the employee.   After the employee has suggested things you could do, offer some of your own ideas about what you might do. Remember, sometimes employees are reluctant to suggest things they actually want really badly, out of a fear that their request will be denied or get them in trouble in some way. So ask yourself the question, 'What are one or two additional things I *could* do that would mean a lot to the employee? If you can, offer to do at least one thing. That one thing may very well be the key to negotiating a successful performance agreement.

However, just as you don't want the employee to feel overwhelmed with too many tasks, you also need to feel comfortable with the amount of work you're committing yourself to. Remind yourself that you and the employee will be paring down your overall list so you can concentrate on a few things that are important to both of you.

6. Strike another bargain. Do the same thing as you did in heading 3 above, only in reverse. Instead of bargaining on the *employee's* tasks, the two of you must try to agree on the things *you'll* be working on.

All the reminders cited in heading 3 are equally relevant here. But there is one more thing to keep in mind (we've mentioned it before). Many managers and supervisors expect their employees to make large, even outrageous, demands on them, but our experience has proved otherwise. Employees usually make small—sometimes even seemingly trivial requests of their bosses. For example, it's much more likely for an employee to ask for a friendly smile and a hello in the morning than a 50 per cent increase in salary. Often, requests that seem the most inconsequential, and are actually the easiest to fulfil on the boss's part, are the most important ones to the employee.

Walking Through an Example

Let's return now to the example from the last chapter, where Tom, the sales manager, was sitting down with Lisa, one of his salespeople. In the last chapter, Tom spent quite a bit of time presenting his analysis of Lisa's work performance. He described the areas where he thought Lisa was performing effectively, citing some specific examples in each area. Then he talked about some of the areas where he thought Lisa could stand to improve, and he talked rather specifically about what she could do to improve in these areas. You may recall that Tom frequently had to use his good listening skills to respond to a number of dips in Lisa's receptivity.

When we left them in the last chapter, Lisa seemed pretty receptive to Tom's suggestions about how she could stand to improve her performance. However, Tom and Lisa had not yet written down the tasks that both of them would be working on over the next several weeks and months.

Let's go back to where we left them in the last chapter to see how Tom negotiates a performance agreement with Lisa:

> **Tom:** OK, Lisa, why don't you take a few minutes to talk about the specific things you'd like to work on over the next few weeks, given all the things we've talked about so far.
>
> **Lisa:** (*Smiling and shaking her head, but saying nothing*)
>
> **Tom:** (*Smiling*) Yes?
>
> **Lisa:** (*Still smiling*) Well, I was just thinking ... perhaps we ought to put the worst first.
>
> **Tom:** (*Looking a little puzzled*) How do you mean?
>
> **Lisa:** I mean those damn reports! (*Starts to laugh*)
>
> **Tom:** (*Laughing loudly*) Oh! Now I know what you're talking about. [You can always tell when there's good chemistry between people. Good-natured teasing occurs, as Lisa was doing with Tom.]
>
> **Lisa:** Seriously, Tom, as I said, I'll make a commitment right here and now to get those monthly reports in on time every month for ... let's say the next six months.
>
> **Tom:** (*Enthusiastically*) I'm not going to argue with that! (*Beginning to take some notes, but still being attentive to Lisa*)
>
> **Lisa:** OK, you've got a deal.
>
> **Tom:** Great. What else?
>
> **Lisa:** Well ... I'd still like to work on this problem of increasing my closing rate, especially with prospects for very large orders.
>
> **Tom:** (*Nodding*) Uh-huh.
>
> **Lisa:** I'm up to about three hundred right now, and I'd really like to get it up to around four hundred, if I could.
>
> **Tom:** (*Nodding and making another note*) OK, so far we've got getting your monthly reports in on time for the next six months and increasing your closing rate for large orders from 30 to 40 per cent.
>
> **Lisa:** (*Looking thoughtful*) Right.
>
> **Tom:** (*Leaning forward slightly*) Good. What else?

At this point Tom realises Lisa's second task, increasing her closing rate from 30 to 40 per cent, even though specific, is a huge undertaking and may even be unrealistically high. In addition, he knows that for Lisa to achieve this goal she'll have to work on some smaller tasks, such as handling objections, time management, and so forth. However, Tom won't interrupt Lisa at this point to suggest that she should break the task down into smaller bites. Instead, he'll wait until after he's had a chance to offer some of his thoughts about what she should work on and they're actually ready to write down Lisa's specific tasks on the performance agreement form. Lisa is much more likely to be receptive at that time.

> **Lisa:** (*Pausing and still looking thoughtful*) I still would like to do a better job of getting interviews with prospects. (*Pause*) I suppose what I'm saying is I want to do a better job of selling the interview as well as selling our product.
>
> **Tom:** (*Nodding*) That sounds good.
>
> **Lisa:** Tom, I know you already think I'm pretty good at getting leads, but it's still something I'd like to work on.
>
> **Tom:** That's fine, Lisa. A little later on perhaps we can talk about how I can help you in that area ... and in any of the other areas too, of course.
>
> **Lisa:** (*Nodding*) Good. I'd like that. (*Pausing and looking thoughtful*)
>
> **Tom:** (*Leaning forward slightly*) Go ahead, Lisa, think out loud.
>
> **Lisa:** Well ... you mentioned earlier that one of the areas where I could improve is getting to know the competition better. As I said, I really agree with that. (*Pause*)
>
> **Tom:** (*Continuing to jot down a few notes*) Good. What else?
>
> **Lisa:** (*Pausing for a few seconds*) I think that about covers it. I can't think of anything else.
>
> **Tom:** (*Glancing at his notes*) OK, let's see what we've got here. You've mentioned a number of things: one, getting all your monthly reports in on time for the next six months; two, improving your closing rate for large orders from 30 to 40 per cent; three, doing a better job of getting interviews; four, being better at getting leads; and five, finding out more about the competition. (*Pause*)
>
> **Lisa:** (*Nodding*) I think that about covers it.

Up to this point no real negotiating has taken place. Tom has simply managed to get Lisa to think about the tasks she'd like to work on. Tom's been very careful not to voice any opinions, one way or the other, about what Lisa has chosen to work on. Now he'll offer his suggestions about what she might work on.

Tom: Good. Lisa, before we actually write down the tasks you'll be working on over the next several weeks, I'd like to add a couple of ideas of my own. (*Pause*) But, before you get nervous about piling too much on your plate, let me say this: after I make a few suggestions, I think we should pare down your list to a manageable size.

Lisa: (*Smiling and looking a little relieved*) Good.

Tom: OK. Let me make my suggestions, and then let's figure out what's actually feasible for you to do.

Lisa: (*Nodding*) Fine.

Tom is really conveying two messages to Lisa here. The first is fairly direct: 'Don't get nervous about having too much to do; we're going to pare down the list to a workable size.' The second message is a little more subtle: 'Let me get my suggestions out without a lot of argument; then we can negotiate what you're actually going to end up doing.'

Tom: Well, Lisa, there are really only two areas I'd like to mention as possibilities for you to work on. (*Pause*)

Lisa: (*Not saying anything but nodding*)

Tom: One is responding to customers' objections, in the way we discussed it earlier. (*Pause*) And the other has to do with time management. You know, making up daily and weekly 'to do' lists to help you establish your priorities. (*Pause*)

Lisa: (*Chuckling and looking a little sheepish*) Oh yes, I must have forgotten about those.

Tom: (*Smiling but not saying anything*)

Lisa: (*Smiling broadly*) It's amazing how some things are easier to forget than others.

Tom: (*Laughing*) That's true, isn't it? (*Taking a slightly more serious tone*) Remember, Lisa, I'm not saying you have to work on these two areas. But I did want to get them down as possibilities.

Lisa: (*Nodding*) Well, I'm glad you did, Tom. I'm not as convinced as you are that I need to work on them, but I'd certainly be willing to give it a try.

Tom: Fair enough. Well, let's see. We've got quite a few things on the list now. Why don't we try to decide on the specific things you'll be working on and get them down on paper?

Lisa: OK.

At this point Tom takes out a sheet of paper and draws a line down the middle. On the top of the left-hand side he writes, 'What Lisa is going to be working on.' On the top of the right-hand side he writes, 'What Tom is going to be working on'. By doing this, Tom communicates two very important messages to Lisa: (a) the agreement, although written, will be informal; and (b) the focus of the agreement will be on both of them, not just on Lisa.

Tom: Well, Lisa, as I said earlier, I think the most important thing for us to keep in mind here is to choose a few, very specific tasks for you to work on. (*Pause*) We want to avoid biting off more than you can chew.

Lisa: (*Nodding and smiling*) Yes, I think that's a good idea. I probably would have a tendency to put down too much.

Tom: (*Smiling*) Good. Let's get started. What should we put down first? [Once more, Tom has given Lisa the responsibility for deciding what she'll be working on.]

Lisa: That's a difficult choice ... but I think I'd really like to work on finding ways to get leads to new market areas.

Tom: OK. How should we put that down?

Lisa: Well, I'm not sure. But I do think it's something you can give me some help on ... (*Pause*)

Tom: (*After about a fifteen-second silence*) Well, how does this sound? 'Spend at least one-third of her weekly meetings with Tom talking about specific ways she can increase her leads to new market areas.'

Lisa: Yes. That sounds good.

Notice that Tom gave Lisa the opportunity to state this task in her own words before he offered the wording. Tom also checked to see that Lisa agreed on the wording before moving on to the next task. Notice also the specific way the task is stated.

Tom: All right, good. What's next?

Lisa: (*Thinking for a few seconds*) I'm not sure, but I know I could work on doing a better job of selling prospects over the phone on granting me an interview.

Tom: All right. What do you think we ought to put down for that?

Lisa: (*Pausing*) I don't know. But there's something I might try with you, Tom, if you're willing.

Tom: Go ahead.

Lisa: Well, I've got some ideas for new techniques, and it would be nice if I could role-play them with you, if that's all right.

Tom: (*Nodding*) Of course. What if I put down this: 'Role-play with Tom some new and different techniques for getting prospects to grant her an interview'?

Lisa: Perfect. That's exactly what I had in mind.

Tom: Great. Well, that's two tasks. How about a couple more?

Lisa: Well, what do we put down about my wanting to increase my closing rate for large orders from 30 to 40 per cent? [Here Lisa has brought up a task Tom thinks is too big to put down, even though it sounds specific.]

Tom: Lisa, that's a pretty broad task. But I think the first two tasks we've got down, the one on getting leads and the one on getting interviews, are going to go a long way towards helping you improve your closing rate. What do you think?

Lisa: (*Wrinkling her forehead a little*) Hmmm ...

Tom: You're not sure you agree with my logic?

Lisa: (*Looking thoughtful*) No, I think I see what you're saying. OK, OK. I agree. I think they will help to boost it. [It's possible Lisa is saying she agrees with Tom here, even though she may not really be in agreement. Only time will tell.]

Tom: All right. What's next?

Lisa: (*Smiling*) Well, I guess we'd better get something down about my getting those monthly reports in on time ...

In the next few minutes Lisa and Tom will be finishing her portion of the performance agreement (see page 235). Notice that the agreement covers nearly all the areas Lisa was originally interested in working on: doing a better job of getting leads and interviews, and indirectly, improving her closing rate. The agreement also covers two areas of concern to Tom: getting monthly reports in on time and learning more about the competition. So far, however, the agreement doesn't include anything on time management or dealing with objections, two other areas where Tom thinks Lisa could improve. But we think Tom should feel very satisfied at this point. The tasks laid out for Lisa's side of the agreement are precisely stated, and she seems quite committed to carrying them out. The fact that Tom didn't get all he wanted in there is fine. It's the natural result of a give-and-take process like this.

Now let's rejoin them as they start discussing the tasks Tom will be working on.

Tom: OK, Lisa, I'd say that's about enough for you to be working on. What do you think?

Lisa: I agree. I think it looks pretty good.

Tom: OK. Why don't we change gear and start talking about some of the things I can do to help you with your tasks ... (*Pause*)

Lisa: (*Nodding*)

Tom: ... And I don't think we should forget about the things you said earlier in the interview when I asked you how I could make your job less frustrating and more satisfying. [It's especially important for Tom to remind Lisa of this question. Whatever he can agree to in the next few minutes will have a powerful motivational effect on Lisa, increasing the chances that she'll do what she's just agreed to do.]

Lisa: (*Smiling*) I certainly can't object to that.

Tom: Good. Well, what are your thoughts on what we can put down for me to do? [Once again, Tom asks Lisa to go first.]

Lisa: (*Looking thoughtful*) Well, to tell you the truth, Tom, you're already involved in three of the tasks we've got down for me.

Tom: (*Nodding*) Uh-huh.

Lisa: (*Pausing several seconds*) Well ... (*Smiling and looking just a little embarrassed*) ... Um, I don't even know if it's that important.

Tom: (*Leaning forward*) Lisa, it sounds as if you're perhaps feeling a little reluctant to tell me what you're thinking? [Let's see if Tom's read back drags it out of her.]

Lisa: (*Sitting up in her chair and talking in a firmer tone of voice*) Well, Tom, actually there is one thing I'd like you to do for me.

Tom: Whatever it is, I'd like to hear it, Lisa.

Lisa: It has to do with the scheduling of our individual sales meetings. (*Pause*) It really annoys me when you hold meetings with me and the other salespeople so late in the day. I must miss my train three or four times a month. [This is obviously a sensitive topic for Lisa, for it's taken her almost the entire interview to get it out. How Tom reacts may have a strong impact on the ultimate success of the performance agreement.]

Tom: (*Pause*) That must be rather frustrating.

Lisa: (*Looking relieved*) It really is! Especially because you once said we could schedule those meetings more or less whenever we wanted to. (*Pause*) If I miss that train, I have to wait over an hour for the next one. It can ruin my plans for an entire evening. (*Pause*)

Tom: (*Nodding*) Well, I'm sorry, Lisa. I wasn't looking at it from your perspective and I didn't realise I was causing you such a problem. What do you think we ought to do about the situation?

Lisa: I think holding the meetings a little earlier in the day would be the simplest solution.

Tom: I can manage that. What about if we put down, 'Hold sales meetings with Lisa earlier in the day, so she doesn't miss her train'?

Lisa: If you'll agree to that, Tom, it would make me very happy. (*Smiling*)

Tom: Well ... I agree. (*Smiling broadly*) What else can I do?

Lisa: Uh ... I think we've already dealt with it, but (*Smiling*) it might be nice to put it down in writing. (*Pause*)

Tom: (*Looking slightly confused*) What's that, Lisa?

Lisa: You know, the matter of the ... (*Clearing throat*) ... ahem ... the 'girls' in the office?

Tom: (*Shrugging his shoulders and raising his palms to the ceiling*) I think you've got me on that one. (*Both laughing*) How does this sound? (*Talking while writing*) 'Tom will no longer use the expression "girls in the office" in Lisa's presence'?

Lisa: (*Half-serious, half-teasing*) Hmm. I was rather hoping it might read something like, 'Tom will no longer use the expression "girls in the office" in *anybody's* presence.'

Tom: (*Feigning outrage*) What! You do drive a hard bargain, don't you? (*Now more serious*) Well, I suppose if you're going to be working on all the things you've agreed to work on, it's the least I can do. [Tom's agreeing to do this should have a powerful motivational effect on Lisa. It's a classic example of a request that's very important to the employee *and* very easy for the boss to do.]

Lisa: (*Smiling*) Thank you, Tom. I really appreciate it.

Tom: Don't mention it, Lisa. Is there anything else you can think of?

Lisa: (*Thinking for a few seconds*) No, that's it. If you do those two things, I'll be very happy.

Tom: OK, I'm glad to hear that. But let me mention a couple of things I've been thinking about ... [Now it's Tom's turn to suggest a few additional things he might do for Lisa. Since she's pretty pleased already, this will be like icing on the cake.]

We'll leave the interview at this point, as Tom and Lisa are wrapping up their performance agreement. The final agreement is reproduced opposite.

WHAT LISA WILL WORK ON:
- Spend at least ⅓ of weekly meetings with Tom talking about specific ways to increase leads to new markets
- Role play with Tom new techniques for getting prospects to grant her an interview
- Submit all her monthly reports to Tom on time for next 6 months
- Meet with Tom on a quarterly basis to review what both of us have learned recently about the competition.

WHAT TOM WILL WORK ON:
- Hold meetings earlier in the day so she doesn't miss her commuter train.
- Will no longer use the expression 'girls in the office' - in Lisa's or anybody's presence.
- Help Lisa, for the next two weeks, set up daily and weekly 'to do' lists. Show Lisa some tricks Tom has learned for getting through his paperwork rapidly.

After they completed the performance agreement, Tom and Lisa agreed to meet in four weeks to discuss the agreement and review the progress they'll have made. In general, scheduling a follow-up meeting about a month later is about right. It's long enough to give people time to make some definite progress and it's short enough for the original meeting still to be in people's minds.

So that's it—a fully negotiated performance agreement. You may be thinking, 'OK, that went very smoothly. But I can't believe they're all going to be this easy.'

We can't really argue with you about that. Some agreements will be harder to negotiate than this one was. And some will be easier, too. But don't forget that you've now begun to develop some good listening skills and other techniques, such as 'stop-look-and-listen', to help you out when the going gets a little rough at any point in the interview.

A Quick Summary

To summarise, negotiating a performance agreement will go more smoothly and effectively if you:

- ▶ keep it informal;
- ▶ make sure there's something in it for both of you;
- ▶ stick to priorities—that is, focus on what's important and don't bite off more than you can chew;
- ▶ be as specific as you can in writing down the tasks you'll both be working on.

Now that the performance agreement has been completed, the hardest work is over. In the next chapter, we'll talk about how to end the interview with the best possible chance that it will lead to improved performance for both of you.

Chapter 15

Step Nine:
Close the Interview

YOU'RE coming to the end of the interview. You and your employee have hammered out a performance agreement that describes the things you're both going to do in the next several weeks. Now you're ready to bring the interview to a close.

Here's what we recommend to make this last stage of the interview go as smoothly as possible:

► Ask for the employee's overall reaction to the interview.
► After listening to the employee's reactions, offer some of your own thoughts and feelings about how things went.
► Schedule a specific time, date, and place for a follow-up meeting to review how well you and the employee are living up to the agreement you've just reached.
► End the interview on a positive note.

Ask for the Employee's Reaction

It's not a very good idea to end any important life experience abruptly because people often feel a need to talk about what happened. Whether you call it 'processing', 'debriefing', or simply 'talking about what happened', it's often very important for people to review and reflect on significant life events after they've occurred. Since performance improvement sessions definitely fall into the category of significant life events, they're no exception to the general rule.

Here's an example of how you might ask for an employee's reactions at the end of the meeting:

'Well, Pat, we certainly covered a lot of ground today. Before we finish though, I'd like to get your reactions to today's meeting. (*Pause*) I'd be especially interested in hearing how the meeting compared to what you expected, what you think we accomplished and didn't accomplish, your general feelings about where we go from here, and anything else you'd like to mention.'

A comprehensive, thought-provoking question like this should get the employee talking. If the person's response to the question is entirely positive ('I'm really glad we did this' or 'This has been a super experience'), you're in good shape. You can say you're glad the employee feels that way and move on to offering your reactions.

But it's very possible the person could have a mixed reaction, or even a negative reaction. For example, the employee could be upset about something you said earlier in the interview, but held back from showing it at the time. Now he might say:

'I've been thinking about what you said earlier about my lack of motivation. I think what you said was unfair and untrue, especially when you compare me with the others around here.'

Or the employee might have second thoughts about the performance agreement. Maybe she feels the agreement is unbalanced and that she's agreed to do a lot more than you agreed to do. She might say:

'Well, I've been thinking about what we both agreed to do over the next month or so. I don't know, the more I think about it, the more it seems kind of unfair. (*Pause*) I'm going to be doing so much more than you are.'

Think for a minute or two about how you'd respond to these two reactions. Then compare your responses to our suggestions. Our thoughts about dealing with negative reactions at this stage of the interview should sound familiar to you by now:

1. Whenever employees seem angry, irritated, or upset, give them room to talk about what's on their minds. Don't argue with them or interrupt. Don't tell them they shouldn't feel the way they do. Patiently listen to what they have to say. Ask open-ended questions, probe for specificity, use encouragers, and use good attending skills. When they finish talking, read them back and be prepared to hear even more. When they've finally finished, then it's your turn to talk.

2. Whatever the complaint, ask a dissatisfied employee to come up with ideas about how to solve the problem. Calmly and without frustration in your voice, ask the employee for suggestions about how to resolve the problem. Responsibility for solving problems should be on the employee's shoulders as well as your own. Once again, listen. Also be willing to bend a little. If you can live with the employee's suggestions, make the necessary changes in the performance agreement.

3. If you and your employee have very different ideas on how to proceed, don't get involved in a win-lose struggle. Use the 'Stop-look-and-listen' technique, if necessary. Remember, it goes like this:

▶ *stop* the interaction as soon as you notice the discussion is becoming argumentative or unproductive.

▶ *look* squarely at the problem by describing it succinctly and objectively.

▶ *listen* for suggestions you both can live with for resolving the problem.

Here's an example of how these suggestions could be used by a supervisor at this stage of the interview:

Supervisor: Well, we've covered a lot of ground, Len, and before we pack it in, I'd like to get your reactions to what we've accomplished here today. (*Pause*) I'd be interested in anything you have to say.

Employee: (*Hesitating*) Well ... um ... I suppose we've made pretty good progress. Uh ... It went a lot smoother than I had expected. I don't know ... I suppose it went quite well.

Supervisor: (*Leaning forward*) So, in some respects it went better than you thought it would. But something still seems to be on your mind, Len. (*Calmly*) What is it?

Employee: (*Fidgeting*) Well ... um ... I didn't mention it earlier, and I probably should have, but I don't think putting that agreement down in writing makes a lot of sense.

Supervisor: (*Pausing to make sure employee has finished*) So ... you're feeling rather uncomfortable at the idea of putting it in writing?

[Good listening particularly good reading back is usually all that's necessary to get employees to 'open up' and tell you what's bothering them.]

Employee: (*jumping in quickly*) Yes, I suppose I am. I don't know. It just seems so formal and legal and all. Why on earth can't we just agree to do those things and shake hands on it. I'm going to remember what I agreed to. And I'm sure you will too.

Supervisor: (*Pausing for just a moment*) So what you're saying is that writing our agreement down on paper has made it seem impersonal and legalistic ... and very different from the informal way you like to do things? [Notice how the employee builds on each read back. Again this is typical.]

Employee: Yes, that's certainly a very strong part of it. Look, I know this is your show, but ... well, you just never know who's going to lay their hands on a piece of paper like that. I know it's not going to go in my personnel folder, or anything like that. But, things like that have a way of being seen by people who have no business seeing them.

Supervisor: I think I see what you're saying. (*Pause*) Just having a piece of paper means there's a possibility of someone seeing it. (*Pause*) I'm also wondering if you're thinking I may show the agreement to someone else? [This is not a read back, even though it looks a bit like one. It's what we call 'checking out a hunch.' Sometimes it's a very useful communications tool, but don't do it too often. It was very helpful in this case, because the supervisor's hunch was wrong.]

Employee: No, that's not right! I believed you when you said it was just between you and me. I don't know. Maybe I'm just overreacting and taking this whole thing too seriously. But I'd still like to make it a verbal agreement. What do you think?

Supervisor: (*Noticing that the employee's receptivity has gone up*) Well, Len, I can certainly appreciate your feelings. As a matter of fact, I often get a little concerned that some of the other people I supervise will show copies of our agreements to other people. And that makes *me* feel uncomfortable! (*Both laugh*) As I think about it, though, I've got to say that I'd like to keep the agreement in writing. I supervise about a dozen people now, and if I don't put things in writing, I'd forget about half of what I agreed to. (*Pause*) But I want to respect your feelings on this issue, as much as I can. What suggestions do you have for how we can resolve this matter of your discomfort with a written agreement and my strong need to have one? [Notice how the supervisor continues to push for a written agreement, but invites the employee to think about a solution both can live with, a 'win-win' solution.]

Employee: (*Looking very thoughtful*) Hmm ... good question. Well ... um ... I don't know. (*Eyes brighten*) Well, one possibility is just crossing out our names from the top of the page. That way, if anybody sees it, they wouldn't know whose it was. But since we came up with the agreement, we'd always know it was ours. What do you think?

Supervisor: Excellent! (*Rubbing out names*) Great suggestion, Len! Any other reactions to what we've done today ...?

Share Your Reactions with the Employee

After listening fully to your employee's reactions, you should share some of your own thoughts and feelings about how things went in the interview. Of course, what you say and how you say it will depend on how you feel the interview went. You'll either have positive reactions, not-so-positive reactions, or a combination of the two.

Positive Reactions

If you feel pleased or satisfied at the end of the interview, say something positive about the experience to your employee. Here's an example.

'I've got to tell you, I feel very good. I think we accomplished a lot here today. (*Looking thoughtful*) To be honest, I think we accomplished much more than I had hoped. I was especially pleased with the way you came to the interview so well prepared. You did a thorough job of examining your own work performance and had a number of helpful suggestions for how I could make your job more satisfying. (*Pause*) I was very pleased at how we were both willing to bend a little when we had that slight disagreement on how to proceed earlier in the meeting. I'm also very happy about the things you've agreed to do to improve your work performance. I think you've set your sights high, but not too high. (*Pause*) And, finally, I'm really looking forward to doing the things I agreed to do, because just doing those things will make me a better supervisor. Thanks for helping to make this a worthwhile experience.'

Don't be afraid to express your thoughts and feelings in some depth. The employee will almost certainly be interested in your reactions. And it'll be good for you to do it as well. Whoever said keeping all those thoughts and feelings inside was a good idea, anyway?

Not-So-Positive Reactions

Sometimes, at the end of an interview, you may feel that the employee hasn't been very co-operative, despite your best efforts. Or maybe, as the meeting is coming to an end, you feel you've had to take several giant steps just to get the employee to move an inch. In situations like these, we suggest you try the following.

1. Be honest about your feelings without being punitive or losing your cool. You have a right to your feelings, just as the employee does. And you'll feel better if you express them directly and forthrightly. However don't use your words as weapons to hurt or punish the employee in some way.

2. Don't blame the employee for what happened. It's possible to talk about feelings of disappointment, frustration, and even anger without blaming others or making them responsible for your feelings. So try to express your thoughts and feelings effectively, without overreacting, lecturing, or using emotionally loaded expressions.

3. Start with the positive. Try to find something the employee said or did during the interview that was positive or made you feel good. Start with that and then move to the not-so-positive aspects.

4. Describe the problem briefly and objectively. Describe what happened from your perspective, as calmly as you can. Be brief. Be factual. Be objective. When you finish describing the problem, tell the employee how it made you feel. Ask the employee for suggestions on how the problem might be resolved, either today or in future meetings. Look for win-win solutions. And, once again, be prepared to shift back and forth from presenting to listening.

Here's an example of a supervisor demonstrating these points:

Supervisor: (*Having just heard employee's reactions to interview*) Well, Diana, I have to admit, my reactions are also rather mixed. Let me begin by mentioning some of my more positive feelings, and then I'll mention some that aren't so positive. (*Pause*)

Employee: (*Looking thoughtful*) OK.

Supervisor: On the plus side, I'm very happy we had this meeting. I realise we had some trouble scheduling it and had to postpone it twice because of bouts of flu. So, it's nice to have it behind us. (*Pause*)

Employee: I've got to agree to that.

Supervisor: (*Leaning forward*) Another thing I'm happy about is the thorough job you did of identifying your strengths. You helped make me aware of some things you're capable of handling that I hadn't really seen before today.

Employee: (*Smiling*) I'm glad to hear that. I've been itching to get some new, more challenging assignments.

Supervisor: That's another thing I'm pleased about, Diana—that you want to take on more responsibilities. (*Pause*) On the other side of the coin, though, I've got to say I was surprised and a little disappointed when you said you couldn't think of any ways you could improve your performance. Compared to the complete and thorough job you did in identifying your strengths, I was hoping to get the benefit of your thinking in that area too. (*Pause*) [Notice how the Supervisor does this diplomatically—yet honestly—and doesn't use any emotionally loaded language or try to blame the employee in any way. Imagine how badly things would have gone if the supervisor had said, 'I thought it was ridiculous when you identified only strong points and came up with no areas needing improvement.']

Employee: It was a bit unbalanced, was it?

Supervisor: Well, yes it was. Now, that may be because this is the first time I've asked you to do something like that. And people usually get better at it the second time around. (*Pause*) The next time we get together, I'd like to find a way out of this problem of you focusing exclusively on your strengths and me identifying all the ways you can improve. Any suggestions?

Employee: Well, that was rather how it went today. Um ... it seems I've been concentrating on my strong points and ignoring the weak ones. (*Pause*) And maybe you've been focusing on both, but putting a little more emphasis on the things I could be doing better. Maybe ... um ... maybe next time we get together, I could just focus on how I could improve and you could just focus on my strong points. How does that sound? [Employee can only make this kind of admission—and recommendation—when she feels 'safe' enough to do it. It would have never happened if the employee felt under attack or threatened in some way.]

Supervisor: That sounds worth a try. We'll both be concentrating on an area we didn't focus on as much as we should have today. Any other suggestions ...?

Sharing your reactions with the employee, especially if they're not positive, means taking some risk. However, as long as you're ready to shift from a presenting mode to a listening mode to deal with any dips in employee receptivity, you should be able to manage the situation pretty well.

Schedule the Follow-Up

After you and the employee have discussed your reactions to the meeting, schedule a follow-up meeting to review your progress. You should do this in broadly the same way as you set up the original performance improvement interview (when you first asked the employee to meet with you in Step Two). Here's what we recommend:

1. tell the employee the purpose of the follow-up meeting and explain briefly what's going to happen when you meet;
2. tell the employee how you plan to prepare for the follow-up meeting and suggest how the employee can prepare for it;
3. schedule the meeting;
4. answer any questions the employee may have about the meeting.

Here's an example of a supervisor arranging a follow-up meeting with the employee near the end of their first performance improvement interview:

Supervisor: Even though we'll be talking informally almost every day, Max, I'd like to schedule a follow-up meeting in three to four weeks to review our progress. (*Pause*)

Employee: Three to four weeks? OK, that sounds good.

Supervisor: As I see it, the purpose of the follow-up meeting will be to review how both of us are living up to the terms of the agreement we reached earlier. In that meeting, I'd like to take a careful look at how well we've both accomplished what we set out to do, discuss any problems we've run into, and talk about where to go in the future. (*Pause*)

Employee: (*Nodding*) OK.

Supervisor: I plan to review my copy of the performance agreement at least once a week, just to make sure I stay on top of things. You might want to do the same. (*Pause*) So, when we meet, let's plan to use the agreement as a springboard for discussion. How does that sound?

Employee: (*Smiling*) Yes, that makes a lot of sense.

Supervisor: All right. Before we schedule a specific time and date, though, what questions do you have?

Employee: Hmmm. I can't think of any right now.

Supervisor: Fine, but if you think of anything, just ask. OK? (*Pause, employee nods*) So, how about Thursday, the 21st at, say, 2 p.m., here in my office?

Employee: (*Looking at calendar*) That suits me.

The exact timing of follow-up meetings will vary from situation to situation, but they shouldn't be put off too long. They should probably be scheduled within about one month of the original interview. If too much time passes, there's a tendency to lose the momentum you built up in the first meeting.

End the Interview on a Positive Note

Try to end the interview on a positive note, especially if it had some difficult moments. Here are some suggestions:

1. Make a positive concluding comment about the interview. Here are several examples.

'I'm glad we had this meeting. I think we made a lot of progress today.'

'Well, it was a hard, but productive session. I'm glad we met.'

'I always seem to learn so much in meetings like these. And this one was no exception.'

2. Usher out the employee in a friendly, easy manner. Stand up, smile, walk the employee to the door, and shake hands. It's the kind of thing any good host or hostess would do.

3. Thank the employee for meeting with you. For example you might say:

'Thanks for working as hard as you did in today's meeting, Ted. I really appreciate the effort you made.'

'Thanks for the suggestions you came up with, Helen, I'm going to start putting some of them into practice right away.'

'Thanks for spending as much time on this as you did, Tim. I know the effort will be worth it in the long run.'

4. Say you're looking forward to the follow-up meeting. But don't overdo it or you'll sound insincere.

Here's an example of a supervisor ending the interview on a positive note:

Supervisor: (*Standing up and smiling*) Well, that about does it for today, Bob. I really enjoyed this meeting. (*Pause*)

Employee: (*Smiling and also standing up*) Yes, me too! I have to confess, it went a lot better than I thought it would.

Supervisor: (*Hand on employee's shoulder, walking towards the door*) Me too! But a large part of the reason it went so well is because you got so involved in the process. Thanks. I appreciate it.

Employee: Well, you certainly helped too. I appreciate that.

Supervisor: Thanks. (*Shaking the employee's hand warmly*) I'm looking forward to meeting with you again on the 21st. Take care.

That concludes the actual interview. You've heard your employee's reactions to how things went, shared some of your own reactions, arranged for a follow-up meeting, and ended on a positive note. Now you can turn your attention to the important task of following up.

Chapter 16

Step Ten: Follow Up

THE INTERVIEW is over, after a lot of time and effort. Let's review what's happened. You prepared for the meeting by reading this book and analysing the employee's performance. You asked the employee to meet with you, suggesting some ways both of you could prepare for the session. In the meeting, you orchestrated a complicated human interaction in which a number of sensitive and important topics—the employee's work performance, your performance as a supervisor, your relationship with the employee—were discussed. You called upon a variety of listening and presenting skills to get the perspectives of two people out on the table. You eventually carved out a performance agreement between the two of you. What you've done, quite frankly, is a lot of hard work.

Even though the interview is over, in many ways your work has just begun. You and the employee are beginning to work on the tasks you've laid out in your performance agreement. Now, your main obtective is to do whatever you can to make sure these tasks get done—yours as well as the employee's. It's a very important final step in the performance improvement process. We call it following up.

Following up includes both the informal things you'll be doing on a day-to-day basis as well as the formal follow-up meeting you scheduled at the end of the performance improvement session. We'll discuss both types of follow-up in this chapter. We'll begin by describing a variety of informal, ongoing things you can begin doing almost immediately. Then we'll offer some thoughts about how to proceed with the formal follow-up meeting.

Some Frank Advice

Before we discuss these two types of follow-up, we'd like to offer you some frank advice. You, the boss, and an employee have agreed to do some things in the weeks and months ahead. Obviously, you're going to be monitoring the employee's performance. But, guess what? The employee is going to be monitoring *your* performance as well: if you've agreed to do something, do it! The day after the session is over, the employee is going to be very interested in how well you're starting to live up to your end of the bargain. And if you don't do what you agreed to do, you can expect the employee to follow suit.

In some respects, then, the most important advice we can give you at this point is this. Live up to your end of the agreement. That, more than anything, will increase the chances that employees will live up to theirs.

Informal Follow-Up

Informal follow-up refers to all the things you're going to be doing to help employees do what they've agreed to in the performance agreement. As we've said, it begins immediately after the session ends. Informal follow-up is important for several reasons:

1. Immediate reinforcement of any new behaviour is important. The longer reinforcement is delayed, the less likely it is that the new behaviour will become a habit. Waiting several weeks until the formal follow-up interview is too long. Immediate follow-up will help you and the employee take advantage of the momentum you built up in the interview. Both of you will be much less likely to fall back into old habits.

2. You and your employee are likely to be very busy during the next few weeks and you might neglect your agreement. There will be lots of responsibilities, besides what's written on your performance agreement, competing for your attention in the weeks ahead. It will be tempting for both of you to put the agreement on the back burner and concentrate on the nominal demands of your job.

3. Changing behaviour is hard work and periodic encouragement is necessary. Both you and your employee can expect to get a little frustrated and discouraged before the follow-up interview. You'll both need something to boost you up between now and then.

In the rest of this section we'll describe some specific things you can do to follow up informally, beginning right after the performance improvement meeting on up to the follow-up interview:

▶ follow up immediately and keep in touch periodically;
▶ ask the employee to follow up with you;
▶ reward employee effort;
▶ expect to get a little discouraged; and
▶ use other resources to support your efforts.

Follow Up Immediately and Keep in Touch Periodically

It's important to check up with the employee a day or so after the performance improvement interview. For example, you might approach the employee when there are no other employees around and say: 'Hilary, I just wanted you to know that I enjoyed our meeting yesterday. I think it was a valuable and productive session. I'm looking forward to working with you on the areas we agreed on.'

Following up immediately has several advantages.

1. It lets your employee know you meant what you said during your initial meeting. Since many supervisors never follow up, some employees will wait a day or so to work out whether or not you mean business. Following up immediately shows you're committed to improving the employee's performance *and* your performance as a manager.

2. Checking back with employees informally gives them a chance to ask questions that didn't occur to them during the interview. It'll also give them a chance to clear up points that have come up since the meeting. You may even want to probe for questions or comments, saying something like this: 'Well, it's been two days since we met. Are there any questions you didn't get a chance to ask during our meeting? Or any thoughts you've had since then?'

3. Immediate follow-up with the employee is also good for you. It helps remind you that your responsibility didn't end with the interview. And it makes future follow-up contacts that much easier.

It's a good idea to keep in touch periodically with the employee after the first informal contact. There are many ways to do this. You can arrange to take a coffee break or have lunch together. You can even chat briefly in the car park or have a few words when you're both waiting for the lift.

Without giving employees the feeling that you're looking over their shoulders, let them know you're: (a) ready, willing, and able to help them achieve their goals; (b) committed to doing what you agreed to do; and (c) willing to meet with them at any time to discuss the progress, or lack of it, you're both making.

Ask Your Employee to Follow Up with You

As soon as you begin working on your part of the performance agreement, you may even want to consider asking your employee to follow up with you. For example, you could say:

'Listen Jean, I'm going to have to work hard to live up to my part of the bargain and I'd appreciate all the support and encouragement you can give me. So I'd appreciate your asking me how things are going every now and then and maybe even giving me a pat on the back when you see me doing something I've agreed to do. Also, please remind me of anything I might have forgotten. Believe me, any help will be greatly appreciated.'

Involving the employee like this serves several purposes.

1. It establishes a two-way relationship in which you both help one another out. As we've said a number of times before, this is an important relationship you have with the employee. Now you're also partners in a behaviour change effort, so it's important to act like partners.

2. It helps to make sure the spotlight doesn't always shine on the employee. You deserve some attention too.

3. Most important, it will help you do the things you agreed to do. We've already talked about what will happen to the employee's commitment if you agree to do something and then don't do it. You don't want to be the one to fail to carry out your part of the agreement.

Reward Employee Effort

Psychologists and educators often say it's better to praise people for behaving the way you want them to than it is to punish them for behaving in a way you don't. It's called 'rewarding (or reinforcing) the desired behaviour'. This principle certainly applies to employees. So, whenever you catch employees 'doing something right', reward the desired behaviour. Give them some good, old-fashioned, praise:

'That was really nice work, Terry. Good job!'

'I couldn't help but notice how you handled that situation, Dee. Well done!'

'You're really giving this an all-out effort, Alan. Keep up the good work!'

Whenever you praise employees for behaving a certain way— whether it's coming to work on time, handling a difficult customer calmly and patiently, or any other task the employee has agreed to— it increases the chances that they'll behave the same way in the future.

Expect to Get a bit Discouraged

Employee progress after a performance improvement interview is often a mixed bag. You'll see some definite signs of improvement, but you'll probably also see some areas where no progress, or even some backsliding, occurs. That old saying about 'the best-laid plans' is probably going to apply, at least in some ways.

So don't expect perfection and don't get too discouraged if things don't go perfectly. You should also avoid the common ineffective tendencies identified earlier in the book: avoiding, overreacting, complaining, and lecturing. If you see the employee beginning to backslide, your listening skills will also be useful. Sit down with the employee and talk about it. Get the employee's perspective on what's happening. Find out how he feels. Ask her for any ideas and suggestions about how she might get back on track. When receptivity is up, let the employee know that it's normal to see a failure or two at this point. Remind the employee of whatever good progress you have observed. Use your presentation skills to offer your own suggestions and to get the employee thinking positively again. As one of our supervisors put it, 'It's like being a good coach. You accept a temporary failure and concentrate on the future. You rebuild morale and get the players to try even harder the next time.'

Use Other Resources to Support Your Efforts

You and the employee don't have to take on this thing alone. You can take advantage of other resources as well.

1. Seminars, training programmes and other instructional materials that focus on the areas where the employee is trying to improve. For example, you might want to send an employee a copy of an article, 'How to Get Better Control of Your Time', along with a short note that says: 'Thought you'd be interested.' Or you could tell the employee about a forthcoming workshop on time management at your local college. Most performance problems are quite common, so there are many programmes, articles, materials, and workshops available to help people deal with them.

2. People resources within your own organisation. Many companies—especially the larger ones—have training staff, employee assistance counsellors, consultants, psychologists, social workers and personnel specialists available to help employees. For example, you can ask a struggling salesperson to meet with a member of the training staff who's interested in sales training. You can arrange a meeting between the director of your employee assistance programme and an employee whose poor performance seems to be related to a family drinking problem. Or you can involve the management consultant you've been using with a newly appointed supervisor who's having trouble making the transition from the labour force to management. In short, you can act like a matchmaker between the needs of employees and the skills of third-party resource people.

So far, we've been talking about informal follow-up. That is, the variety of things you can do on a continuing basis to support and reinforce the goals you and the employee established at the end of your meeting. Now let's turn to the formal follow-up interview.

The Follow-Up Interview

You and your employee scheduled a formal follow-up meeting at the close of the performance improvement interview. At that time, you told the employee it would be a good idea to sit down in several weeks to review the progress both of you had made towards the goals laid out in the performance agreement.

In many respects, the follow-up interview is just another version of the ten steps of the performance improvement process. Basically, the same skills and techniques apply. Here's the sequence of steps:

1. analyse your employee's performance and your own performance;
2. remind your employee of the follow-up interview;
3. begin the interview;
4. find out how things are going;
5. review your progress;
6. review your employee's progress;
7. decide 'where to go from here';
8. close the interview.

In elaborating on these steps, we'll try to avoid repeating what we've said already. However, reviewing some of the earlier chapters may be helpful as you go through the follow-up procedure.

Analyse Your Employee's Performance and Your Own Performance

Just as you prepared for the initial meeting with your employee, it's important to get ready for this one, too. Look over the performance agreement carefully and review the progress you've both made over the past few weeks. As you do this, ask yourself:

'Has the employee accomplished the goals that were set? Have I? Which goals were accomplished and which were not?'

'In what specific ways has the employee exceeded or fallen short of her goals? How about me?'

'If goals were not accomplished, why not? What factors can help to explain the employee's and my performance? What events have occurred in the past few weeks that can help put things in a better perspective?'

Remind Your Employee of the Follow-Up Meeting

Remind the employee about the follow-up interview several days prior to the meeting. As you did when you arranged the first interview:

1. approach the person when there are no other people around;
2. remind your employee that the follow-up meeting is approaching and briefly review the purpose of the meeting;
3. tell your employee how you plan to prepare for the meeting;

4. suggest how your employee can prepare for the meeting;
5. confirm the date, time and place of the meeting;
6. end on a positive note.

Here's an example.

Supervisor: (*Out of earshot of others*) Well, Len, the follow-up meeting we scheduled at our performance improvement session last month is coming up next week and I wanted to remind you of it. (*Pause*)

Employee: (*Looking a little surprised*) It's coming up already?

Supervisor: Yes, I could hardly believe it either. Doesn't time fly? (*Pause*) Listen, Len, I'm going to prepare for the meeting by carefully reviewing the performance agreement we wrote up. (*Pause*) And I'd like you to prepare for the meeting by doing the same thing. How does that sound?

Employee: (*Nodding*) Fine. Actually, I've been looking at it on and off quite a bit this month. But I'll give it a careful look before the meeting.

Supervisor: Good. My calendar shows that the meeting is scheduled for next Tuesday morning at 10.30 in my office. (*Pausing, looking at employee*)

Employee: I'll be there.

Supervisor: Good. I'm looking forward to it. See you then.

You may run into some problems when you remind employees of the follow-up meeting, especially if they're feeling guilty about not doing what they set out to do. It may be helpful here to review the strategy for asking your employee to meet with you in Step Two and the listening skills in Chapter 8.

Begin the Interview

To get the follow-up meeting off to the best possible start, here are a few suggestions.

1. Set the stage for a private meeting, with as few distractions and interruptions as possible.
2. Make the person feel comfortable and welcome. Get out from behind your desk, give the employee a warm greeting, sit down face-to-face and engage in a bit of casual chat before getting down to business.

3. 'Structure' the meeting. Remind the employee of the purpose of the meeting. Then give the employee a preview of what's going to happen in the rest of the session. Tell the employee how you'd like the two of you to approach the session and what you hope to achieve.
4. Respond to the employee's questions and concerns, but don't get thrown off track. If you ignore the questions or emotional concerns of the employee, you'll pay the price of reduced involvement and co-operation.

Here's an example of a supervisor getting a follow-up interview off to a good start.

Supervisor: (*Having just reviewed the purpose of the meeting*) There are a number of things I'd like to cover today, Gerry. Let me just mention them briefly so you'll have an idea of what to expect in the rest of the meeting. (*Pause*)

Employee: (*Nodding*)

Supervisor: First, I'd like you to begin by telling me how things are going, in general, at work and if you're experiencing any problems you think I should be aware of. (*Pause*)

Employee: (*Acknowledging agreement*)

Supervisor: After that, I'd like us to discuss how well we've accomplished the things we set out to do when we met about a month ago. We can use the performance agreement we came up with as a guide. (*Pause*)

Employee: OK. I brought my copy with me.

Supervisor: Good. I have mine here too. (*Pause*) When we get into it, I'd like us to begin with a review of how well I've done and, when we finish with me, we'll move on to an analysis of your performance. How does that sound?

Employee: (*Nodding*) That sounds good to me.

Supervisor: Just as we did last time we met, I'd like us to be frank and open with each other. That was very helpful last month and I'd expect it to be helpful again today. After we've reviewed each other's performance, I'd like to talk about where to go from here. We'll probably come up with another agreement about what the two of us can do in the future, much like the one we came up with last time we met.

When a meeting is 'structured' this way, the employee gets a preview of what's going to happen in the meeting and a chance to get on the supervisor's wavelength before they actually get down to business. For more information on getting the interview off to a good start, you may want to review how to begin the performance improvement interview in Step Three.

Find Out How Things Are Going

As you begin the follow-up meeting, it's a good idea to find out how things have been going for your employee since your last meeting. Here's how you might do it:

> 'Well, Sally, before we review the progress we've made, I'd like to spend a few minutes talking about how things are going, in general, on the job for you. And I'd also like to hear about any problems you're having. (*Pause*) So, how have things been going?'

Asking how things are going at the outset of the follow-up interview serves several purposes:

- ▶ it eases employees into the interview by getting them talking about things that are important to them;
- ▶ it gives employees an opportunity to discuss problems that may be important to them but don't seem to have much to do with the purpose of this meeting;
- ▶ it gives you a chance to show, once again, that you're interested in what employees have to say.

A couple of problems may surface at this stage of the interview. Employees may want to keep talking about how things are going or about some of the problems they're experiencing. Or they may make some critical remarks about you or the performance improvement process, possibly because they haven't accomplished what they set out to do. If this happens, keep your cool and use your listening skills. For a review of how to handle problems such as this, review the strategy for finding out how things are going in Chapter 9 and the listening skills in Chapter 8.

Review Your Progress

It's best to review *your* progress before taking a look at how well your employee has fared. By beginning with yourself, you let your employee know you're taking the process seriously and that you're standing behind the commitments you made. You can start things off by saying something like this.

Supervisor: All right, let's begin by reviewing my progress first. What I'd like to do is take each of the things I agreed to last month and discuss them one at a time. I'd like to get your reactions first and then I'll offer my own thoughts. (*Pause*)

Employee: I'm ready whenever you are.

Supervisor: OK. (*Looking at a copy of performance agreement*) Well, the first thing I said I'd do is try to do a better job of controlling my temper and stop making critical comments about you in front of other people. What are your thoughts about how well I have achieved that goal? (*Pause*)

At this point, shift into a listening mode. As your employee responds be sure you:

▶ use good attending behaviour;
▶ probe for specificity or more information when you hear something that's not clear;
▶ read back the employee's remarks to make sure you've heard things accurately;
▶ be sure the employee's completely finished before offering your own views.

The employee's analysis of your performance might go as follows:

Employee: (*Thoughtfully*) Well, I suppose I'd have to say you did quite well. (*Pausing, adding nothing*)

Supervisor: (*Leaning forward*) Tell me a little more, Don. I'm not quite sure what you mean.

Employee: Well, I won't say you completely accomplished your goal, but I'd have to say you came pretty close. (*Pause*) I can only think of one time you lost your temper for a moment and shouted at me in front of some other people. (*Adds nothing*)

Supervisor: (*Pausing for a moment*) So, with perhaps that one exception, you'd say I was more or less able to stop criticising you in public?

Employee: (*Slightly more animated now*) Yes, you remember? When the machine got jammed and you let Fred and me know—in no uncertain terms, I might add—what you thought of how we got ourselves into that mess. (*Pause*) But I've also got to say I really appreciated how you came up later and apologised to both of us for blowing your top.

Supervisor: (*Slowly and looking directly at employee*) So, my apolo gising for the incident sort of took some of the sting out of it?

Employee: I'd say it took *all* of the sting out of it. If you hadn't apologised, I think I would've been pretty resentful. I certainly would've stewed over it for a while.

Supervisor: (*Smiling*) I'm glad you didn't have to. And I want you to know I appreciate your comments. (*Pause*) Any other thoughts about this area before I offer my thoughts on the subject? (*Pause*)

When the employee gives you the signal that you've heard things correctly, it's your turn to talk. When presenting your own views about the progress you've made:

▶ try to be specific and factual;
▶ build as much as you can on the employee's analysis;
▶ when you agree with the employee, say so;
▶ when you disagree, let the employee know you have a different view without attacking or disparaging the employee's view;
▶ if the employee's receptivity drops while you're offering your view, stop talking and start listening. When receptivity goes back up, start talking again.

When you finish reviewing your progress in the first area, summarise the discussion and make a transition to the second area by saying something like this:

'All right, it sounds as if we both agree that I did a pretty good job of living up to my agreement to control my temper and not criticise you in public (*Pause; employee nods assent*) A little later in the interview I'd like us to talk about what I might continue to do in that area. (*Pause*) But now I'd like to move on to the second thing I agreed to do, which was ...'

Discuss the goals laid out in the performance agreement one at a time. In each instance, get your employee's reactions, then give your own. When you've finished reviewing your progress on all your goals, briefly summarise the entire discussion before moving on to the employee's side of the agreement. Here's how you might make the transition:

'All right, that was very helpful. (*Pause*) Let me try to summarise what the two of us have said about the progress I made living up to my part of the performance agreement. In the first area ...'

While you give a summary read back like this, check carefully to see if the employee is in agreement on all the main points. Then make the transition to the employee's part of the agreement:

'OK, I think that just about does it. What would you add to what I've said before we move on to a discussion of the progress you've made?'

Review Your Employee's Progress

Once again, you're going to ask your employee to do a self-analysis before you present your analysis. A good way to move into a discussion of your employee's progress is to say something like this.

Supervisor: OK, now that we've finished with me, let's take a look at the progress you've made in the past month. (*Pause*) Why don't you take each of the goals we set down in the performance agreement and tell me how well you feel you've accomplished each of them. (*Pause*)
Employee: (*Nodding*)
Supervisor: After you finish reviewing your progress in all four areas, I'll offer my thoughts. All right?
Employee: Fine. That sounds like a good way to do it.
Supervisor: All right, let's begin with the first one. How well do you think you accomplished what you set out to do in that area?

When the employee begins to talk, everything we've said about listening applies. Don't argue or interrupt, even if you disagree. Just draw the person out, fully and completely. Your goal is to get the employee to do as complete an analysis as possible. When the employee has finished, briefly summarise what you heard and give the person a chance to build on your read back. Then it's your turn to talk.

For additional help with this portion of the follow-up interview, you may want to review the strategy for asking your employee to do a self-analysis in Chapter 11.

When presenting your analysis of the employee's progress, pay attention to the presentation skills you learned in Chapter 12. Especially remember to stop talking and start listening when you notice your employee's receptivity drop. In addition, think about the following.

1. As much as you can, build on the employee's analysis. Try to establish as much agreement as you can between your analysis and the employee's analysis.

2. Start with the positive. Begin by talking about those areas where the employee met, exceeded, or came very close to the goals that were established. Be specific; use examples to back up your points. Then move on to any areas where the employee didn't make as much progress as you had hoped. Once again, be specific. Describe what happened; don't criticise.

3. Wait until you've presented your entire analysis before worrying about next steps. This will be especially difficult if the employee hasn't made much progress. However, it's important to finish describing how much progress the employee has made in each area before talking about where to go from here.

4. Get your employee's reactions when you've finished. Ask for an overall reaction to your analysis. Encourage your employee to think out loud about what you've said. This will give your employee a chance to express any agreement or disagreement and also give you a chance to make sure the person has understood what you said.

Review the strategy for presenting your analysis of the employee's performance in Chapter 13 if you have any questions about how to proceed.

Decide 'Where to Go from Here'

Having reviewed your progress and the employee's, now you need to answer the question: 'Where do we go from here?' In this section we'll offer some suggestions on how to answer this question in three different situations, where:

1. your employee has made a lot of progress;
2. your employee hasn't made much progress (perhaps because of mitigating circumstances) but has put in a lot of effort;
3. your employee hasn't made much progress and hasn't put in much effort.

1. A lot of progress. This is what you're looking for. Your employee has lived up to the terms of the performance agreement, and you're satisfied with the person's progress. In this situation, we recommend that you and the employee agree on some new goals for both of you and set a long-range follow-up meeting to review those new goals.

The goals that you and the employee set for each other may be extensions of your original goals, completely new goals or a combination of the two. The important point is that the two of you are off to a good start. You've set the tone for a positive working relationship. Our advice is to keep doing more of the same.

Although you may want to meet again fairly soon for another formal follow-up session, you can probably afford to schedule the next formal meeting several months from now. Keep up informal follow ups though; they're essential. But try to reserve most of your formal follow-up meetings for employees whose progress has not been so good (without giving short shrift to the good performers).

2. Little progress—a lot of effort. Sometimes employees make little progress even though they put in a lot of effort. For example, let's say you're a manager working with a newly appointed supervisor who's technically skilled, but rough around the edges when it comes to dealing with people. Although he's tried very hard, let's say he just hasn't improved very much in getting along better with his employees.

You have a number of options in a situation such as this.

▶ You can decide simply to renegotiate the same agreement for another month or so to see if the person can improve with more time. Sometimes just a little more time is all that's really needed.

▶ You may decide that you set your original sights a little high and that you'll aim for more modest goals in a renegotiated agreement. Then you can revise the employee's goals and set up another follow-up meeting to review progress on these new goals in about a month.

▶ Maybe you've got enough evidence that the person doesn't have what it takes to 'make it'. But let's say the person is technically skilled and motivated, and you don't want the organisation to lose such an employee. In this situation, we'd recommend thinking about 'restructuring' the person's job to take advantage of his strengths and to reduce the demand on areas where he's not so capable. We'll talk more about the alternative of restructuring in the next chapter when we'll help you answer the question, 'What do I do if none of this works?'

Sometimes, circumstances will prevent employees from making real progress, even when they try. For example, injury and sickness, company labour problems, material shortages, equipment malfunctions, and many other obstacles may interfere with an employee's progress. If this is the case, give the same performance agreement another try. Schedule another formal follow-up interview in a month. If the mitigating circumstances—whatever they may be—are still likely to be a problem, then renegotiate the agreement to focus on aspects of the employee's performance that are more under the person's control.

3. Little progress—little effort. Sometimes employees don't make much progress or put in much effort. This may signal the beginning of the end. At this point, it may even be more appropriate for you to consult the next chapter, 'What do I do if none of this works?' Before you do, though, you may want to give it one last try. But, once again, you don't have to work out what to do all on your own. Put some responsibility on the employee's shoulders as well. Ask the employee to help arrive at a solution to the problem. You might begin in this way.

> **Supervisor:** (*Calmly and slowly*) Leslie, let's stop for a minute and take a look at the situation here. (*Pause*) About a month ago we both decided to do some things that would help improve your job performance and also increase your job satisfaction. (*Pause*) Earlier today, we both agreed that I seemed to carry out my part of the agreement pretty well. However, when we reviewed your progress, we both agreed that you came up rather short in accomplishing what you set out to do. (*Pause*) I'm disappointed in the progress you've made as well as in what seems like a lack of effort on your part. (*Pause*) However, I'd like to put that behind us now and come up with a new agreement that has a better chance of succeeding than this one did. What suggestions do you have about how to proceed from here? What would you do if you were me and I were you?

Here you ask the employee to think about the problem from your point of view. Then listen to the employee's suggestions, using all the skills we've talked about throughout the book. If the employee doesn't come up with any good suggestions, it's time to get a little tougher. You may want to identify some of the consequences if the employee continues to make little effort and little or no progress. Here's an example.

> **Supervisor:** OK, Leslie, I'd like you to put yourself in my position. Imagine that it's six weeks from now and there's still no progress in these areas. What would you do then if you were me?
>
> **Employee:** I don't know. (*Pause; supervisor leans forward*) Um, I suppose you'd have a right to be upset. Maybe you could give me a warning?
>
> **Supervisor:** Yes, I could put you on probation by giving you a formal warning letter. (*Calmly, without a threatening tone*) As you know, that's the first step of our dismissal process here. Any other ideas?
>
> **Employee:** (*Hesitating*) Um ... I can't think of anything else.
>
> **Supervisor:** OK. Let me see. (*Pause*) I could also recommend that you don't get an increase during the next salary review period. (*Pause*) Any other ideas from you?
>
> **Employee:** (*Looking a little concerned*) I hope you don't have to do that, but I can't think of anything else.
>
> **Supervisor:** Well, Leslie, I'll do what I have to do, but it's pretty much under your control. (*Pausing for effect*) I want you to know, though, that I'm prepared to take strong action if I don't see any progress within the next six weeks ...

Sometimes a discussion like this *will* get the person's attention. When faced with the prospect of dismissal or some other serious negative consequence, some employees will turn around. It's at least worth a try before throwing in the towel.

To review, in this section we've identified several different ways to plan your next steps with the employee, depending on the person's progress. Whichever course of action you choose, you'll come up with a second written agreement—much like the first one—stating what you'll both be working on in the future.

Close the Interview

Once the performance agreement has been fully discussed and a new agreement negotiated, it's time to bring the meeting to a close. Here's a guide:

1. get the employee's overall reaction to how things went;
2. offer your reactions;
3. schedule another follow-up meeting to review how well the two of you are living up to the new agreement you've reached;
4. end the interview on a positive note, or as positive a note as is possible under the circumstances.

For example, you might want to say:

'I'm glad we had this meeting, Mike. Even though we encountered a few difficult moments, I really value the opportunity to sit down and put our heads together. I'm looking forward to our meeting next month.'

The follow-up interview is the last step in the performance improvement process. But, in reality, unless you decide that 'none of this works' for a given employee, there is no formal end to the process. To be helpful to the employee—and to you—it has to be an ongoing process. You've got to keep following up, formally and informally, with the employee to keep things moving forward. Your goal, which you've had from the very beginning, is to work towards the most productive and satisfying working relationship the two of you can achieve.

If you follow the advice we've offered in these pages, we strongly believe you'll achieve that goal with most of your employees, and even with some 'problem' employees you were almost ready to give up on. But it won't work with everyone. That's when you must answer the question, 'What do I do if none of this works?' That's the focus of our next, and last chapter.

Chapter 17:

'What Do I Do If None of This Works?'

IF YOU skipped over some of the previous chapters to read this one, we wouldn't be surprised. Helping employees—especially the problem ones—improve their work performance can be a pretty tough job. It's easy to get frustrated and wonder if you're not just wasting your time.

Even though it sometimes works wonders, the performance improvement process doesn't always work as well as we'd like it to. In fact, with some employees it won't work at all. When it doesn't, you'll want to ask the question, 'What do I do if none of this works?'

In this chapter, well try to help you answer these three questions:

▶ How do you come to the conclusion that 'none of this works' for a particular employee?
▶ What are your options if none of this works?
▶ How do you choose among the options?

We'll describe four options that are available to you. We'll also give you some practice in choosing among them. They are:

▶ firing;
▶ transferring;
▶ restructuring;
▶ neutralising.

First, though, let's talk about how and when to decide that the performance improvement process hasn't worked with a particular employee.

How Do You Decide You Are Wasting Your Time?

When you decide that 'none of this works' for a particular employee, you conclude that it's no longer worth your time and energy—or that of your organisation—to try to help the employee improve (at least in the employee's current job). But how will you know when it's no longer worth your time or effort? Unfortunately, there's no way to be absolutely certain. But there are some important things to consider when making this important decision.

In our opinion, there are four kinds of employee performance that, after at least one follow-up interview, indicate the process has not worked:

1. the employee's performance is worse than before;
2. there's been no change at all;
3. there's been minimal change;
4. the employee's performance improved temporarily, but the improvement was short-lived.

Things Actually Got Worse

Not too often, but every now and then, an employee's performance will actually get worse after a supervisor has conducted a performance improvement interview. Of course, you may have to take a lot of the responsibility for this outcome. It's possible you did or said something during the interview that confused or upset the employee. Or maybe you committed yourself to something in the performance agreement and failed to live up to your end of the bargain. Whatever the case, the fact that the individual's performance got worse, not better, is something you can't ignore. It will have to be a factor in your decision to stop the performance improvement process and consider other alternatives.

No Change At All

You may go through the entire performance improvement process with your employee without seeing any change in the person's behaviour. Although this failure could also be partially your fault, it too is evidence you can't ignore.

A Little But Not Enough

A little change is much more likely than a change for the worse or no change at all. In fact, from the outset, you may expect only a little change in an employee. For example, you wouldn't expect a miserable receptionist to become warm and effusive overnight. Or you wouldn't expect a sloppy and disorganised service technician to become the picture of order and neatness right away. And you wouldn't expect a salesperson with poor presentation skills to sound like an eloquent orator in a month.

As time passes, however, you should expect to see *some* improvement as the employee approaches an acceptable level of performance. If the initial small changes in performance don't eventually lead to larger and more significant changes, you may have to accept the fact that you're never going to get the kind of performance you need to see from the employee.

Temporary Improvement, But Short-Lived

Sometimes the employee will make some dramatic changes almost immediately after a performance improvement interview. Instead of arriving ten minutes late every day, the employee turns up twenty minutes early. Those reports that were overdue for months appear neatly typed, on your desk when you arrive on Monday morning. Instead of being a grouch on the phone, the employee does an about-turn and is suddenly courteous and helpful.

Dramatic changes like these look great, but often don't last very long. After a week or so, you may see the employee fall back into the old patterns and habits. Now the employee seems to be performing at the same level as before.

This flash-in-the-pan change in an employee's performance is not always a sign that the person is no longer worth trying to save. But people who make these kinds of abrupt and dramatic changes in their behaviour often aren't committed to changing. They're making changes for you rather than for themselves. They seem willing to put a great deal of effort into making the changes you want, and right away too. But if those changes don't lead to an immediate increase in their personal job satisfaction, they return to their old habits.

Let's say you've made the decision that it just hasn't worked for an employee. What are you going to do now? What *do* you do if 'none of this works' for a particular employee?

In a situation like this, most managers are not fully aware of the options available to them. In the remainder of the chapter we'll describe four options in detail: firing, transferring, restructuring, and neutralising. We'll also talk about how to decide among the four options. Finally, we'll cover some important points to keep in mind when implementing each option so things will go as effectively and as smoothly as possible for you, the employee and the organisation.

Firing

Firing is the action an organisation takes to sever or terminate the relationship between itself and an employee so that the employee no longer receives payment for services rendered to the organisation. The usual means of firing is for bosses to inform employees that they're dismissed from their jobs and will not be offered any other position in the organisation. However, there are some dismissal proceedings that may be easier or more palatable for you and your employee than a simple dismissal. Laying off an employee—making him redundant— is one alternative; asking the employee to resign is another.

Laying off is sometimes a euphemism for firing, and sometimes not. For example, in large manufacturing industries and many other segments of the economy, it's common to lay off workers (both union and management) when business drops. When business picks back up, people are rehired. The same pattern holds true for seasonal industries such as construction and tourism.

There may be several reasons an employer decides to lay off rather than fire an employee: (a) to make it easier for the worker to collect unemployment insurance benefits; (b) the employee won't have the stigma of being fired; and (c) the employer doesn't have to document or defend a performance problem as the reason for dismissal. An important note: redundancy does cost the company money.

Asking the employee to resign is often another way of trying to make the dismissal process a little easier for the person being let go. You're still firing the person, but you're just giving the individual the opportunity to do it with a little more dignity.

Why Bosses Are Reluctant to Fire Employees

Anyone who's ever been a boss knows that firing an employee is not easy. Apart from the many administrative and legal considerations, the vast majority of managers and supervisors find firing an employee an unpleasant and emotionally difficult task. As a result, most bosses are *very* reluctant to fire employees, even problem employees who should have been dismissed long ago. Here are some reasons why:

1. They feel guilty. Most bosses view being fired as a shameful and embarrassing experience for an employee. Generally, the last thing they want to be is the 'bad guy' who puts an employee through such an unpleasant experience. In our view, this is even true of tough, ruthless types of bosses.

2. The thought of sitting down with an employee to deliver the bad news makes most managers nervous. The prospect of looking the employee right in the eye and saying, 'Pat, I'm sorry, but we've decided to let you go' is very distasteful. So they put it off until next week. Or next month. Or next year.

3. Many bosses engage in 'catastrophic thinking'. They immediately think of the worst things that could happen to them if they fire someone, such as getting involved in a protracted legal struggle, having the decision overturned by a superior, or losing the respect and friendship of other people in the organisation. Sometimes they also imagine the worst that could happen to the employee. They ask themselves such questions as, 'Will he be able to find another job?' 'What will happen to her family if she can't get another job?'

4. Many supervisors put off firing an employee because they think they won't be able to find a better replacement. This isn't just true for jobs requiring a high level of technical skill. Regardless of the job vacancy created by a dismissal, many employers fear they'll have enormous trouble filling the job with a new employee who's qualified or motivated. Here's what we often hear them say:

> 'Do you have any idea how hard it is to find a skilled and experienced accountant (or systems analyst, legal secretary, machinist, etc.) these days? I'll admit this fellow's not the greatest. In fact, at times he's pretty bad. But I'd rather have him than nobody at all.'

Each of these reasons is understandable. Firing someone is an emotional topic, and it's hard for anybody to approach it in a completely rational manner. However, while there are problems associated with firing employees, there's a positive side as well.

Positive Aspects of Firing

Although we don't ever expect it to become an easy task, it's possible to adopt a more positive outlook toward firing. Here are some reasons why.

1. It can be a great opportunity. Although being fired is a bitter pill for an employee to swallow, it's possible to view it as an opportunity for growth rather than as a shameful and embarrassing experience. As psychologists, we know that it often takes a crisis to spur people on to bigger and better things. The life histories of many very successful people are filled with stories of how they got fired early in their careers. For many of them, getting fired had an attention-getting effect. But even when employees don't do much soul-searching and self-improvement, we've noticed that many people who've been fired still move on to better, higher-paying, more satisfying jobs anyway. As a result, they show a dramatic improvement in their level of self-confidence and self-esteem.

2. Firing an employee is never easy, but it's much less difficult if you have the kinds of good communication skills we covered earlier in the book. Part of the reason firing is so difficult is because most bosses don't have the necessary interpersonal skills to help employees through this difficult and delicate process. The presentation and listening skills you've learned will help make the task of firing an employee much smoother and a lot less painful.

3. Don't buy the argument that a problem employee with scarce technical skills can't be fired because it will be too difficult to find a replacement. We think the time and effort expended to replace such an employee will be outweighed by the damage caused by your own frustration, the employee's lack of productivity, and lowered morale among other employees in your work unit that would result from not firing the person.

You may be saying to yourself, 'Yes, firing somebody is an unpleasant and distasteful task and I may be more reluctant to do it than I should be. On the other hand, how do I decide when it's time to fire somebody? What rules of thumb should I use?' We'll try to answer this question below.

Performance Problems that Warrant Firing

As we'll point out later in the chapter, there are any number of differences among organisations, employees, and supervisors that make firing, or any of the other three options, appropriate in one situation but not in another. However, we have some strong opinions on the kinds of employee behaviour and performance that *should* lead to dismissal.

1. Dishonesty.   There are certain kinds of dishonesty that any supervisor would agree are grounds for immediate dismissal, such as forging company cheques, taking backhanders, stealing money or property, or selling confidential information to a competitor. But there are other kinds of employee dishonesty that, although less obvious, can be just as destructive, if not more so:

▶ lying, especially repeatedly, about anything having to do with work;
▶ talking behind your back in a disparaging manner; that is, making negative or derogatory remarks about you to other people, but never confronting you directly;
▶ behaving pleasantly and congenially in the presence of other employees, but making negative or derogatory remarks about them as soon as they leave; and
▶ saying positive things about the organisation in your presence and in the presence of other managers and supervisors, but running down the organisation when no managerial personnel are around.

These more subtle forms of dishonesty are, admittedly, more difficult to document than more blatant forms, such as stealing property or embezzling funds. But we feel strongly that employees who behave dishonestly, whether subtly or blatantly, are destructive elements in any organisation. The quicker you get rid of them, the better.

2. Absenteeism.   Absenteeism is a major problem in British industry. Each year millions of pounds of potential profit go down the drain as a result of employee lost time. All of us—consumers, employers, and employees—feel the impact of absenteeism, either through the quality of goods and services we purchase or in the frustration, dissatisfaction, and drop in morale we experience at work.

Almost no organisation will tolerate frequent and continuous absence from an employee. However, most organisations wait far too long to do anything about an absence problem. And they often fail to make employees suffer any consequences for further absence once a warning message has been delivered. We think this is a mistake.

Unless there are extenuating circumstances, frequent employee absence is an unacceptably bad habit. Like most habits, unless its arrested in its early stages, it's likely to worsen as time passes. It's important to make it clear to employees who've just begun a pattern of absenteeism that their lack of attendance is a real problem that needs to be corrected *right away*. Supervisors should begin to take immediate steps towards dismissing employees whose attendance remains poor after they've made a firm commitment to correct the problem.

3. Substance abuse.   Employee alcoholism has been an obstacle to the productivity of organisations for a long, long time. Beginning in the 1960s organisations have had to face a related, if less pronounced, problem—drug abuse.   And the last fifteen years has witnessed a continuing struggle over the general consumption of a wide variety of illegal and legal substances, including alcohol, marijuana, cocaine, heroin and a plethora of prescription drugs.

To combat substance abuse and the host of other personal problems that hinder worker productivity, many organisations, especially larger ones in the United States, have set up employee assistance and substance abuse treatment programmes. The basic message these employers send their substance-abusing employees is a good one: resolve your problem and you'll continue to have a job here. We strongly support these kinds of programmes; they're long overdue. They have the potential for making a strong impact on the pain and suffering of millions of people, as well as on the productivity of the organisations that employ them.

In spite of our strong support for these programmes, we feel that managers and supervisors have to be coldly realistic about how difficult it is for alcoholics and drug abusers to overcome their destructive habits. As much as *you* may be willing to help an employee give up drugs or alcohol, the employee is the one who must be motivated to stop. Yes, you should care about the employee; but your responsibility as a supervisor demands that you pay attention, first and foremost, to work performance. That, as they say these days, is the bottom line.

The Misuse of Drugs Act 1971 makes it an offence to possess, supply, offer to supply or produce controlled drugs without authorisation.   It is also an offence for the occupier of premises to permit knowingly the production or supply of any controlled drugs or allow the smoking of cannabis or opium on those premises. Under common law it is an offence to 'aid and abet' the commission of an offence under the Misuse of Drugs Act. In certain circumstances, an employer who does nothing about a drugs problem may also be liable to charges under the Health and Safety at Work Act 1974.

With many employees who have drug or alcohol problems, you'll end up facing the tough fact that your efforts and the organisation's efforts to help have been in vain. The employee's habit continues, and job performance remains poor, or gets worse. Finally, you're left with one choice—to fire the employee. However, get advice. According to ACAS (Advisory, Conciliation and Arbitration Service), it may be appropriate to treat the problem as one of illness. Be careful, and keep accurate, confidential records of instances of poor performance or other problems. ACAS recommends that organisations should have clear rules on the use of alcohol, and suspected cases of alcohol misuse should be fully investigated before deciding on appropriate action. If you have any queries, consult: ACAS, (See page 275 for their address). We believe that, hard as it may be to do, firing is the best thing for you and the organisation. And it's unquestionably the best thing to do for the employee. If you have any doubts about this, talk to a recovering alcoholic or cocaine addict who 'went straight' only because some employer had the good sense finally to fire them.

4. Insubordination.   This is a word that isn't as commonly used as it once was. As it has become more socially acceptable for all of us to stand up to and disagree with authority figures—parents, bosses, government leaders—words such as *insubordination* and *disrespect* seem rather old-fashioned.

It's our strong opinion that employees not only have a right to disagree with and express their opinions to their supervisors, we think employees *should* do these things. On the other hand, we think there's a big difference between assertive openness and downright insubordination. For example, we think it's *healthy* for employees to:

▶ ask their supervisors why certain tasks need to be performed (especially if the boss doesn't offer a reason);

▶ offer opinions, especially in private, that differ from their boss's ideas, values or philosophies;

▶ suggest new ways of doing things, even if those new ways are different from procedures instituted by their supervisors;

▶ tell their supervisors, in private, that they're upset, embarrassed, hurt or otherwise disturbed as a result of something the supervisors did or said.

However, we definitely do *not* think it's good for bosses to put up with employees who:

▶ flatly refuse to do certain things that supervisors request;
▶ ignore instructions to perform certain tasks and proceed with their own methods, without first checking with their managers;
▶ openly disapprove of or disparage what their supervisors are saying or doing in a group setting (especially if members of the group don't belong to the supervisor's work unit);
▶ go around complaining about their boss to anybody who'll listen to them.

Keeping an employee who is openly and flagrantly disrespectful of your authority as a supervisor is a losing proposition. Your other employees will lose respect for you, and more important, you'll lose respect for yourself. It just isn't worth it!

5. General lack of productivity. From the standpoint of general effectiveness and overall productivity, employees can be roughly divided into the following three categories:

▶ self-starters and problem-solvers;
▶ people who do only what they're asked to do; and
▶ non-performers.

When you give self-starters and problem-solvers a task to do, they often get it done ahead of time and with a higher level of quality than you expected. They also anticipate tasks that need to be done and do them without being told. They're always coming to you with suggestions and ideas about how to improve things and how to increase productivity in your work unit.

In contrast, if you don't keep close tabs on people who do only what they're asked to do, their performance is likely to fall off. But, you can usually count on them to get the job done, even if you have to 'motivate' them now and then.

The non-performers of the work world are a constant source of frustration. Unfortunately, it seems as if there are more of them around nowadays than ever before. These are employees who:

▶ hardly ever get their work done on time;
▶ do what they're told to do and absolutely nothing more;
▶ give you all kinds of excuses why they can't do something (and, of course, never tell you how something *can* be done); and

▶ show up for work day in and day out and don't do anything unless they're given a specific task to perform.

It's always worth a try to help non-performers improve their performance. But even optimists like us have to confess: they're frustrating to work with, and often the best solution is to fire them.

Important Things to Keep in Mind About Firing

As a result of rapidly changing social conditions, as well as changes in the law, it's a lot harder to fire an employee these days than it used to be.

Legal problems aside, you should also be prepared for some personal unpleasantness. As we've said, firing somebody is tough; there are no two ways about it. It's always a distasteful emotional experience; for you, the employee and often for other employees as well.

Here are some things to keep in mind when you consider firing an employee:

1. Explore your dismissal options with some people 'in the know.' It's often helpful to consult with more experienced people before doing something for the first time, and this is no exception. Identify people in and around your firm who might know more about this area than you do (the firm's personnel director, your boss, the owner of another company in your industry, a staff member from your firm's trade association, a company solicitor or even a consultant). Briefly explain the situation and then interview the resource person on what to do. If you do a good job of 'picking the brains' of these people, you should end up with a much better understanding of the situation you're in and a solid array of alternatives.

If you have any doubts as to the correct procedure, contact ACAS (Advisory, Conciliation and Arbitration Service), Clifton House, 83-117 Euston Road, London NW1 2RB. Telephone: 071-388 5100. Fax: 071-388 9722.

2. Reduce the possibility of legal action with documentation. If you do one thing, and one thing only, you can virtually guarantee you'll never lose a dismissal case: you must be able to prove that you took reasonable steps to help an employee improve and that those steps did not result in substantial improvement.

Documentation means keeping records of each time you speak to the employee about deficiencies in work performance and subsequent actions you take to help improve the individual's performance. These records can take various forms. Here are some examples:

▶ Write a *memo to file* stating that you spoke to the employee about a certain matter on a certain date. Note the specific actions or efforts you agreed to make and those the employee agreed to make. You should also write a memo to the file whenever somebody makes a major complaint to you about the employee's performance.

▶ Keep a copy of any performance agreement you and the employee work out and then write a memo to the file on how successfully—or unsuccessfully—the agreement was carried out.

▶ After several unsuccessful attempts at coaching the employee, write a memo or note to the employee directly, stating that you're displeased with the employee's performance, why you're displeased, specifically what you expect the employee to do to improve and the possible consequences if there's no improvement in a reasonable period of time.

▶ Give the employee a formal warning as part of the formal dismissal process in your organisation. This will place the employee on some type of probationary status pending improvement in performance.

Whatever form of documentation you use, it's important to follow these guidelines:

▶ Keep a copy of the documentation in the employee's personnel folder.

▶ Make sure the employee receives a copy of all communications directed to him or her. (This does not include a memo to file.) In describing the employee's deficiencies, be as precise as you can be, noting specific, observable behaviour.

▶ Make sure all appropriate personnel (especially your supervisor) receive copies of all documentation. You should also speak to these people in person, in addition to giving them written copies.

▶ Unfortunately, some people have a tendency to 'forget' when things get a little tight. You don't want to be left carrying the can if your efforts to dismiss an employee end up in a legal battle or in unwanted publicity.

3. Be prepared to 'tough it out' for a number of months. Remember that old saying about the wheels of justice grinding slowly? In large organisations and government agencies especially, the process is likely to take a while. Whatever your situation, it'll probably take longer than you expect.

4. Be prepared for the 'reverse sympathy' phenomenon. As the supervisor of a problem employee, you'll get plenty of sympathy from people. 'I don't know how you can be so patient with him', 'if I were you, I'd have fired her a long time ago', and other supportive statements are common enough—until you begin the dismissal process. Then, many of these same people will change their tune, and you—not the employee—will end up wearing the black hat. If you *anticipate* this reversal it won't take you by surprise, and it'll be a lot easier to cope with.

5. By now, you've developed a good array of listening and negotiating skills to help you through the process. It's not out of the question to discuss the various options with the employee. Sit the person down, lay out the options, and ask for the employee's reactions, using the skills we've discussed throughout the book. It'll even work in the case of the 'reverse sympathy' phenomenon. If people say something like, 'I just can't understand why you let Terry go, especially after all he's done for you,' you can simply read them back. Try saying, 'It sounds as if you're pretty upset about the way I handled the decision about Terry' and let them talk further about how they feel. When they wind down and their receptivity to what you've got to say has been built up, then you can offer your perspective. Doing something like this is so much more effective than getting defensive, snapping back in an angry way, or explaining for the umpteenth time why you did what you did.

6. Try not to take the whole process too much to heart. Firing somebody is not a light-hearted matter, but it doesn't have to be deadly serious either. And if you go about the process effectively and without a whole lot of mistakes, the unpleasantness will pass quickly after the employee leaves. Besides, you should look at the whole process as a good solution to one of your most pressing problems and a major opportunity for growth for the employee.

Transferring

Transferring means reassigning an employee from one position to another position in the same organisation. As we apply the term here, transferring also means the employee is assigned to a different work unit (section, department, or division) under the supervision of a different manager. It also means the employee's new job has roughly the same responsibility and pay as the original job.

The decision to transfer an employee is very different from the decision to fire an employee. Transferring implies that you feel the employee can make a worthwhile contribution to the organisation, but the contribution should be made in a different job. Firing, on the other hand, implies that you feel the employee is not worth trying to salvage in any job in the organisation.

There are two guidelines that should help you decide whether an employee should be transferred rather than fired:

1. the employee has some especially strong or unusual skills that could be used in another position in the organisation.
2. the employee's skill deficiencies probably would have little or no impact in the new position.

To help you get a feel for applying these two guidelines, here are two examples of employees who we think should be transferred.

Tony is the general manager of a large metal-working plant in the North. He's been in this position for about six months. Before that he had worked for over ten years as a project engineer.

During his time as an engineer, Tony had very little supervisory responsibility. Almost all his efforts were devoted to initiating production line innovations to increase efficiency and productivity. Tony was extremely effective at this and probably saved the company several millions of pounds over the ten-year period he worked in that position.

Since his promotion to general manager, however, Tony has run into a lot of problems. The supervisors who report to him are beginning to grumble and complain. They're saying such things as, 'He never really comes out and says what he wants me to do', 'I thought he was supposed to be the general manager, but he still acts like an engineer', and, 'He's got all the technical knowledge in the world, but he doesn't know how to handle people'.

Tony's boss, the founder and president of the company, has had several 'sit-down' sessions with Tony, but they haven't resulted in much improvement. He's thinking he may have made a serious error in promoting such a technically-orientated person to such a people-orientated job.

Tina has worked for a large transport company for about five years. For the first four and a half years she worked as a recruiter in the employment section of the company's personnel department. About six months ago, she received a promotion to a job in the salary administration section of the department.

When she was first promoted, Tina's new boss was very excited about having her join them. She had developed a reputation in the employment section as a first-rate recruiter, and everybody seemed to be singing her praises. But as the months have gone by, her supervisor has changed her mind about Tina. Tina is very likeable and extremely hardworking; there's no doubt about that. But there is a lot of numerical and statistical work in her job, and it's become obvious that Tina and numbers don't get along very well. She's made a number of errors that Tina's boss was able to catch, but if she hadn't, the mistakes would have been costly and embarrassing.

Tina's supervisor has discussed the demands of the job with her and, frankly, is not optimistic that she'll be able to acquire the necessary skills, no matter how hard she tries. In fact, her boss is beginning to wonder if she didn't make a mistake in promoting Tina in the first place.

From our vantage point, both Tony and Tina seem to fit the guidelines for transferring fairly closely. Tony has some strong and well-demonstrated technical skills, and he's saved the company a lot of money over the years. Tina also has a strong track record as an employment recruiter and has gained the respect of a lot of people in and outside the company. In addition to being very skilled in some areas that are important to their organisations, both Tony and Tina have some very specific 'weaknesses', or areas of ineffective performance. Tony lacks the people skills to be a good manager and Tina lacks the quantitative skills to be a good wage and salary analyst. The important point is this: their areas needing improvement are narrow enough that they probably wouldn't pose a problem in many other jobs within the organisation.

Important Things to Keep in Mind About Transferring

In our view, the most important thing to remember when transferring an employee to a new position is to be honest with and helpful to the employee's new supervisor. So, when you're discussing the transfer, be truthful; don't mislead the potential new boss in any way. In fact, it's a good idea to meet and, as objectively as you can, tell the person everything you know about the employee's strengths and areas needing improvement. Offer suggestions that will help the two of them get off on the right foot together.

In many organisations, it's common for managers to sing the praises of problem employees they're trying to get rid of, in the hope that some unsuspecting manager in the firm will pick them up via a transfer. This is referred to—crudely, we'd add—as 'passing the rubbish'. So remember this when exploring the transfer option: being untruthful is a disservice to the employee and the new supervisor. And it'll probably come back to haunt you.

Restructuring

Our third 'What do I do if none of this works?' option is called restructuring, and it's similar to transferring. While transferring involves assigning an employee to a new job under a different supervisor in another section of the organisation, restructuring involves modifying the employee's current job. Both options are designed to get an employee working in a job that will *maximise* the employee's strengths and special skills and *minimise* the areas needing improvement.

Here are two examples of employees who are good candidates for job restructuring.

Georgia works as a research scientist for a research and development company that specialises in government research contracts in the human sciences. Georgia has been with the company for over fifteen years and has distinguished herself as an excellent proposal writer. She's also helped other researchers—especially those who have poor writing skills—to prepare technical articles and final reports for publication.

Georgia's one major problem in her job over the years has been face-to-face contact with government contracting officers and technical representatives. Georgia is incredibly shy, especially with strangers, and has great difficulty expressing herself verbally in front of a group. It's not that she hasn't tried to resolve her problem either.

She's tried seminars, assertiveness training classes and personal therapy. But she still has lots of trouble when she has to make a presentation in front of a group of government officials. Georgia's boss believes her extreme shyness and lack of good presentation skills have lost the company a number of contracts that would've been won by a more outgoing and assertive research scientist. However, he doesn't want to lose Georgia because her other skills are enormously valuable to the organisation.

Georgia is a good candidate for job restructuring. Because the company is continuing to expand, it wouldn't be difficult to rebuild Georgia's job so that she spent all her time writing proposals and reports and helping other staffers write theirs—both of which she loves to do—and no time dealing face-to-face with government representatives or putting on critical group presentations.

Clarence is nineteen years old and has been working for about a year for a medium-sized dry cleaning operation in a large city. Clarence's boss, the owner of the operation, had strong reservations about Clarence when he first hired him. He was worried Clarence might have an attendance and an attitude problem. It hasn't turned out that way, however. Not at all. Clarence hasn't missed a day of work in six months. In fact, he's usually waiting at the door when the owner arrives in the morning. He's especially good with customers; in fact a number of them have commented to the owner on what a pleasure it is to come in and talk to Clarence.

However, Clarence runs into problems when he's out the back working on machines all by himself. There's nobody to talk to and, after a while, he has a tendency to get bored and make mistakes. He's trying to improve, but he's not making much progress.

The owner is seriously considering restructuring Clarence's job to take better advantage of his very strong people skills and reduce the demand on his attention-span problems (that only seem to come into play when he's working by himself). The operation has a huge backlog of overdue accounts from old customers who've been extended credit. The owner thinks it might be a good idea to cut back Clarence's time on the machines and have him spend several hours a day on the telephone acting as an in-house bill collector. He's tried him out on a few calls, and Clarence has been able to sweet-talk everybody he's called into paying up right away. Because he's so popular with customers, the owner is also thinking of using him more and more in a sales capacity as time goes by.

While Georgia and Clarence are good candidates for restructuring, there are obviously many situations where it will be impossible to restructure an employee's job. But we think it's an option that could be used more frequently than it currently is. All that's required is a little creative thinking and a willingness to be flexible when thinking about the contribution employees can make. When done effectively, restructuring can be an effective way of turning a marginal worker or a problem employee into a productive and satisfied member of your work unit.

Important Things to Keep in Mind About Restructuring

Restructuring is the only one of the four options in which you and the employee continue to work together. For this reason we think it's important for the two of you to sit down and have an in-depth discussion about how the person's job should be restructured. The basic outline for such a discussion might go something like this.

▶ Begin the discussion by mentioning that you've been thinking seriously about ways to rebuild or restructure the employee's job in the company. Say that your goal is to try to create something that will take better advantage of the employee's strengths (certainly better than the current job does).

▶ Pause and actively listen to the employee's reaction to this idea.

▶ Present your thoughts and ideas on how the job can be restructured. Once you've finished, use your listening skills to draw out the employee's reactions and alternative suggestions.

▶ Use the negotiating skills you learned earlier to arrive at a mutually satisfying agreement with the employee on how the job can be restructured to satisfy both of you.

Neutralising

Our fourth and final option—something we call neutralising—is an option we don't like very much, because it means keeping someone around whom you'd rather fire. However, there are some situations in which neutralising may be the only sensible option for a supervisor who has a problem employee who's no longer worth trying to change.

Neutralising means restructuring the jobs of problem employees in such a way that their weaknesses, liabilities, or areas needing improvement have as little negative impact as possible on you, other employees, and customers or clients. We see neutralising as an alternative to firing. In fact, it should be used only if the difficulties involved in firing problem employees would be greater than the problems you'd face by neutralising them.

There are two kinds of organisations for which neutralising may sometimes be a more sensible option than firing. The first is the family owned business, where often the problem employee is a member of the immediate family or an in-law. The second is the organisation in the public sector—government department or agency. As an example of the dilemma that a manager faces in this second situation, we recently heard about a civil servant who spent so much time and effort trying to dismiss one of his employees that his own job performance ratings suffered as a consequence.

Here are three supervisors who chose the neutralising option:

Charles Waylon is the chief executive officer of an old and established manufacturing firm in the south-west. Charlie's problem employee is Harry Grant, his sister's husband and, of course, his brother-in-law. Charlie has tried Harry out in a variety of jobs in the company, all with very little success. 'The problem with Harry is threefold,' said Charlie. 'He's very sociable, he doesn't like to work very hard, and he doesn't really have any marketable skills. If he weren't my brother-in-law, I'd fire him tomorrow. But I just can't do that to my sister and her children.' Charlie has since given up trying to get Harry to change. Instead, he's solved the problem by making Harry his director of special projects. Now Harry is kept busy every day on what many people consider to be 'make work' projects. But he's happy, and he's no longer in the way of employees who are making money for the company.

Ruth Bradford is a supervisor for a job counselling project sponsored by a city council. When she took the job, Ruth inherited a staff counsellor who she felt was emotionally unstable and who had no business working with clients. Ruth immediately began dismissal proceedings, but soon realised it would take at least six months to get the counsellor off her staff, *if* her attempt was successful. In the meantime, Ruth stopped assigning clients to the counsellor and gave him the responsibility of going to the public library and some local college libraries to do research for an annotated bibliography she needed for an information resource centre she was trying to establish. Although the counsellor was not terribly effective at this task, he seemed to enjoy it, and he was able to collect some useful information for her. Most important, Ruth was able to isolate him from clients, her principal objective in the first place.

Laura Haskill is a newly appointed information director for the public relations department of a city council. Laura supervises a publicity officer named Bill Richford, who is fifty-eight years old and has been working for the city for thirty-five years.

Right after she was appointed, Laura said, 'If Bill weren't protected by his long service, not to mention some of the political heavyweights in this city, I'd let him go. He's gone into active retirement. He always comes in on time and leaves on time, but I just can't get any work out of him. It's frustrating.'

After wrestling with the problem for a while, Laura found one thing Bill can do well, and actually likes to do: editing the press releases that juniors in the department have written and giving them suggestions for improvement. Laura would still like to fire Bill, but at least she's found something productive for him to do.

Important Things to Keep in Mind About Neutralising

As we said, neutralising is not an option we're particularly fond of. However, in some circumstances, it may be the only real alternative. So, if it's not feasible to fire a problem employee, the following list of do's and don'ts may be helpful to you.

1. Don't try to drive the person away. Don't harass problem employees in an effort to get them to resign or seek a transfer. This hardly ever works. The employee will try to strike back at you in ways that could be embarrassing and painful. Besides, the ultimate result of such a campaign is the undermining of morale in your whole work unit.

2. Don't assign the employee tasks that are crucial to the effectiveness of your work unit. This may seem obvious, but some supervisors tend to get a little stubborn about this and adopt the attitude, 'Well, if I've got to keep him, he's going to pull his weight like everybody else.' Yes, it would be nice if he would pull his weight, but all the evidence suggests he won't. So don't be short-sighted and ask him to do things you know he won't or can't do.

3. Keep trying to help the employee change. We're firmly committed to the view that most people can and will change for the better if we just open the right doors for them. So, as hard as it is to do it, always try to convey an attitude of supportive helpfulness to the employee. Strongly reinforce any signs of positive change. Let the employee know how pleased you are with whatever improvement you see. Whenever possible, ignore faults and concentrate on strengths.

4. Enlist the aid of other people in coming up with ways to help the employee make positive changes. It's a good idea to view helping the employee change as 'a challenge for all of us'. Don't say, 'Look, we all know she's a complete idiot but we're just going to have to put up with her'.

How Do You Choose Among the Four Options?

To some extent, we've already talked about how to choose among the four options. We've described each of them in some detail—firing, transferring, restructuring and neutralising—and we've talked about when each is appropriate. But, so far, we haven't given you much help in deciding how to choose an option, given that your situation and circumstances are always unique.

The task of deciding among the options will be a little easier if you consider these three sets of factors:

1. the organisation;
2. the employee; and
3. you.

First we'll describe the implications of these factors in choosing among the options. Then we'll give you an opportunity to consider these factors in deciding what to do with some hypothetical employees.

The Organisation

Organisations are a lot like people. They have much in common with each other, but they also differ in many ways. How your organisation differs from others in three important ways—size, policies and traditions, and financial situation—will have an effect on which option you choose for a particular employee.

1. Organisational size. From the standpoint of what to do about a problem employee, there are at least two significant ways large organisations differ from small organisations:

▶ except at the highest managerial levels, the impact of an employee's poor performance on the overall productivity of the organisation is less in a large organisation than in a small one;
▶ large organisations tend to have a much greater variety of specialised jobs than small organisations.

These differences have several implications for supervisors trying to decide what to do about a problem employee. In a larger organisation you're more likely to have the 'luxury' of working with a problem employee longer than you would in a smaller organisation. Although the employee's poor performance may be equally frustrating for you, your organisation will feel the impact of the employee's ineffectiveness less if it is large. Also, larger organisations have not only more jobs but a greater variety of specialised jobs than smaller organisations, making the possibility of a transfer easier in a bigger company. Most people, even problem employees, have some skills. If you're a supervisor in a large organisation, your chances of locating a position where the employee's skills could be put to good use are greater than if you work in a small organisation.

2. Policies and traditions. Your organisation's policies and traditions are undoubtedly going to have some effect on which option you select. For example, if you work for a government agency, the option of firing a problem employee probably poses more problems than if you work for a private company with a long history of quickly dismissing unproductive people. You'll have an easier time restructuring an employee's job if you work for a company that allows its managers some flexibility than you will if you work for a more tightly controlled organisation. There's nothing wrong with picking an option that's inconsistent with the company line. However, it's important to be realistic about the obstacles you'll encounter if you make such a choice.

Here's one way to help ensure that you're being realistic. Take a piece of paper and draw a line down the middle. At the top of the left side write, 'Advantages of choosing this option'. On top of the right side write, 'Disadvantages of choosing this option'. If you take the time to fill in both sides conscientiously and honestly, you'll end up with a much clearer sense of whether or not you still want to choose a particular option, especially if the option is inconsistent with the organisation's policies and traditions.

3. Financial status of your organisation. How your organisation is doing financially may have a big effect on the option you choose. When profits are up and budgets are fat, you generally have more flexibility. During periods of austerity, your options are much narrower. In a time of relative prosperity, you might decide to transfer an employee, or restructure the individual's job. However, you might decide that firing or laying off the same employee is the only sensible option when the company is tightening its belt.

The Employee

As there are different kinds of people, there are also different kinds of problem employees. In attempting to choose among the four options, it's important to make a rough distinction between two broad types:

▶ problem employees who are generally and broadly ineffective; and

▶ problem employees who are narrowly and specifically ineffective.

Employees in the first category are candidates for firing, or neutralising if firing is not a feasible option. Because of bad habits or a general lack of skill, or a combination of the two, these people would have difficulty performing effectively in any job in the organisation.

Employees in the second category are generally good candidates for transferring or restructuring. While they have a specific skill deficiency or negative characteristic that keeps them from making a worthwhile contribution in their current jobs, their particular liabilities may not get in the way in a different or restructured job. In the right positions, they're people who can still make a contribution to the organisation.

For example, employees in the first category might include those people who are absentee problems, openly disrespectful to their supervisors, constantly complaining or offering excuses for why things can't be done, hampered by a drinking or drug problem, or guilty of dishonest behaviour. Employees in the second category might include those people who are poor at delegating authority and responsibility, not good at verbal or written expression, unable to handle a task related to the rest of the job, have poor quantitative skills or are apt to get completely flustered when work pressures mount up.

You

Probably the biggest factor in choosing among the four options won't be the organisation or the employee. It will be *you*—who you are as a person and your situation in the organisation. Like the organisation and the employee, you're unique. What's even more important, the employee and the organisation notwithstanding, it's you who'll be making the choice.

Here are some things about you that are worth considering.

1. Your philosophy about human behaviour change. Even if you're not a psychologist or a philosopher, you probably have some definite opinions about the likelihood of successfully persuading other human beings to change their behaviour. You may be pessimistic. You may be optimistic. Or you may fall somewhere in between.

Let's say you're pessimistic. If you are, you're probably not going to try too hard to help employees improve their performance. You may think, 'That's just the way it is and there's not a lot I can do about it'. Your tendency will be either to put up with the poor performance of problem employees, or to try to get rid of them. You probably won't waste your time trying to get them to change.

On the other hand, let's say you're an optimist when it comes to the idea of getting people to change. If so, you're likely to give the performance improvement process some extra effort. You may be reluctant to give up on employees until the evidence is overwhelming that they're not going to change. Even then, you may walk that extra mile. That's the way it is with optimists.

If you fall somewhere in between optimism and pessimism, as we do, then you're likely to make a strong initial effort to get employees to change. But you'll also be ready to 'cut your losses' if you don't get some fairly immediate evidence of improvement. You'll give it a good try, but you're not going to hang around for ever waiting for someone to change.

None of these philosophies is right or wrong. But there are a couple of important things to remember here. One, try to be open and flexible enough to modify your philosophy. In the case of some new evidence of improvement, re-examine your pessimistic tendencies. And in the case of no evidence, reconsider whether you're an optimist or a dreamer. At the same time don't abandon your philosophy too easily. If you do, you'll cause yourself a lot of conflict by getting caught in the trap of second-guessing yourself, which can end up being very uncomfortable.

2. Your relationship with your boss. The relationship you have with your boss will definitely have some impact on your choice among the options. In fact, when we first wrote this book, we said, 'An entire book, longer than this one, could be written on the different types of bosses and on how best to get along with them'. We went on to write a book just like that a couple of years later, *Problem Bosses: Who They Are and How To Deal With Them.*

In terms of what to do about a particular problem employee, however, the most important characteristic of your relationship with your boss is the amount of general support and freedom given to you for the decisions you make. If your boss allows you to be independent in the decisions you make, you can rely on your own feelings and opinions in choosing an option, though you might want to use him as a sounding board. If your boss is always looking over your shoulder, it's probably best to involve her in the decision-making process from the beginning. If you don't, she's likely to challenge, or even veto, your choice of options.

3. Your 'chemistry' with the employee. We believe in getting down to the level of specific, observable behaviour in deciding why an employee is not performing effectively and what you need to do about it. However, the quality of a relationship between two people is often extremely difficult to describe in specific, behavioural terms. Because of reasons we may never fully understand, we can get along famously with one person and absolutely miserably with another.

The same holds true for bosses and employees. In addition to the employee's actual performance, it's important to pay attention to how the two of you actually get along. Do you seem to enjoy each other's company and have a basic liking for each other? Or do you have a tendency to avoid and maybe even dislike each other? Do you enjoy each other's sense of humour? Or do you both tend to shudder when the other person makes an attempt at being funny? Is the atmosphere fairly relaxed when you're together? Or does it tend to be stiff and formal?

The answers to these and similar questions will have a lot to do with how comfortable either of you feels about the option you choose. Let's say you work for a government agency and have a problem employee you'd like to fire. If the chemistry between the two of you is pretty good, in spite of the employee's poor performance, you might look towards the transferring or neutralising option rather than go through a painful and protracted firing process. If the chemistry is bad, however, you might decide to endure the long firing process rather than continue working with someone who causes you so much discomfort.

Now let's give you a little practice in choosing among the options.

Practise Choosing Options

Up to this point we've talked about the four options and the factors —the organisation, the employee, and you—that will affect the one you choose. Now we'd like to get you involved in trying the options on for size. The form on pages 292-4 will give you a chance to practise choosing.

In this chapter we've tried to describe four options—firing, transferring, restructuring, and neutralising—that are available when you decide the performance improvement process hasn't worked for a particular employee. In addition, we've given you some guidelines for selecting among these options and some practice in choosing them.

We strongly hope that the ten-step performance improvement process we've described in this book will reduce the number of times you'll conclude that 'none of this works' for an employee. But when you do reach that conclusion, we hope our suggestions in this chapter will make your task a little easier.

A Concluding Note

Being a manager or supervisor isn't easy; you don't need us to tell you that. Being 'the boss' is always a tough job, and one for which most of us are not very well prepared when we first step into the position. But we believe it can be a tremendously rewarding job. Although we're interested in helping you increase the productivity of your employees, we also see some humanistic fringe benefits you'll get from using the performance improvement process outlined in this book. Perhaps the most important reward will be watching people develop. For us, being a part of the growth process of another human being is a very satisfying. Perhaps it's the same for you.

If you adopt the attitude, 'How I can help unlock this person's door to growth?' with all the employees you encounter, you may not always find the key, but you'll feel good as a result of having tried. And your skills as a developer of people will get better all the time.

Finally, everything we've said in this book about you and your employees applies to your other important relationships as well. For example, even though we've written an entirely different book on the subject of problem bosses, we think the approach we've recommended here for dealing with employees can be just as effective in dealing with bosses. So, whether you consider your boss a 'problem' or not, try to apply what we've said in this book to that relationship as well. You may be pleasantly surprised at the results.

On a more personal level, since writing this book, we've learned that a number of husbands and wives have used the ten-step approach to improve their relationships with each other. And with some real success, too. We've even learned that some parents have used the performance improvement process during some difficult and tumultuous times with their teenage children. Also with some pretty good success.

Obviously, we've been pleased—very pleased—to learn from people that 'this works' with employees, bosses and family members. But, to be honest, we're not surprised. Why? Because we use the same basic approach in our relationship with each other as best friends and business partners ... and in our personal lives as well. Who knows? Maybe you should try it, too.

Choosing the Best Option

Below are descriptions of hypothetical situations for four problem employees. In each case, their supervisors have decided that 'none of this works'. For each employee, decide which of the four options—firing, transferring, restructuring, or neutralising—you'd choose. After you've made your choices, compare your decisions with the ones we would have made.

1. **Sam** is a senior level civil servant who's recently been assigned to your unit. He's about fifteen years older than you are and has been in government service for over thirty years.

Sam's reputation as a technical expert in his field is excellent. Although his level of professional activity has subsided quite a bit in the last ten years, he's turned out lots of articles and papers that have received world-wide recognition. He still receives quite a few invitations to speak at professional conventions and conferences.

In spite of Sam's reputation, you're not very impressed with him. At staff meetings he holds forth on his ideas to the boredom and exasperation of the other members of your team. He doesn't get tasks completed on time. And when he does get them done, they don't look at all like what you expected. In the performance improvement interview you've had with Sam he's made it pretty clear that he thinks you should give him a lot more free rein so he can make better use of his real talents. When you express your side of the story, it is obvious that he's not listening to you.

Option you'd choose: _____

2. You're in the process of setting up a new sales office in a provincial area after having been transferred from London. The first person you hired when you got there was Caroline, your personal secretary.

When you hired Caroline, you were extremely pleased with her. She had superb secretarial skills, in addition to being a friendly and vibrant person. But she's been with you about two months now and your estimation of her has dropped considerably. During that period she got into a shouting match with one of your recently hired salespersons when you were out of the office. Shortly after you had individual talks with both the salesperson and Caroline, you learned that Caroline had phoned the company's director of personnel to complain about you. When the director called you to tell you what Caroline had told him, it was apparent that she had distorted a lot of facts and had said some pretty damaging things about you. When you confronted Caroline with what you'd heard from the personnel director, she acted in a very charming and friendly manner and tried to persuade you that she was just a little upset at the time and needed somebody to talk to.

Option you'd choose: _____

3. You're the manager of the customer accounting department for a large transport company. The function of your department is that of an internal bill collector. You have a staff of about twenty-five customer account representatives whose job it is to call delinquent accounts to get them to pay their bills.   *Continued*

Nancy has been on your staff as an account rep. for about five months now. At this point you're really torn about Nancy. If you look at it one way, she's the best you have. She's very persuasive and has been able to settle some delinquent accounts that nobody else (including you) has been able to do. On the other hand, Nancy is about to give you an ulcer. She's so incredibly bad with numbers that her records are almost incomprehensible. Your boss has told you bluntly that he can't put up with any more of her mistakes because he's starting to get heat from *his* boss.

Option you'd choose: _____

4. You're the manager of sales training for a large electrical corporation with headquarters in the north-east. One of your principal responsibilities is the supervision of young management trainees just out of college.

You took Jim under your wing about three months ago when he expressed a strong interest in sales engineering. You decided to take Jim into the sales training programme primarily on the basis of his excellent engineering degree from a top university.

Now that you've had an opportunity to observe Jim in a number of different kinds of selling situations, you're pretty well convinced that he's never going to make it as a salesperson. His knowledge of engineering principles and application is remarkable for someone so young, but he obviously lacks a lot of the people skills that you feel are so important for selling. In spite of several coaching sessions with him, he still doesn't smile very much, give a good firm handshake, talk enthusiastically about his products and so on.

At this point, you're beginning to wonder whether you should even go through the motions of running him through the last six months of the training programme.

Option you'd choose: _____

Choosing the Best Option: Answers and Discussion

Here are the choices we would've made for each of these employees. When you compare your choices with ours, it's important to remember that there are no right or wrong answers—just different consequences.

1. **Fire or neutralise Sam.** We're not 100 per cent certain what we'd do about Sam. We know we wouldn't transfer him or try to restructure his job, but we're not sure whether we'd try to fire him or try to neutralise him.

Our final choice would probably come down to something like this: if Sam were really arrogant and constantly challenging our authority, we'd probably try to fire him in spite of the tremendous effort it would take to make that happen. On the other hand, if Sam were just rather independent, but not really abrasive, we'd probably be more inclined to neutralise him. Even though the choice of putting Sam out in a corner would be distasteful, it probably wouldn't be as unpleasant as the long drawn-out process of trying to get him fired. *Continued*

2. **Fire Caroline.** We don't have any doubts here. We'd move quickly to fire Caroline. She's given us some pretty strong evidence that she's deceitful, if not downright dishonest. We think that not getting rid of her quickly and deliberately would be courting disaster.

3. **Restructure Nancy's job.** Nancy obviously has some real strengths and some areas that definitely need improvement as a customer representative. She's very skilful at getting people to pay their bills, but she has an absolutely terrible time with figures.

We'd be inclined to restructure her job to take advantage of what she does well and to minimise the effect of what she does poorly. One way to do this would be to make her a troubleshooter—that is, restructure her job so that she's responsible for helping other representatives with particularly troublesome accounts. This would allow her to put her persuasive skills to good use, but her lack of skill with numbers would no longer be a problem because the representative in charge of each account she worked on would be responsible for all paperwork and arithmetic.

4. **Transfer Jim.** We'd begin to think pretty seriously about a transfer for Jim. He seems to be very technically competent. In such a large organisation, there are probably any number of engineering positions where his skills and abilities could be used, and where his poor interpersonal skills would not be the drawback they are in selling.

Questions and Answers

AFTER our workshops, many participants have questions about the the performance improvement process and other aspects of our approach. We've included some of these questions—and our answers—below.

Question: My company has a performance appraisal system with a rating form that has to be filled in on each employee at least once a year. The approach you recommend is a little different. What do you think I should do?

Answer: We don't like performance appraisal rating forms. They ask you to evaluate the employee from unsatisfactory to exceptional (the words may differ, but they mean the same) on a long series of global traits, such as dependability, ability to get along with others, quality of work, and so on. They don't get at the heart of employee performance because they don't get down to specific behaviour. Another reason we don't like them is because the boss rates the employee, but not the other way round. What kind of a 'system' is that?

After an appraisal where one of these forms is used, employees often end up feeling like school children who've just been given their reports. If their marks are high, they feel pretty good. If their marks are low, they feel bad.

We think you should try to get around these forms. Here's how.

1. During the performance improvement interview, tell the employee you don't approve of the rating form approach, but you have to send in some kind of completed form. Schedule a separate meeting to get the form out of the way.
2. When you meet with the employee, say that the purpose of the meeting is to get the form taken care of quickly because you don't feel it's a helpful tool.
3. Ask the employee to fill in the form. If you can live with these self-

ratings, tell the employee that's exactly how the form will be turned in. If you can't live with them, use your negotiating and listening skills to arrive at ratings you can both agree on. (Always give the employee the benefit of the doubt.)

By the way, if you work in an organisation where many managers get away with not filling these forms in, join the ranks. They're a waste of time, and we're convinced they do more harm than good.

Question: I'm the CEO of a family-owned business. Most of the people who report directly to me are relatives or in-laws. How would you modify your approach to handle this kind of situation?

Answer: We wouldn't modify it at all. Our work with a number of family-owned businesses has taught us that our approach can be especially helpful to somebody in your situation. It's informal, task-orientated, and personalised. It involves employees appropriately in the process of improving performance, theirs and yours.

Question: How long should these performance improvement interviews last? And how often should they be held?

Answer: The interviews should probably last between an hour and an hour and a half. If you take less than an hour, you are probably rushing things a bit. If you take more than an hour and a half, you may be getting bogged down in one area. (Though it's much better to err on the side of too much time than too little.)

As you begin to use this approach with employees, you may find yourself taking well over an hour and a half. The main reason will probably be that your employees have a lot to say because they haven't had the opportunity to talk in this manner before. The extra time spent should be worth it.

You should hold a comprehensive interview with each one of your employees at least once a year, with several more formal follow-up sessions. But more important than formal meetings is using these skills and techniques on an informal, continuing basis. You can find out how things are going in a ten-minute conversation in the hall. You can give employees constructive, helpful feedback in just a few minutes in your office. You can get employees to talk about problems they're experiencing over lunch or while walking to the car park after work.

The more you use the skills, the sharper they'll get and the more helpful they'll be to you.

Question: I'm a manufacturing supervisor with thirty-one people who report directly to me. How can I possibly do what you recommend with so many people? I'd spend all my time in meetings.

Answer: You're right. It's impossible to do what we recommend with that many employees and still do all the other things you have to do. We suggest that either you try to reduce the number of people who report directly to you or you interview only on a priority basis.

Let's take the first option. Supervising thirty-one people violates a management principle called 'span of control', which states that managers ideally should only supervise between five and ten people. Supervising any more than ten people makes it difficult to keep track of what everybody's doing; supervising thirty-one makes it impossible.

We'd suggest that you talk to your boss and ask to have four or five of the thirty-one promoted to supervisory or 'lead' positions, in which they would report directly to you. Each of them, in turn, would have six or seven people to supervise.

If you work in an industry where profit margins are close, you'll definitely get some objections to this kind of proposal. The major argument you'll hear is, 'If I promote these people to supervisors, they're not making money for us; they're an expensive overhead item.' And your argument (after using your listening skills to build up receptivity) should be that productivity will go up, not down, with a properly supervised production force.

But let's say your argument fails. The second option is to interview only workers who meet certain criteria, such as:

▶ Hard-core problem employees;
▶ The real star performers (who will probably get promoted anyway);
▶ Workers who are new and need a lot of feedback.

Even if you have to choose this second option, don't give up on the first. Keep trying to get your supervisory load reduced.

Question: I work in an area where there aren't really any enclosed offices, only partitions and room dividers. It's almost impossible to carry on a private conversation. What suggestions do you have?

Answer: We take a strong stand on this issue: if you want to conduct an effective interview, you've got to find somewhere to do it where people can't overhear you.

If you don't have a private office, you might try the following:

▶ Use the conference room or some other community space where you can close the door and hold a private conversation.

▶ Ask if you can borrow your boss's office (or the office of some other senior person) for an hour or so. It's for a good cause, and it'll give your boss an excuse to get out of the office for a while.

▶ Come in early or stay late to conduct the interview (giving the employee some compensatory time if you use this approach);

▶ Leave the building if you have to. Go to a quiet restaurant, or another relatively private place.

Be persistent. You'll find a solution.

Question: I'm very new in my job, and I'm much younger than most of the people I supervise. They haven't really accepted me yet as a supervisor. What can I expect if I begin to use this process with them?

Answer: We've found that a major complaint of older workers about their younger supervisors goes something like this: 'My boss doesn't really value and respect my knowledge and experience.' They say things such as:

'I know this place inside out and he doesn't even know where the loos are yet.'

'There are all kinds of things I could tell her that she really needs to know. But if she isn't asking, I'm not telling.'

'He's making mistakes that are so obvious, but he doesn't pay much attention when we try to give him advice.'

'She's got a good head on her shoulders, but she really doesn't know anything yet. I could really help her out, if she were interested'.

The performance improvement interview—especially if you use your listening skills—is an excellent opportunity for you to show older workers that you do value and respect their experience. Simply by being a good listener, you should be able to get them to tell you all kinds of things you ought to know about the organisation, like the best ways to cut through red tape, things to look out for, and so on. You show them—without giving up your authority as a supervisor—that you're interested in what they have to say and that you want to benefit from their experience.

Question: What do you do when it comes to the follow-up meeting and the employee has done everything he agreed to do and you haven't?

Answer: This will happen sometimes. When it does, go ahead and hold the follow-up meeting anyway. Don't give in to the temptation to postpone it until you've had more time.

Here are some suggestions on how to handle the situation.

1. Without feeling or sounding guilty, tell the employee why you failed to live up to your end of the bargain. If appropriate, apologise.
2. Without blaming anybody or making excuses, mention any special problems you had in accomplishing what you agreed to do.
3. Get the employee's view of the situation and ask for suggestions on how to improve things in the future.
4. Renegotiate a performance agreement that has a better chance of succeeding than the last one. And don't make the same mistake again, or you'll regret it as you see the employee's morale and performance start to deteriorate.

Question: You say that the performance agreement is for the use of the supervisor and employee only, and that copies should not go in the employee's file. But you also say that documentation is necessary if an employee is going to be fired. Isn't that a contradiction?

Answer: This is a sensitive issue. If you tell the employee, 'The performance agreement is just between you and me,' then it's probably not ethical later to use the agreement against the employee in the dismissal process. As a supervisor, however, you're responsible if the employee doesn't live up to the performance agreement—even if that action leads to firing.

Here's what we suggest:

1. keep the original performance agreement as a confidential document between you and the employee.
2. if, in your follow-up meeting, it's clear the employee has violated the agreement, tell the employee that future agreements will not necessarily be kept confidential. Say that these agreements will be put in the employee's personnel file and may be used to build a case for dismissal if that becomes necessary.

Question: What should you say when you ask the employee to meet with you to discuss work performance and the employee says, 'Are we going to discuss my salary in this meeting?' This happened to me and I didn't know what to say.

Answer: We think you should keep discussions of salary and work performance separate for two reasons:

1. If you include salary in a discussion of work performance, the employees will focus on how much money they're going to get, not on how work performance can be improved. This is especially true when employees feel they're not getting the pay rises they deserve. No matter what you say about the positive aspects of their performance, dissatisfied individuals are likely to walk away thinking, 'Well, I suppose that's all they think I'm worth.'

2. Although an employee's salary is certainly related to work performance, there are other factors that affect salary and salary increases, things that don't have anything to do with performance. Here are some examples:

▶ Budget constraints. Often it's impossible to give even a superb performer more than a small pay rise because of poor profits, budget cutbacks and other fiscal problems beyond your control.

▶ Job market competition. There are many technical areas in which the supply of skilled workers is scarce. Even though it seems unfair to employees in other job categories, it's often necessary to offer larger salaries and annual increases to attract and keep these workers.

▶ Internal equity. A typical problem in organisations that employ union personnel is called compression. That's what happens when the wages of hourly union employees begin to approach (or surpass) the salaries of the non-union management personnel who supervise them. To keep things equitable, organisations automatically increase the salaries of these supervisory personnel, regardless of their performance.

When you have a meeting to discuss an employee's salary, a lot of the steps and techniques covered in the book will apply. The most useful skill you've learned for this kind of discussion, however, is the ability to listen actively. Employees are often dissatisfied with their pay and their pay rises. Give employees an opportunity to talk about this dissatisfaction without offering all kinds of explanations and reasons why their dissatisfaction is unjustified. Just listen. They'll feel better and so will you.

Question: I agree with you that the performance analysis form should be filled in thoroughly and completely. Is it also OK to get the employee to fill in the same form?

Answer: We think it's better to keep the form for your own use. If you ask your employee to fill in the same form, the person is likely to be very curious about how you filled in your copy and will probably expect, if not ask, to see it.

This can cause some problems. The language you use on the form is likely to be somewhat blunt and straightforward on the 'needs improvement' side. Unlike you, the form can't monitor the employee's receptivity. It can't stop talking and start listening if receptivity drops. Besides, once the person has read the form and feels unfairly judged by you, it's difficult to undo the damage. It's better not to let it happen in the first place. As an alternative, ask employees to write down (not just think about):

▶ The areas where they think they're performing effectively;
▶ The areas where they think they could stand to improve; and
▶ Their thoughts about how you could make their jobs less frustrating and more satisfying.

We've found that employees who write these things down before the interview are better prepared for, and get more involved in, the meeting than those who are only asked to think about these things.

Questions: I'm concerned about asking the employee, 'How can I make your job less frustrating and more satisfying?' I know you said it wouldn't open up Pandora's box, but I'm not sure I agree. Won't I get some strange requests if I do ask it?

Answer: This is one of the most common questions supervisors ask us. They fear employees will make all kinds of unreasonable requests, like two-hour lunch breaks or six-week holidays.

We think your question is part of the very human tendency to expect the worst. In our experience, though, employees rarely make unreasonable or irrational requests when they get asked this question. Just think about what you'd say if your boss asked you the question? Are your requests unreasonable? Would your requests open up Pandora's box? Probably not, but that's what *your* boss would probably be worried about too.

When outrageous requests are made, they tend to be made in jest. In such cases, the best response is to say, 'OK, anything else I can do for you?' The serious requests will usually follow.

One final word of caution. Don't avoid the question just because you expect the worst. You'll deprive yourself of some very useful information if you do.

Question: Throughout the book you use the phrase, 'areas where the employee could stand to improve'. Why not just use the simpler expression, 'weakness'?

Answer: For a couple of reasons:

1. The word *weakness* is an emotionally loaded expression that's likely to lower the employee's receptivity;
2. It's not a very useful concept. Its focus is negative, not positive. You don't get as much useful information when you ask, 'What are the employee's weak points?' as you do when you ask, 'How could the employee stand to improve?'

Question: I know what you say about listening skills is important. But will it really work with the silent types? I've got a man in the office who hasn't said 'Boo' in two years. How, all of a sudden, is he going to start talking in a performance improvement interview?

Answer: Lots of supervisors express this concern about getting employees to 'open up' in an interview. Most of the time they come back later saying:

'It was really incredible. He just started talking and didn't stop.'

'You know, this really works.'

'I thought she was just going to sit there and say nothing like she usually does, but she opened up. I was really surprised.'

When employees don't open up, it's usually because their supervisors aren't being very good listeners. Most bosses tend to talk too much and sometimes even monopolise conversations with employees. They often ask closed-ended questions and don't wait very long for an answer. And when the employee doesn't start talking right away, they'll often just answer the question themselves and keep on talking. To make things worse, they often interrupt whenever they disagree with what the employee's got to say.

If you're this kind of listener, you'll have to work especially hard to get the shy, retiring types to talk. Comprehensive questions are often very good with quiet people. Plan to use a lot of encouragers when they do start talking. Do the other things regarding listening skills we suggested in Chapter 8. Use good attending skills. Ask questions that give the employee plenty of room to respond. Read the employee back. If you listen skilfully, the employee will talk. We guarantee it.

Question: I not only have problem employees, I also have a problem boss. I can see the value of your approach for dealing with my employees. Do you think it could be adapted for use with my boss?

Answer: Yes. We know some people who've done it. Here's a possible adaptation:

1. Analyse your boss's performance following the same basic approach for analysing your employee's performance in Chapter 4.
2. Ask your boss if you can meet to talk about some ways both of you can improve the quality of your working relationship. (If your boss balks, use your listening skills.)
3. Begin the meeting by explaining the following.

▶ The purpose of the meeting as you see it.

▶ Your ideas on how to proceed. For example, your boss could start off by giving you feedback on your performance and then you could give your boss some feedback. Then the two of you could come up with an agreement on what you're both going to do to improve the relationship in the future.

▶ Ask your boss to give you feedback on your performance, starting with the things you're doing well and moving to the areas where you could stand to improve.

▶ Do the same for your boss. The most important thing to remember is *stop talking and start listening* if your boss shows even a hint of defensiveness.

4. Negotiate a performance agreement if you can (preferably in writing, but don't press it) and try to arrange a follow-up meeting.
5. End the meeting on a positive note, saying how pleased you are that you had a chance to talk about things.
6. Try to follow up both formally and informally, using the techniques discussed in the chapter on following up.

Even our final chapter on 'What do I do if none of this works?' can be adapted to a problem boss. You can't very well restructure your boss's job or neutralise your boss, but you can 'fire' your boss by resigning or getting a transfer. Good luck.

Index